OSHUN, *LEMONADE*, AND INTERTEXTUALITY

UNIVERSITY PRESS OF FLORIDA

Florida A&M University, Tallahassee
Florida Atlantic University, Boca Raton
Florida Gulf Coast University, Ft. Myers
Florida International University, Miami
Florida State University, Tallahassee
New College of Florida, Sarasota
University of Central Florida, Orlando
University of Florida, Gainesville
University of North Florida, Jacksonville
University of South Florida, Tampa
University of West Florida, Pensacola

OSHUN, *LEMONADE,* AND INTERTEXTUALITY

Afro-Atlantic Religion in Black Cultural Production

Sheneese Thompson

UNIVERSITY PRESS OF FLORIDA

Gainesville/Tallahassee/Tampa/Boca Raton
Pensacola/Orlando/Miami/Jacksonville/Ft. Myers/Sarasota

Cover: *Ore yeye o*, by Andreyaa Hora, www.andreyaahora.com.

Publication of this work made possible by a Sustaining the Humanities through the American Rescue Plan grant from the National Endowment for the Humanities.

Copyright 2025 by Sheneese Thompson
All rights reserved
Published in the United States of America

30 29 28 27 26 25   6 5 4 3 2 1

DOI: https://doi.org/10.5744/9780813079387

Library of Congress Cataloging-in-Publication Data
Names: Thompson, Sheneese Shereena, author.
Title: Oshun, Lemonade, and intertextuality : Afro-Atlantic religion in Black cultural production / Sheneese Thompson.
Description: Gainesville : University Press of Florida, 2025. | Includes bibliographical references and index.
Identifiers: LCCN 2024057039 (print) | LCCN 2024057040 (ebook) |
   ISBN 9780813079387 (hardback) | ISBN 9780813081106 (paperback) |
   ISBN 9780813074061 (pdf) | ISBN 9780813073866 (ebook)
Subjects: LCSH: Beyoncé, 1981—Criticism and interpretation. | Afro-Caribbean religions. | Black people—Caribbean Area—Religion. | African American arts. | Women and literature—America. | Caribbean Area—Religion. | Africa—Religion. | BISAC: LITERARY CRITICISM / Women Authors | LITERARY CRITICISM / Subjects & Themes / Religion
Classification: LCC BL2565 .T46 2025 (print) | LCC BL2565 (ebook) |
   DDC 200.97—dc23/eng/20250113
LC record available at https://lccn.loc.gov/2024057039
LC ebook record available at https://lccn.loc.gov/2024057040

The University Press of Florida is the scholarly publishing agency for the State University System of Florida, comprising Florida A&M University, Florida Atlantic University, Florida Gulf Coast University, Florida International University, Florida State University, New College of Florida, University of Central Florida, University of Florida, University of North Florida, University of South Florida, and University of West Florida.

University Press of Florida
2046 NE Waldo Road
Suite 2100
Gainesville, FL 32609
http://upress.ufl.edu

GPSR EU Authorized Representative: Mare Nostrum Group B.V., Mauritskade 21D, 1091 GC Amsterdam, The Netherlands, gpsr@mare-nostrum.co.uk

Òṣun, yèyé mọ'rọ̀
Ọ ṣá mi na l'ayé o

Ẹ kọ́
Òṣun, mother who builds wealth
You selected me first to have the world
You educate

CONTENTS

Acknowledgments ix

Introduction 1

1. When Life Gives You Lemons, Add Honey 21
2. Don't Hurt Yourself: Odù Ọ̀ṣẹ́túrá as a Method for Analyzing Fault, Retribution, and Accountability 48
3. Water Always Returns to Its Source: Oshun's Medium as Guiding Principle in Narratives of Healing 78
4. Honey in the Hive: Oshun and Yemaya in Celebration of the Black Feminine 102

Conclusion: Reflections 122

Glossary of Terms 129
Notes 133
Bibliography 145
Index 155

ACKNOWLEDGMENTS

I would like to acknowledge Olodumare, as God blessed me with the faculties, opportunities, and fidelity to complete this book. I would like to thank Orisha for their benevolence on my behalf. I would like to thank my mother, Abeena Hollis, for her love, sacrifice, and unwavering support. I would like to thank her mother, my Nana, Thelma Hollis, for her wisdom, patience, and continued protection after her transition to becoming an ancestor. I would like to acknowledge all my ancestors on my maternal line—the Sims, the Jameses, the Jacobs, and the Hollises, who have passed on—as it is their shoulders on which I stand. I would like to thank my paternal grandparents, Regina and Hollie Thompson, as well as my paternal ancestors—the Thompsons, Blackwells, and Nelsons who have passed on—as it is they who paved the way for me.

I want to acknowledge my godmother, Iya Gheri, my *ajubona*, Iya Diane. For all the spiritual and life lessons you have taught me, I am eternally grateful. This book is especially not possible without the religious training you have imparted to me, as well as the reverence for Orisha and our traditions that I have learned along the way. Thank you, specifically for your contributions to this project, and encouraging me to keep going, but most importantly for accepting me as your goddaughter and for guiding me on the path of Orisha. I want to thank my godfather, Baba Joe, for his kind heart and protective nature, as well as my god-brothers and -sisters who continuously checked in on me during the writing process.

I would like to acknowledge Sian Hunter, my wonderful editor, who saw potential in the project immediately and guided me throughout the process graciously. And, last, I would like to acknowledge many people who are not named and yet are indispensable in making this book possible.

Introduction

Bí òní ti rí, ọla le má rí bẹ́ẹ̀; ìyẹn ni babaláwo fi ńdífá ọrọrún
Tomorrow may not be like today; hence, the divination consultation is carried out every fifth day
—Yoruba Proverb

On April 23, 2016, Beyoncé Knowles-Carter released her sixth studio album, *Lemonade* (2016). The visual album boasted a free promotional debut with Home Box Office (HBO) that could be viewed free of charge from the debut and on demand through the Monday following. Unlike the albums that preceded it, *Lemonade* is a coherent conceptual visual album, as opposed to discrete visual accompaniments, that explores twelve stages of the emotional and narrative development of a woman working through the complex feelings that accompany infidelity and reconciling difficult relationships. Beyoncé draws on a variety of different elements to tell a story that centers herself and yet is bigger than herself, including the landscape of Louisiana (especially New Orleans), the poetry of Warsan Shire, and the art of Laolu Senbanjo, and perhaps most relevant to this analysis, many iconographic elements associated with the Yoruba riverine goddess, Oshun: especially the color yellow and water.

Through the use of imagery broadly associated with the Yoruba goddess Oshun—sweet water (rivers), the color yellow, love, sensuality, sexuality, abundance, and beauty to name a few—Beyoncé's visual album incorporates these iconographic features of Oshun, I argue, with special attention to the ways Oshun and the imagery associated with her support the narrative goals of the album that I understand here to be confronting turmoil, rebirth, transformation, and reconciliation. Further, I read *Lemonade* between Black women authors Ntozake Shange, Jamaica Kincaid, Erna Brodber, and others who also use Afro-Atlantic religion—namely, Lucumí—in their texts to expand possibilities for thinking through what the trials of Black womanhood and exploration of self-defined sexuality can mean and do and whose "artistic creation[s] often act as a conduit for their collective personal and public struggles."[1] For this reason I have chosen to read *Lemonade* intertextually alongside Ntozake Shange's *Sassafrass, Cypress & Indigo* (1982), Jamaica Kincaid's "At the Bottom of the River" (1983), Spike Lee's updated and serialized *She's Gotta Have It* (2017, 2019), Julie Dash's *Daughters of the Dust* (1991), Beyoncé's *Black Is King* (2020) as well as Ifá and Diloggún divination verses and other Yoruba ritual and rhetorical practices that serve as pre-text and intertext for the visual album. Each of these narratives maintains the centrality of Oshun and her iconography as catalysts for positive change on behalf of the protagonists. Finally, I assert that Beyoncé's *Lemonade* does the work of effectively employing the iconography of Afro-Atlantic religion on the global stage in generating a narrative about repossessing herself in the face of external definition, generational trauma, and emotional violence. Here, iconography should be understood denotatively and is applied to the images, symbols, implements, and characteristics broadly associated with Oshun.

What follows is primarily an application of what I term an "Oshun epistemology," which I define as the organization of information, or ways of knowing, embedded in Oshun's "mythistorical archive," to borrow Keith McNeal's term, composed of cosmogonies, oral histories, and ritual practices. I argue that this epistemology can and should be applied theoretically to explicate meaning from cultural and social phenomena and do so here alongside Moyo Okediji's theory and method of "semioptics" to analyze the presence and narrative import of Oshun's iconography and other Yoruba ritual and rhetorical practices in *Lemonade* alongside the other primary narratives mentioned above. This is an empirical study as much as it is a theoretical one concerned with making the layers of Oshun's presence and influence legible. I have chosen *Lemonade* as the central text of analysis given both its timelessness and popularity. While blogs and websites have mentioned Beyoncé's homage to Oshun in *Lemonade,* to date only a few academic writings have addressed the intersection between the visual album and Yoruba textuality inclusive of Oshun, other Orishas, and rhetorical practices like *oríkì* (praise poetry). Omise'eke Tinsley's *Beyoncé in Formation: Remixing Black Feminism* (2018), Kinitra D. Brooks and Kameelah L. Martin's *The Lemonade Reader* (2019), and Christina Baade and Kristin McGee's *Beyoncé in the World: Making Meaning with Queen Bey in Troubled Times* (2021) are three edited volumes that address the Afro-Atlantic religious influences in *Lemonade,* though the edited volumes do not focus exclusively on this topic.

Limitations

While the subjects of this study are Black women, this study is not a feminist or "womanist" study of their subjectivity. With respect to the long genealogy of Black womanist and Black feminist intellectual inquiry, the priority of this study is to excavate Oshun's narrative influence over the protagonists in the narratives I've chosen to analyze. I do not concede that, by virtue of the subjects' femininity or my own, feminist pedagogy is either compulsory or even a more effective tool of analysis given this project's focus on constructs and experiences of womanhood and femininity. While Oshun is often discussed in terms of feminist theory and pedagogy as in the cases of Teresa N. Washington, Diedre Badejo and others, here I do not equate Oshun's feminine archetype, or her intervention of behalf of women characters, as intrinsically feminist in nature. I assert that Oshun's epistemology is both inclusive of and broader than feminism. The contentious debates around Orisha, Oshun in particular, and their representative incorporation into feminist discourse will be discussed in more detail in chapter 2. Similarly, this project is not grounded in ethnomusicology and does not seek to analyze the sonic elements of the album from that perspective. I analyze the sonic and musical elements as they are relevant to the broader exploration of Yoruba iconography and cultural influence.

Given Beyoncé's celebrity, I will also note here that my reading of *Lemonade* is not marked by fandom, despite her immense talent. As an Africana Studies scholar who focuses on Black popular culture, my decision to analyze the visual album has less to do with Beyoncé herself, and more to do with the composite elements that make up the entirety of *Lemonade*, particularly those elements that are informed by Yoruba cultural forms, and the ways in which Beyoncé uses them to manipulate the sacred to "encode, in art and ritual, vital knowledge about meaning, values, epistemologies, and history" for her storytelling purposes.[2] And while I have a distinct reverence for Oshun as a practitioner, this research is anchored in the application of Oshun's religious implements and iconography to *Lemonade* and the other texts. My positionality allows for the excavation of Oshun's elements that are not readily legible to laypersons.

Lucumí, Oshun, and Other Orishas

What follows is a summary of the Lucumí religion, Oshun's attributes relevant to the analysis of the primary texts featured in this book, and other pertinent Orishas and spiritual forces. The summary makes no attempt at being exhaustive, as the history of Lucumí, Oshun's attributes, and their symbolic import across the many geographies of her worship constitute a book-length project of its own. The other Orishas featured in the summary meaningfully interact with Oshun in her stories of origin such that an absence of their description would limit understanding. Further, I have included Orisha who work alongside Oshun, and those whose iconographies are also featured in the texts discussed in the chapters to follow. These summaries appear here to avoid distracting digressions in later analyses.

The term *Lucumí* as it pertains to its current use to refer to the religion and its adherents has its roots in the transatlantic slave trade.[3] Yoruba-speaking people who endured the depravities of the Middle Passage to be disembarked in Cuba referred to one another as "oluku-mi" meaning "my friend."[4] It is important to note that through the term originated among Yoruba-speaking peoples it was applied to non-Yoruba speakers who may have been shipmates, and later those who would become cultural and religious converts. The large influx of Yoruba-speaking people into the Americas via the transatlantic slave trade follows the collapse of the Oyo Empire between 1816 and 1836.[5] Like other ethnic groups imported into Cuba, the Yoruba-speaking population brought not only their language, but also their socioreligious structure given that people from all strata of society were captured.[6] Lucumí is premised upon three Yoruba-derived religious tenets: ancestor veneration,[7] belief in Olodumare as the creator (which is to say, monotheism),[8] and Orisha worship.[9]

In the Lucumí system, it is believed ancestors can intervene on behalf of living family members and are venerated for this reason, but also for their own elevation in the spiritual realm. For this reason, not all ancestors are celebrated, but only those who lived well and returned to Olodumare.[10] While belief in Olodumare is foundational in the religious structure, direct ceremonial worship of Olodumare is not.[11] There are conflicting views as to why this is true. Some are of the opinion that Olodumare is too distant from earth and human interaction as well as too expansive to be comprehended by humans.[12] Others attribute this to the lack of physical shrines dedicated to Olodumare; however, it is important to note that Olodumare is given high praise in Lucumí ceremonies and prayers. Olodumare is omnipotent, omniscient, and the creator of all things including his emissaries, the Orisha.[13] Orisha are benevolent deities that intervene on behalf of human beings and serve as intermediaries between humans and Olodumare.[14] Orisha can be separated into three categories including primordial divinities (Irunmolé), deified ancestors, and personifications of natural forces.[15] Oshun, however, occupies both categories of primordial divinities, as a member of the Irunmolé and personifications of a natural force, fresh water.

Oshun is simultaneously one of the most popular Yoruba Orishas and one of the most mysterious, and perhaps the most written about. With festivals in her honor from Ọṣogbo to Salvador, Philadelphia, Havana, Miami, and New York, Oshun is celebrated and worshipped widely, likely contributing to academic interest in the Orisha and her practitioners throughout the Yoruba diaspora. Here I will discuss Oshun's popular iconographic and symbolic associations, placing particular emphasis on the ones that anchor my broader analysis of the visual album: water, the colors yellow and gold, honey, sweetness, and her ritual dance.

Oshun is a primordial Orisha, sent to earth by Olodumare to aid in the creation of the human world alongside sixteen other Orisha referred to as the Irunmolé. The *odù* (divination verse) that tells the story of Oshun's participation, or lack thereof, is Ọ̀ṣẹ́túrá, which explains in short that "without female participation, the whole life cycle is arrested."[16] Though the contents of this odù will be discussed at length in chapter 2, it is important to note that Oshun's presence at the time of creation informs her significance among the pantheon of the Orishas, and the cautionary tale of her exclusion provided by Ọ̀ṣẹ́túrá solidifies it. Additionally, though Obatala is credited with sculpting the human form, this, too, would have been impossible without Oshun's waters to soften the clay.[17] Oral histories suggest that Oshun originally resided in the ocean with her sister (also seen as mother) Yemaya, ruler of all water, but eventually grew tired of the ocean. Consequently, Yemaya furnished her sister with a river of her own in which to dwell.[18] It is worth noting that Yemaya and Oshun are considered sisters because of their similarities, though there are many differences between them. One difference worth noting is that Yemaya is generally considered motherly and more conservative than Oshun. Although they have similar ritual implements, Yemaya's are typically cast in silver or stainless steel whereas Oshun's are cast in brass. The collective work of the sister goddesses is explored in detail in chapter 4. It is with the cosmological development of Oshun's departure from the sea that she becomes associated with sweet (fresh) waters and the sweetness/pleasures of life, love, sex, and abundance, and Yemaya becomes associated with the ocean and, for Africans in the diaspora, the Middle Passage. While pleasure is absolutely Oshun's domain, it is not her only domain as she is also associated with social organization and is a formidable warrior on behalf of herself and her children. Though at times Oshun is associated with the extremity of pleasure, even vice, she is more accurately described as the balance of fortune and misfortune, seeing the good that can and may come from a seemingly bad situation, or colloquially, "turning lemons into lemonade."

The colors associated with Oshun are yellow, amber, shades of gold, and orange. Oshun's number is five as well as multiples of five. Following the proverb in the epigraph, the fifth day is the divination day. Oshun is closely associated with divination because of her marriage to Orunmila, the Orisha of divination. Though Orunmila is associated with Ifá, Oshun is associated with Diloggún, a sixteen-cowrie-shell divination system made up of the first twelve odùs of Ifá, which has sixteen odùs and their combinations totaling 256 possible divinatory outcomes.[19] Historically, it has been argued that Orunmila brought the wisdom of Ifá from heaven to earth, but Wande Abimbola argues that the odùs reflect that it was Oshun, not Orunmila, and that Diloggún precedes Ifá.[20] This is significant given that Diloggún is "said to be less complex than Ifá divination and less revered among the Yorùbá in West Africa but more esteemed than Ifá in the Americas, where it is ubiquitous and more often used," making Abimbola's assertion controversial among those who are gender-biased in their interpretation of the interplay between Oshun and Orunmila as well as their interpretation of ritual which can be exclusionary to women.[21] Diloggún's priority in Lucumí and Candomblé (its Brazilian counterpart) "may [also] be explained by its relative simplicity; the popularity of Ṣango, Yemọjá, Ọṣun, and other òrìṣas with whom the sixteen cowries is associated; and that it can be practiced by both men and women."[22] While views on this vary by geographical location of practitioners, it is important to note that in Lucumí and Candomblé alike, "Ifá divination [is] considered the purview of men," and these religious practices are predominated by women that necessitated the development of a divination system that could be used equitably.[23]

Oshun's primary tools or implements are those of water, mirror, and fan. Water serves as her abode, an elixir with which she can cure the ill, and path by which she can guide her wards to safety. Alone, water can be used to cool a fever and in conjunction with another one of her tools, honey, that can cure other illnesses as well. As mentioned in Robert Farris Thompson's article "Orchestrating Water and the Wind: Oshun's Art in Atlantic Context," Oshun "cures without fee, she gives the honeyed water to the child."[24] There are many *patakís* (oral histories of the Lucumí religion) that tell of Oshun's ability to both guide her devotees home, if that is where safety resides, or to a new place of founding where safety can be established.[25] These patakís will be discussed in full detail where they are necessary to flesh out the analysis of Oshun's use of water to intervene in or even stabilize the lives of her devotees, as well as the characters explored in the following chapters, but it is important to introduce water as both abode and ritual implement here. Additionally, mirrors are important tools for Oshun. On the surface, they represent her vanity, but given a second look, mirrors also signify Oshun's ability to help her devotees see themselves or healthily (re)construct their self-images.[26] Symbolically, reflections, or doubling, then become an important feature of Oshun's analytical framework. This is especially true given her cosmological birth of twins, Orisha Ibeji. Finally, her fan is as much an accessory/status symbol as it is a tool to cool herself and disputes. Oshun's complexity is reflected in both the breadth and depth of her domain as well as her relationships with other Orishas.

Elegba is also well represented in literature regarding African diasporic spiritual and cultural practices. Elegba is enigmatic as the guardian of the crossroad and divine messenger of the Orishas.[27] He is often characterized as a trickster, but he would be more accurately described as test/catalyst. Elegba holds people accountable by testing or tricking them, and quite often, the test is a catalyst for dispensing with behaviors or habits that no longer serve peoples' best interests or have become dangerous. Elegba shares many interesting relationships with Oshun. For one, Ọṣẹ́túrá suggests that he is Oshun's son, born to restore balance to the world.[28] In another pataki, Elegba uses his divine trickery to hold Oshun accountable to a promise she made to marry the first suitor to bring her a nine-tailed monkey.[29] Presenting his gift to her as a vagabond, he challenged her fidelity to the promise, which she kept.[30] Others suggest that he was simply a good helper and protector of Oshun. Elegba's colors are red and black, and his number is three.

Shango, warrior-king of Oyo, is the thunder god. Shango is one of few Orishas who is believed to have lived a human life and then became a deified ancestor. Shango's origin story informs his ritual iconography. The story goes that "Shàngó was recklessly experimenting with a leaf that had the power to bring down lightning from the skies and inadvertently caused the roof of the palace of Oyo to be set afire by lightning. . . . Half crazed with grief and guilt, Shàngó went to a spot outside his royal capital and hanged himself from the branches of an ayan tree. He thus suffered the consequences of playing arrogantly with God's fire, and became lightning itself."[31] Indicative of his intimate relationship with fire, thunder, and lightning, Shango's colors are red and white, his number is six, and he is widely represented by the double-sided axe.[32] Though Shango has three principles wives, Oba, Oya, and Oshun, patakís differ between which he favors, though many suggest it is Oshun. Oshun and Shango's passionate relationship produced the divine twins, Ibeji.

Oya, the whirlwind, mother of mystery and sudden change is also one of Shango's wives, making her a sister-wife of Oshun.[33] In Orisha lore, she and Oshun compete to be Shango's favorite wife. Like Shango, she fights with thunderbolts and is also said to have the ability to breathe fire.[34] Despite her association with the whirlwind and storms, Oya is still considered a riverine goddess in Nigeria, but lives at the cemetery gates in the Americas underscoring her critical role in escorting *egun* (ancestors) to the afterlife.[35] It should be noted here that egun are essential to the Lucumí tradition, and bloodline ancestors are often considered the first line of defense for any practitioner, as they are able to intervene quickly on their behalf if they are venerated regularly, not just in times of trouble. Little is written about Oya in the academic discourse of Yoruba religions in the New World, which I attribute to her characteristic mystery. Her name meaning, "She tore," underscores the quickness of her intervention and the severity of the change that she implements. Oya's number is nine, and she is associated with both maroon and multicolor based on her relationship with egun.[36]

Aganju, whose name means "Wilderness or uninhabited plain or forest," is represented by the molten magma of a volcano.[37] Aganju has a close relationship with Shango and in many cases he is characterized as Shango's father, but other patakís characterize Shango as Aganju's uncle.[38] Some patakís indicate that because of Aganju's relationship union with Oshun, he was elevated to the status of Orisha.[39] Though Aganju is one of the more obscure Orisha's, his relationship with Oshun is one aspect of his lore that has been well documented.

Finally, Ajogun are considered "purveyors of doom—death, disease, destruction and loss."[40] I refer to Ajogun here because misfortune in Yoruba and subsequently Lucumí traditions is characterized as spiritual imbalance or, in worse cases, malevolent attack from the Ajogun. Here, I characterize the hardship of the characters analyzed in the following chapters as Ajogun activity. Interestingly enough, "Ọṣun is believed to have a soothing effect on [Ajogun] so that they can benefit humankind."[41] For example, death, particularly young or unexpected deaths are considered an attack of ikú (death). However, death is necessary for the burgeoning of new beginnings, for which Oshun is famous. Since Elegba is the leader of the Ajogun, Oshun's ability to soften them is due in part to her close relationship with him as well as her cooling fan and soothing waters.[42] Other Ajogun include

Àrùn (Disease), Ẹ̀gbà (Paralysis), Ọ̀ràn (Serious Trouble), and perhaps most importantly here, Òfò (Loss) and Èpè (Curse).[43]

Other Yellow Things: Yoruba Tricolor Chromacy

Like Western conceptions of primary colors, Yoruba culture traditionally recognizes three colors and their gradations, but Yoruba culture differs in its classification of what it considers primary colors: *dúdú* (black), *funfun* (white), and *pupa* (red). *Dúdú*, which is black or any color similarly deep in hue like navy blue and purple in the Yoruba cultural understanding, represents a host of symbolic meanings depending on the context, varying from mystery and the occult to unpredictability.[44] The color perhaps most universally signifies "profound depths," particularly those of water that is conceptually significant given *Lemonade*'s use of water as a narrative guide.[45] Babatunde Lawal defines the sociocultural as well as the ritual import of funfun, writing that "[p]ure white is associated with transparency, light, the sky, especially the cirrus and cumulus clouds (*ikùkù*). Hence the color signifies the celestial and sublime, indirectly connecting humanity with Olódùmarè [the supreme God]."[46] Yoruba conceptual understandings of funfun undergird my analysis of the color white's visual significance throughout the film in lighting and staging, but also in costuming. Last, pupa, "in general, refers to the vitality that the blood-stream generates in the body," or the power to bring things into fruition.[47] While red has its own place in the production of the visual album, pupa is perhaps the most important of the three given that the colors yellow and gold are considered secondary colors categorized under pupa and the symbolic meanings associated with it. Additionally, yellow's titular significance is anchored in the color's ritual iconographic association with Oshun.

One patakí details the complicated relationship with the color yellow. The story goes that:

> Oshún was a very beautiful woman. She wore the finest dresses. Golden bracelets jangled at her wrists. A mirror was always in her hand so she could admire herself.... One day, Oshún arrived at a güemilere [ceremonial drumming]. The drummer was a big man. Sweat rolled down his muscled arms as he coaxed screams and moans of passion from the other drummers. "Who is that?" asked Oshún. "That is Shangó," she was told.... Oshún chased after Shangó. She gave him gifts. She cooked for him. She sang for him. She made Shangó fall in

love with her. They became the perfect lovers. . . . The sad thing is that nothing lasts. The perfect romance ended in bitter fights. Shangó and Oshún went their separate ways. Shangó's life changed for the worse. He lost all of his wealth. . . . One day, Oshún asked her friends, "How is Shangó? I haven't seen him in a very long time." Her friends told her, "Shangó is sleeping in the gutter." A spark of love flared to a flame in her heart. "I must go to him," said Oshún. "I will show him one person still cares for him." Oshun sold her dresses and bracelets. She sold her pumpkin fields. She took the money to Shangó and said, "[T]his is for you. . . ." When all of Shango's debts were paid and all his enemies pacified, there was no money left. Oshún and Shangó lived in a small shack. They were so poor that Oshún only had one dress. She wore it every day and washed it every night. The dress lost all of its color and became a yellowish rag. This is why Oshún's "children," her devotees, wear yellow clothing.[48]

Though the details of the pataki can and often do vary, as oral histories do, one consistency is that Oshun experiences hardship and that a dress of hers (usually white) eventually turns yellow due to frequent washing. Though Lydia Cabrera also records the story in the inverse, that a yellow dress became white, yellow maintains its centrality and association with Oshun.[49] Aside from the broader symbolic meaning associated with pupa, yellow takes on additional symbolic meaning in relationship to Oshun. Because of the precarity of her situation, yellow is ritually understood to remind Oshun of hardship and is therefore a taboo for many of her devotees. Although the dress is the focal point in the pataki, it is only one of many *things* that associate yellow with the deity. Despite the Orisha's tenuous relationship with the color, the majority of *elekes* (beaded necklaces consecrated to Orishas) made for Oshun incorporate yellow (if sparingly) alongside amber, other yellowish colors, as well as highlights of green, coral, orange, red, and, less commonly, blue, depending on the specific needs of the road/path of Oshun being represented. Elekes iconographically associate practitioners with the Lucumí religion, but specifically associate them with the Orisha's eleke that they may be wearing, yellow exclusively representing Oshun. Other jewelry items including the golden bracelets referenced in the pataki, which are also associated with Oshun's initiated devotees, are typically yellow gold or brass, which the Yoruba consider one of the most precious metals. It is worth noting that the use of brass precedes the use of gold in making tools for Oshun, and that gold is still used quite sparingly given its costs.

Other implements for Oshun, like the mirror, or fan, are also fashioned out of brass adhering closely to cosmogonic and ritual import of yellow and yellow things in honoring her.[50] The use of other metallic variants associated with other Orishas because of their color can also be evidenced in the case of Obatala, whose principle color is funfun, consequently his implements are made of lead or silver, which is also considered white in Yoruba tricolor chromacy, and copper in the case of Oya whose principle color is maroon, both of which are considered pupa for the redness of its hue.[51]

Another yellow *thing* that is salient to the analysis of Oshun's visual and conceptual influence in *Lemonade* is honey. The color of honey operates on one symbolic level since it is in the yellow "family," though closer to the warmth of amber. Additionally, the substance is used by Oshun in many of her patakís to win over her adversary or prevail in a difficult situation. In her case, "honey is the knife," and can on one hand be a healing salve, and on the other a formidable weapon.[52] It is used in both supplication and in battle as evidenced by the following oríkì (praise poetry), "*Yeye moro oyin, a be iwa oyin* (Mother knows the tradition of honey) / *Oyin a bẹ̀*. (We beg [the goddess] with honey)."[53] As Robert Farris Thompson argues, the second line of the oríkì can also be "*Oyin a bẹ́*." (With honey we cut [through danger]).[54] Decades before Moyo Okediji's theory of semioptics regarding the spatial organization of individual characters, or, "language as semioptic text," Thompson engages the linguistic complexity of tonality in Yoruba language that must be translated through the specific arrangement of diacritical marks to assign proper meaning.[55] Hence, arrangement of *bẹ̀* and *bẹ́* presents a semioptic crossroad between the verbal (aural) and visual (textual), as well as the historical and cultural as far as oríkì is concerned. Given its material application, honey has come to represent the sweetness that Oshun brings into the world and the lives of her devotees, particularly after hardship, with which she is intimately familiar, as well as a tool that she uses to protect and defend them. This understanding of honey's ritual and symbolic import anchors my use of it as an analytical tool to think through Oshun's interventions on behalf of Beyoncé, Nola Darling (the protagonist of *She's Gotta Have It*), and Sassafrass.

Yellow *things* will emerge as focal points of analysis throughout the book, employing an object-oriented method of autoethnography.[56] While autoethnographic methods of analysis will be discussed in detail in the next section, it is important to preface why I have committed to referring to these items as "things," and analyze them as such in the chapters that follow. In her article "Autoethnography as Object-Oriented Method," Desireé D.

Rowe asserts that object have the capacity, or power, to deepen the practice of reflexivity in autoethnographic storytelling.[57] Rowe writes that "[a]n object-oriented autoethnography allows for a broader sense of the multiple critical trajectories that are possible within a single, tangible, *thing*."[58] My analysis of *Lemonade* is as much an analysis of the entirety of the project as it is an analysis of the *things* that make up the whole, including lemonade itself as an autoethnographic reference to the wisdom of her grandmother on behalf of Beyoncé. I would argue that the eponymous drink frames the significance of *things* in the visual album, many of them yellow, and the various "critical trajectories" that are housed in their "thingness."[59]

Methods, Perspectives, and Positionality

While I did not initially intend for this project to be constructed as autoethnographic, it has certainly emerged as an autoethnography twofold. First, in lieu of interpreting and analyzing *Lemonade* as an autobiography, I have decided that autoethnography is ultimately more apropos description of the visual album given its commitment to "social, cultural *and* personal narrative truth."[60] As James B. Haile III writes, "[A]utoethnography situates individuals within a specific historical and cultural context out of which they generate their theories and their concepts, which troubles the very idea that a theory is either particular or universal, in the absolute individual sense, but reflexive of concomitant knowledge forms."[61] Beyoncé does that work in *Lemonade* by constructing a narrative that specifies her individual historical and cultural context. With her matri-focused incorporation of New Orleans both in the contemporary moment and as a place that has been experienced differently by at least the two generations that precede her, Beyoncé frames her conceptual ways of knowing as contextually specific notwithstanding the possibility of generalization given the relatability of the content. Robin M. Boylorn addresses this in her article "Bitter Sweet(Water): Autoethnography, Relational Ethics, and the Possible Perpetuation of Stereotypes," writing that "Blackgirl autoethnography is blackened, in that it centers and makes claims about particular, but shared, experiences of women of color, but it also troubles traditional (white, male, heterosexual) ways of knowing and being in the world by embracing the tenets of autoethnography which resist singular representations of experience of research. Blackgirl autoethnography also embraces the impulse to critique, theorize, and analyze our lives as we live and reflect on them."[62] *Lemonade*, then, is one long exercise in analytical reflexivity as Beyoncé eschews "traditional" ways of knowing in lieu of Yoruba/New Orleanian diasporic ones to analyze the difficulty in her life and marriage, as well as make sense of the heritability of trauma or generational curses through critical exploration of her foremothers' relationships to their respective spouses, but especially her own mother and father.

My choice to read *Lemonade* as autoethnographic is rooted in Beyoncé and Jay-Z's own transparency after the album's release regarding their marital difficulties, as well as what would become a trilogy of albums offering listeners and fans a snapshot of their lives: *Lemonade, 4:44* (2017) by Jay-Z, and finally *Everything Is Love* (2018), which is a joint album between the two that closes the proverbial book on that chapter of their lives together. In an interview with Dean Baquet of the *New York Times*, Jay-Z is quoted as saying, "[I]t just felt like she should go first and she should share her truths with the world."[63] As is characteristic of Beyoncé, who is incredibly private, she has said little more than what the albums do about her "truths" or their relationship, other than in her acceptance speech for best urban contemporary album where she states plainly that is was her intention "to create a body of work that would give a voice to our pain, our struggles, our darkness and our history."[64] Conversely, her husband did a series of interviews after the release of *4:44* to clarify the album's meaning in relationship to *Lemonade* and consequently shed some additional light on *Lemonade* itself. Other features of the visual album that lent themselves to an autoethnographic interpretation are the incorporation of images and videos from Beyoncé's youth, her own parents, stepfather, grandmother, daughter, and husband in lieu of actors and actresses. Consequently, it might also be helpful to consider *Lemonade* "biomythography" given that "the album's 'truths' are not the verifiable truth of the conventional memoir."[65] The autoethnographic and biomythographic complexity of the visual album require that Beyoncé be read as a character in the narrative produced by *Lemonade*—that is, informed by her person. Additionally, her incorporation footage that is quite intimate, of herself and her family, further anchors the album's construction of a specific sociocultural and historical context from which to analyze the broader condition of women with whom she shares community and similarity of condition, even considering the nature of her superstardom that places a considerable (but not insurmountable) distance between her and most other Black women. *Lemonade* leans on the similarity, which in Boylorn's words is "blackgirlness," or the very humanity of Black women who share two identities that construct them as vulnerable in two directions.

Second, this book unexpectedly became an exercise of autoethnography for me. While I always intended to lead out with my negotiation of insider/outsider, or practitioner/scholar, I did not see the issue of positionality being an issue of method but an issue of perspective, but in many ways, it has become both. First, I do not posture at objectivity and distance from my research, as my practice of Lucumí informs much of the symbolic legibility that makes this kind of analysis of *Lemonade* and, by extension, this book, possible. Much of my task has been identifying embodied knowledge in the context of the visual album, as well as anchoring my own embodied knowledge in the existing academic discourses about the cultural influences of the Yoruba diaspora. I have been careful not to generalize my experience while valuing what my experience brings to the research, including informing where I have chosen to look for information. It has also informed the ways in which I have characterized Lucumí, its practitioners, as well as Oshun and her multitudinous nature, some of which I have attempted to capture here. In writing this, I have led with my responsibility to my religious community to maintain fidelity to our traditions in my academic pursuits, which also means not sharing quite a bit of information for public consumption. In short, I have valued the method and practice of reflexivity that accompanies the proper implementation of autoethnography. Though this book is largely executed through semioptic analysis video and text (as opposed to an ethnographic field study of a group), it locates me as simultaneously inside and outside the texts, and inside and outside Lucumí, which houses the conceptual framework and many of the theoretical tools deployed here. My autoethnographic priority, and academic intervention, is to move seamlessly between praxis and theory in analyzing the cultural and textual phenomena outlined here.

Finally, semioptics, as defined and coined by Moyo Okediji, is "hybridized from 'semeion' and 'optics,' as meaning and vision: it is a 'cultural crossroads' theory. It emanates from a theoretically diasporic discussion of cultures raised in terms of physical or allegorical borders of disciplines, geography, time, and other experiential or conceptual crossing. It measures the borderlines of objects as they display cultural travels and overlaps; as multisectional products and processes; as arterial networks of commercial and aesthetic connections and crossovers."[66] I have chosen to employ semioptics in lieu of semiotics because of semioptics' own intertextuality with the Yoruba visual and rhetorical practices detailed in the next section, as well as such visual and rhetorical practices in *Lemonade, Daughters of the Dust, She's Gotta Have It, Black Is King,* Jamaica Kincaid's "At the Bottom of the River," Ntozake Shange's *Sassafrass, Cypress & Indigo,* and Ibeyi's video for their song "River" (2015). Moyo Okediji, an art historian and visual artist of Yoruba descent, embeds Yoruba conceptual understandings of space as well as interactions between things and people in the four elements of the semioptic system, which he states are Spectrum, Spectator, Speculation, and Spectacle.[67] "Spectrum" "refers to the visible stimuli that trigger the semioptic process."[68] "Spectator" refers to the viewer, and "speculation" "refers to the intellectual process of exclusion and inclusion, reduction and addition, by which the mind constructs a meaning out of what is observed."[69] Finally, "spectacle" "refers to the cognition or recognition—or lack thereof—of the observed spectrum as particular object(s)."[70] The elements of semioptics connect directly with Babatunde Lawal's conception of àwòrán (a representation or spectrum), awòran (beholder or spectator), and ìran (spectacle).[71] In many ways, these terms are synonymous. The difference lies in the use of the term "spectacle" (ìran), where Okediji refers to an intellectual process of observation, Lawal on the other hand asserts that spectacle is when the spectator becomes the spectrum by virtue of speculation.[72] Both are efficacious in their application and deeply inform my own speculation of the aforementioned texts, particularly regarding their concern with the visible and invisible.[73] I use their conceptual understandings of the relationship between art and viewer to explore the layers of symbolic legibility in the various texts, some visible, some invisible without explication analysis.

Okediji's concept of semioptics and Lawal's interpretation of the spectrum that exists between spectator and spectacle also plays nicely with Kimberly W. Benston's analysis of African American drama as a transformational process "from mimesis, the representation of actions, to methexis, the communal 'helping out' of the action by all assembled."[74] Taking the three together builds a theoretical and figurative bridge between continental African and diasporic understandings of the culturally ties that bind the specific phenomenon of Black performance. Beyoncé's own intent for her project to give voice to "*our*" collective experiences, not just her own, evidences her own transition from mimesis to methexis in an attempt to "help out" Black women whose stories are often relegated to the margins by producing a "healing text" that "offers a space for her audience to heal through their identification with the presented themes."[75] About this process, Cheryl Sterling remarks that the "binaries of actor and spectator, self and other, public and private dissolve to generate a shared consciousness, common moorings (or referents) for the spectators."[76] Perhaps more importantly, Benston describes this transformation as both spiritual and technical capturing the distinct features of *Lemonade* (as well as the other texts) that make its iconographic adoption of Lucumí ways of knowing and meaning-making salient to Beyoncé's transformation, but also the transformation of the millions of spectators it touched and moved.[77] My task and intervention then, is to make the iconographic adoptions of Lucumí in *Lemonade* apparent and analyze them through the multivalent theoretical lenses established by Okediji, Lawal, and Benston.

Ante-texts and (Inter)textuality: Yoruba Ritual and Rhetorical Practices

One of the central components of the argument that anchors this project is that *Lemonade* and its intertexts participate in incorporations of Yoruba religious and cultural concepts including Oshun's iconography. I read these iconographic adoptions as instances of intertextuality with other Yoruba cultural and rhetorical practices, primarily ẹ̀tò (progress) and àlàfíà (peace/health). It is important to note that àlàfíà is complete or total, meaning that any disruptions should be immediately redressed individually, socially, or ritually, although these methods are not mutually exclusive.[78] These disruptions are typically addressed twofold: first with divination to clearly identify the source of the imbalance: and then with ẹbọ (sacrifice, offering, or plea to Orishas to intercede on your behalf). While I maintain that *Lemonade*'s narrative structure is nonlinear, there is an attention to sequence and forward progression toward healing that follows Yoruba narrative form in verbal and visual artistic production. Margaret and Henry Drewal explore constructions of seriality, time, and space extensively, writing that "a unit in a series is *eto*, an orderly arrangement of things, from which derives the adverb *leeto-leeto*, implying in an orderly fashion, one after the other."[79] It is worth noting that ẹ̀tò and àlàfíà are not divorced from divinatory practices, as the general purpose for seeking divination is for seeking health, or the restoration of balance. On this, the Drewals write, "In Ijẹbu, a diviner explains individual ritual stages as *aito*, which he links with the term *eto*."[80] In this case, both ẹ̀tò and aito are textually relevant as *Lemonade* has discretely situated chapters, or units, that are complete within themselves but also contribute the forward progression of the broader narrative. I read *Lemonade*'s stages as ritual ones simultaneously, as Beyoncé's (the character, and perhaps the woman) preoccupation with healing, or àlàfíà, is also a preoccupation with breaking a (intergenerational) curse that plagues not just herself but also her immediate family. Beyoncé's own references to magic (as in sleight of hand and illusion, also supernatural influence) in conjunction with the adoption of Oshun's iconographic elements characterizes healing as a ritual process, with a proscribed order, that ultimately concludes with an initiation of its own. In lieu of an initiation to an Orisha, or a cult, I assert that Beyoncé is initiated into a new version of herself that is equipped to break the curses she inherited.

The issue of seriality, or chronology, both within the text and without also shares intertextuality with ìran (spectacle), another Yoruba rhetorical device that anchors *Lemonade*'s narrative and visual structure. "In the Yoruba concept of spectacle (*ìran*) each diachronic unit of the whole is composed of a series of discrete, synchronic elements. More importantly, these synchronic elements convey disparate ideas or meanings so that, within each unit of the whole, there are connected referents. Each unit itself becomes multifaceted or multifocal."[81] This is similarly true of *Lemonade* as each of the twelve chapters are multifaceted and multifocal, engaging poetry and monologue, music, and dance or other forms of movement that add discursive layers unique to each unit and still connect to the external referent, which in this case is Beyoncé's character in the visual album.

Summary of Chapters

In chapter 1, "When Life Gives You Lemons, Add Honey," I argue that the protagonists choose, or are chosen, to take (re)possession of themselves through the guidance of Oshun, and further, I seek to examine how these characters move from victimhood to healing through the influence of Oshun alongside other Lucumí-derived rituals. Moving away from reinscribing narratives of Black women's suffering for suffering's sake, this chapter is interested in how triumph and self-actualization are achieved in the face of a world that often relies on and perpetuates the subjection of Black women. Focusing primarily on *Lemonade* and Beyoncé, Nola's and Sassafrass's narratives are woven into the chapter to allow for the exploration of Oshun's iconographic influence across three different mediums and allow the intertextuality of Oshun's daughters to emerge.[82]

Chapter 2, "Don't Hurt Yourself: Odù Ọ̀ṣẹ́túrá as a Method for Analyzing Fault, Retribution, and Accountability," addresses the Odù Ọ̀ṣẹ́túrá and its analytical implications as it concerns Oshun's hierarchical and social positioning among the Irunmolé (the first seventeen Orishas to descend from heaven to earth), exclusion, and social justice. I employ Odù Ọ̀ṣẹ́túrá to excavate and analyze the ways in which it operates as both guide and method for seeking corrective measures in instances of gender-based (and nongender-based) exclusion or maltreatment. The Odù Òṣẹ́túrá tells the tale of Oshun's own exclusion in making important decisions regarding the development of the world. As the only feminine energy in the Irunmolé, Oshun is not consulted, and consequently the plans fail. Following the lyrics of Beyoncé's song "Don't Hurt Yourself," this chapter applies this *odù* to examine the ways in which hurting and excluding women, hurts everyone. Further, it argues that, as in the case of the odù, Beyoncé constructs a narrative where both accountability and amends are required for stasis (or àlàfíà) to be restored. Linking the developmental stages of *Lemonade* to the conceptual understandings of fair treatment for women specifically and Black people broadly, this chapter explores the ways in which Beyoncé seeks retribution, holds transgressors accountable, and determines what amends are made before forgiveness is conferred and stasis restored.

Chapter 3, "Water Always Returns to Its Source: Oshun's Medium as Guiding Principle in Narratives of Healing," draws on water as a foundational element to analyze the imagery of *Lemonade* and Julie Dash's seminal film *Daughters of the Dust* alongside Jamaica Kincaid's short story "At the Bottom of the River." Though water baptism, ritual cleaning, and initiation, are not exclusive to the Lucumí system, water being Oshun's primary element carries specific weight as it pertains to the structure of the respective narratives. I assert that the protagonists' respective quests for personal, generational, and even social healing are not only based on submersion in water but also guided and punctuated by water. This chapter examines how integral a role water plays in the rebirth of women characters after the experience of trauma. It begs the question, What can be found at the bottom of the river? Using the creative work of Kincaid alongside the analysis of Beyoncé, and an analysis of Yellow Mary and Eula Peazant's characters in *Daughters of the Dust,* I argue that not only is pain and suffering washed away in Oshun's waters, but also that the appearance of water in each narrative signifies beginnings, significant transitions, and ends, and therefore represents both a departure and a return: a departure from turmoil and a return to the self. Finally, I assert that Oshun can be found at varying locations in the river, including most prominently the bottom, but also that the weight associated with strife can be found and must be left at the bottom of the river for the characters to become light enough to float, or return to the surface leaving their burden behind.

Chapter 4, "Honey in the Hive: Oshun and Yemaya in Celebration of the

Black Feminine," explores the continuation of Oshun's iconographic presence in Beyoncé's cultural contributions beyond *Lemonade*. Just as Oshun represents both the bitter and sweet elements of life, this chapter seeks to analyze the importance of divine feminine archetype in celebration of the sweetness of womanhood as well as their necessity for social order. This chapter engages the complex interplay between Oshun and Yemaya, and Vodoun *lwa* Erzulie-Freda in the construction of wholistic divine feminine archetypes. Focusing on Beyoncé's "Black Parade" (2019), *Black Is King* (2020) as well as season 2 (2019) of *She's Gotta Have It*, I argue that these women characters embody Oshun in times of triumph and to do the necessary work to pay the blessing of healing forward. This analysis is driven by the assertion that in health and happiness these characters seek to embody and extend the elements of Oshun that helped them on their own journeys to the community to spread the love.

The conclusion, titled "Reflections," includes both a synthesis of my findings, relevant connections to events that occurred in the wake of *Lemonade*, as well as suggestions for ways in which the field of African Diaspora Studies can incorporate Afro-Atlantic religion beyond its cultural influences, and perhaps incorporate its utility for reconceptualizing and intervening in Black material realities, especially those of Black women. Finally, I suggest ways in which academic interventions can be made in diasporic debates regarding the capacity for the internet and social media to create linkages, mediums of exchange or shift power dynamics between practitioners. This is particularly true as African Americans' participation in Yoruba spiritual practice has become both more popular and visible as compared with Afro-Cuban and Afro-Brazilian populations, focusing special attention to the unique ways in which American Black people contribute to maintaining and expanding the Yoruba cultural diaspora.

A Note on Orthography

This study moves geographically and linguistically between Nigeria, Cuba, and the United States. Consequently, the spellings vary between anglicized, spanglicized, and contemporary Yoruba spellings of terms, and place-names. Where terms are spelled with "sh" in the anglicized or "ch" in the spanglicized, it replaces the "ṣ" sound in Yoruba. Because the study is anchored primarily by Lucumí as it is practiced in the United States, the author uses common Lucumí spellings used by English-speaking practitioners of the religious tradition when referring to Orisha, Lucumí ceremonial elements, implements, and regalia. Where terms, concepts, and ideas are quoted, original use of tonal marks are reproduced and consistent throughout. Names of authors are consistent with the tonal marks of the original publication being cited.

1

When Life Gives You Lemons, Add Honey

I'ma reign, I'ma rain on this bitter love. Tell the sweet I'm new
—Beyoncé Knowles-Carter, "Freedom"

Bitter Love: Locating Black Women's Suffering

While Beyoncé, Nola, and Sassafrass are all forced into contact with Oshun through some form of suffering, the trespasses against these women serve as catalysts for them to seek and achieve healing. In this chapter I argue that they choose, or are chosen, to take (re)possession of themselves through the guidance of Oshun, and, further, I seek to examine how these characters move from victimhood to healing through the influence of Oshun alongside other Lucumí rituals. Moving away from reinscribing narratives of Black women's suffering, for suffering's sake, this chapter is interested in how triumph and self-actualization are achieved in the face of a world that often relies on and perpetuates the subjection of Black women. Focusing primarily on *Lemonade* and Beyoncé, Nola and Sassafrass are woven in to allow for the exploration of Oshun's iconographic influence across three different mediums that allow the intertextuality of Oshun's daughters to emerge.

Lemonade, opens with the sound of "underwater thumping" and a quick tight shot of Beyoncé's profile, slightly obscured by the grandeur of her fur sleeve, the still of which was used for the cover art of the album.[1] Her iconic honey blond hair is braided in long cornrows as she leans on a vehicle, which cannot be made out, in the Royal Parking Garage located in New Orleans' Central Business District.[2] The camera moves quickly from the decidedly urban setting of the parking structure toward the pastoral scenes of Louisiana's Fort Macomb.[3] Beyoncé's vocals, sounding very much like a woman struggling to breathe, or waiting to exhale, seem to glide in as the camera takes us to a staged Beyoncé in front of heavy red curtains, facing the audience. Dressed in all black as if in mourning, Beyoncé is kneeling in prayer. While the clothing itself is contemporary—a head wrap and half-zipped hoodie over a dress or what closely resembles a tiered flamenco skirt—it follows closely the broader visual connection to Victorian women's aesthetics throughout the film. Additionally, the color black, or dúdú, in the Yoruba cultural understanding represents a host of symbolic meanings depending on the context varying from mystery and the occult to unpredictability.[4] The color perhaps most universally signifies "profound depths."[5] Both Victorian and Yoruba conceptual understandings of colors, their symbolic meaning, and attachment to ritual take import throughout the duration of the visual album. The debut song of the visual album, "Pray You Catch Me," begins to detail a woman in confrontation with both herself and an unfaithful and dishonest spouse. After the completion the first verse, the music fades out into the ambient noise of Louisiana—leaves blowing in the breeze, crickets chirping—while the camera pans from the stage, changes from full color to black and white, and captures two women whose faces are obscured, dressed in Victorian dresses. The camera cuts quickly to a yard, filmed from the roots of a tree. In the background lies what is likely an outhouse on the grounds of the Madewood Plantation House as the word "Intuition" appears on the screen to announce and punctuate the adapted work of Kenyan-Somali-British poet Warsan Shire.[6]

Madewood Plantation serves as an important setting in the narrative of the visual album as it recalls the ancestral nature of the work itself by implying the presence of the many Black people who would have occupied that space under enslavement and therefore serves as an appropriate location to collapse time, expel ghosts of the past, unpack the trauma of the present, and lay a foundation for a brighter future. In using the plantation as the backdrop of the film Beyoncé recasts "the conventional narrative of the plantation as a site of pain and sadness . . . [and] presents this historical space as one of rebirth and Black feminist communion."[7] On the one hand, the plantation is and has been characterized as the setting for scenes of subjection and subjectivity, but Katherine McKittrick's cartography provides a useful remapping of plantation as places to be explored as sites of Black meaning-making, joy, and pleasure that inform the present of Black Americans today and the futures of enslaved Black people then, despite the inhumane conditions of enslavement.[8] This recasting of the plantation is further underscored by the wardrobe choices that place an array of Black women in the finest Victorian-era clothing, which their forbears would not have had access to, reclaiming the fashion antebellum period in the present to pay homage to the past.

The word "Intuition" gives language to the embodied knowledge that women often have drawn on in times both good and bad, but here, addresses an inexplicable "knowing" in relationships with men uninterested in fidelity. It also draws on the long history of "women who know things" in a spiritual sense, making intuition also an out-of-body experience of embodied knowledge that often comes in the form of dreams (both waking and sleeping) and in real time.[9] The camera gradually pans from a hooded Beyoncé in tall grass to an assemblage of women donning Victorian dresses staged in different locations at the Madewood Plantation House, as the singer gracefully recites, "I tried to make a home out of you but doors lead to trap doors, a stairway leads to nothing. Unknown women wander the hallways at night."[10] In speaking truth to herself and her unfaithful partner, Beyoncé, the performer and the character she constructed to reflect autoethnographic events, locates the source of her suffering and the suffering of generations of women before her: a suffering, which in this case—and in the case of the other women characters discussed in this chapter, Nola Darling (DeWanda Wise) of Spike Lee's, *She's Gotta Have It* (2017), and Sassafrass of Ntozake Shange's novel, *Sassafrass, Cypress & Indigo*—serves as a catalyst for seeking healing through the energy of Oshun. While the sources of their suffering are different, they are linked through their nature: violent acts against women's bodies, minds, and spirits at the hands of men both known and unknown.

Unlike Beyoncé, Nola Darling's (DeWanda Wise) dismay is at the hands of strange men. Spike Lee reworked the 1986 film and released *She's Gotta Have It* as a Netflix series. The first episode, titled "#DaJumpoff (DOCTRINE)," introduces the characters using hashtags, paying special attention to the new and younger audience that the series targets: Millennials. Nola Darling's name itself is a nod to the setting of *Lemonade,* as New Orleans is often shortened to NoLa by its residents, creating immediate intertextuality between the two narratives, and reflects the jazziness of her parents, Septima (Joie Lee) and Stokely (Thomas Jefferson Byrd), who are both artists. Nola's romantic partners, #JamieOverstreet (Lyriq Bent), #GreerChilds (Cleo Anthony), and #MarsBlackmon (Anthony Ramos), are all given enough screen time to highlight their character features or flaws: Jamie, serious, mature, and gainfully employed as an investment banker; Greer, vain, self-important, and a sought-after model; and Mars, a playful boy-next-door who is both representative of what Fort Green was as a community and what it will no longer be if the gentrification continues.

Foreshadowing Nola's unfortunate encounter later in the episode, Nola breaks the fourth wall and walks the audience through the difficulty of navigating the treacherous streets of New York as a young woman. A tightly shot montage ensues, focusing on the faces of different men and queer women hurling indecent language and sexually charged compliments at an off-screen Nola Darling. Feeling accomplished in relaying the problematic nature of street harassment, Nola carries on with her life, painting, teaching art, and walking dogs to make ends meet, arranging rendezvous with her lovers, and even having birthday cocktails with her friends to have fun. After a spat with a rather possessive Jamie, she goes over to the house of her former roommate and friend, #ClorindaBradford's (Margot Bingham), to blow off steam. Upon her departure, Clorinda and Nola embrace, and like any good friend Clorinda says, "I know you live down the block, but call me."[11] Mockingly, Nola responds, "Thanks, mom," but is made to regret her snide remark.[12]

Though only a short distance between the two apartments, as indicated by Clorinda's remark, Nola is first catcalled and then physically intercepted by a stranger, a large, dark-skinned Black man in a black leather jacket, who completely ignores Nola's disinterest. Unsatisfied with Nola's refusal to entertain his catcalling, the strange man on the street physically grabs Nola by the wrist tight enough to make it challenging to pull away, and as it is later revealed, tight enough to leave a bruise—marking Nola's body with evidence of the encounter long after its conclusion. After punching the assailant and screaming for her life, the man finally lets her go, but not without calling her, "a muthafuckin' black bitch."[13] Having gotten loose, Nola runs full speed to her Brooklyn home without looking back. Visibly shaken and tearful when reaching her destination, she reaches for and lights a pre-rolled joint to calm her nerves. After regaining her wits, Nola decides to attack the issue of street harassment and sexual assault head-on, through an anonymous poster campaign. Written over the faces of Black women and girls of various shades and hair textures are the words "My Name Isn't" followed by dehumanizing epithets like, "Yo Ma," "Sweetheart," "Baby Gurl," and perhaps most significantly for Nola, "Muthafuckin' Black Bitch."

Nola Darling's fictional work is inspired by Tatyana Fazlalizadeh's salient project "Stop Telling Women to Smile."[14] Fazlalizadeh's project caught Spike Lee's attention and led to Fazlalizadeh becoming the art consultant for *She's Gotta Have It*.[15] Fazlalizadeh reflects on her own work in relationship to Nola's reproduction, noting that for her, "being an artist who works with street harassment, who has a real-life art series about this, who is a painter of women, who feels really close to the character of Nola, I wanted the work to be as realistic as possible."[16] Fazlalizadeh's intentionality in Nola's character construction, given the intimacy that she shares with the both street harassment and public art, underscores the importance of highlighting not just the kinds of violence visited upon Black women, girls, and femmes, but also the kinds of work Black women do to address and redress these harms for themselves and for their communities. Nola Darlings's "My Name Isn't" campaign becomes an extension of Fazlalizadeh's voice, which is featured even more prominently in season 2 as she evaluates the meaning and value of Nola Darling's art as herself.

After confiding in her three beaux in the second episode, "#BootyFull (Self Acceptance)," Mars, who is of African American and Puerto Rican descent, recommends that she receive a cleansing from his sister, Lourdes (Santana Caress Benitez), a Yoruba priestess. In his characteristic playful tone and with an added serious edge rooted in care for Nola's well-being, he says, "Look, you sit with her, you get a cleansin.' Trust. You're gonna wanna wash off all that stink."[17] Initially resistant, and sure she would not be residually affected by the harrowing experience of the assault, Nola finds herself both shell-shocked and off-kilter after mistakenly macing a man simply trying to compliment her poster art one night, and unexpectedly yelling at a maintenance man inquiring about her and Clorinda's presence in the art gallery where she will soon display her work. After acknowledging that she needs to address her trauma, and Clorinda's suggestion to see a therapist (to which she is also resistant), a quickly cut montage ensues of her seeing a psychic with a crystal ball who attempted to overcharge her to banish negative energy, and another energy worker, perhaps attempting Reiki, who didn't seem to get the job done, all scored to Hamsa Lila's song "Oshun."[18]

Although nothing else in the episode indicates that she will move in the direction of seeking guidance from Lourdes or Orisha, Hamsa Lila's song underscores these failed attempts at a quick fix to the disarray in her life. The song works as subtext, marking Oshun's presence and intervention in Nola's life, even though she (and perhaps the audience) is unaware of that fact. Though it might appear at first glance that the Orishas are not involved in Nola's life until she concedes and consciously seeks them out, the introduction of this song at this place in the narrative can be read as both an interception on behalf of Oshun and a foreshadowing of the intervention to come. It is not uncommon for Orisha to send people down a roundabout path that ultimately leads them to the very place that they need to be. Consequently, I read Lee's choice to score Nola's misadventures to Hamsa Lila's song as indicative of Oshun's intervention, specifically sending Nola on a path of dead ends that guide her to Lourdes, and ultimately to the wisdom and abundance offered by Orisha. And through Lourdes, it also marks the intervention of Yemaya, who often works in tandem with Oshun for the benefit of those, particularly women, in need. Oshun and Yemaya's collaboration will be discussed at length in chapter 4 as more explicit connections between the two as it pertains to Nola's development are made clear in the second season of *She's Gotta Have It*.

When Nola finally yields to Mars's persuasive suggestions to consult his sister, Nola remarks to Mars, "I hope this works," underscoring her interest in an immediate fix and a disinterest in the arduous work and faith that accompanies spiritual healing.[19] Nola enters the small Brooklyn apartment to Lourdes sitting on a straw mat (also called *esteras* in ritual contexts) to the left of her stately shrine dedicated to Yemaya, and dressed in all the trappings of a *santera* (priest): a white head wrap, a white dress, consecrated beaded necklaces (elekes), and two beaded bracelets (*idés*) on her left wrist to represent Yemaya (cobalt blue with red and white accents, probably to mark her specific path of Yemaya), and another for Orunmila (green and yellow), the Orisha of divination. Like dúdú, funfun, or white, also takes on specific ritual meanings defined in the introduction. Given the color's association with purity and transparency, there is "[l]ittle wonder that many Yoruba priests and priestesses dress in white attires to emphasize their roles as mediators between the human and divine."[20] Lourdes is in accordance with many other priestesses who wish to signify their mediumship in this way, but also addresses some of the (im)material need for wearing white in ritual contexts. Because of the color's light and reflective properties, it is often the first line of defense against lingering negative or dark energy often carried by clients seeking to dispel negativity from their own lives. In this, Nola and Lourdes's client-practitioner relationship is not different. Therefore, Lourdes's attire, including and perhaps most importantly her head wrap, since the head (*orí*) is both the most powerful and most vulnerable, reveals her as prepared for the seriousness and unpredictability of the ritual undertaking in which she is about to engage, thus signaling her own engagement with body-praxis. Lourdes's "embodiment functions as a pathway to knowledge, a talking book," from which Nola can glean information about her current predicament.

To translate the talking book and gather information regarding Nola's dismay, Lourdes uses the sixteen-cowrie-shell divination system, Diloggún, to consult with Elegba, the messenger of Orisha. Diloggún uses the combinations of the first twelve odùs of the Ifá divination system, which includes sixteen total combinations of the odus. The divination requires open cowrie shells, which can land facing up (convex side up) or down (concave side up). The respective numbers of up- and down-facing shells each correspond to an odù, or a story that will shed wisdom on the situation at hand. As M. Jacqui Alexander writes, "For healing work to be undertaken there has to exist some understanding of cause, the precision of which is gained through a consultation of the Ifá oracle, or the Dillogun in the case of Santería."[21] The falling of the shells confirms that Nola does have a dark energy following both her and her artwork in the form of a shadowy black spider. Though she is skeptical, Lourdes assures Nola by stating her own faith, remarking that "it's not my job to prove this, that this is real and this actually works. Because you'll see. Eleggua will show you."[22] Sure enough, Mar's discovers while biking through the city, that Nola's posters have been vandalized by a graffiti artist, reawakening her feelings of violation, and confirming the content of Diloggún reading session.

This development brings her into full awareness of the depth of her trauma and pushes her toward seeking counseling from the Black woman therapist that Clorinda recommended, #DrJamison (Heather Headley). It is revealed in the sixth episode of the series, "#HeGotItAllMixedUp (DYSLEXIA)," that the person responsible for spray-painting over her work, Onyx, or Dean Haggin (Danny Hoch) as he introduces himself rather awkwardly to Mars in the men's bathroom of the gallery, is responsible for vandalizing Nola's poster art. With harmless enough intent, Haggin gifts Mars with a tagged napkin that Mars uses to identify the similarities between the napkin and the words crudely spray-painted over Nola's posters. A white male artist, Haggin also attempts to capture the "female Black form" and is introduced to the viewer beside a Black natural-haired wife and daughter who serve as visual markers of his questionable commitment to Blackness, both in his art and his politics, repeatedly remarking that its "nation time."[23] The shots of him prominently feature a spider tattooed on his hand, recalling Eleggua's warning about the dark energy haunting her work. Mars's discovery is a major breakthrough but is forced to take a backseat to Nola's anxieties about her material realities (needing to sell her work), having her art publicly displayed and judged, all three of her uninvited lovers showing up to the gallery, and finding out that the motel butt injections of her friend Shamekka (Chyna Lane) exploded because of a fall during her debut dance routine, causing her to be hospitalized and diagnosed with a blood infection. Having been hit from all angles, Nola becomes ready to acknowledge the lack of control she has over her own life and having been shown what she needed to see with her own eyes, Nola is convinced of both Lourdes ability to divine and her need of the guidance of Orisha. She returns to receive the cleansing, in the form of an Oshun bath, initially recommended by Mars, to remove the "stink," and truly begin the work of healing and (re)possession of herself.

Hilda Effania's oldest daughter, Sassafrass, of Ntozake Shange's novel, *Sassafrass, Cypress & Indigo*, also finds her way to Oshun through suffering at the hands of her mate. A weaver like her mother, she finds herself in Los Angeles far away from her South Carolina home, in love with a musician, Mitch. Deeply in love with Mitch, Sassafrass attempts to remain steadfast in her relationship through substance abuse, heroin being his drug of choice. Breaking "the only promise he ever made" to Sassafrass—no dope—Mitch gets high and physically assaults her for the first time, with his instrument—a horn.[24] After finding a bloody mess in the bathroom and Mitch nodded out, Sassafrass lovingly tells him, "You're a lousy, stinkin' junkie, Mitch. I haveta go now."[25] She leaves the home that they built together to find refuge with her sister, Cypress, a popular socialite and professional dancer.

Though Sassafrass finds a life full of freedom, and a new lover, Leroy, at the news that Mitch called and told Cypress "Tell Sassafrass to get her ass home," she follows her heart back to Mitch with the hope that both his addiction to heroin and his habit of hitting her would be cured by her absence.[26] To her surprise, he has earned himself a paying gig and for the moment dispensed with his drug habit, the perceived catalyst for his abusive behavior. She persuades him to help her sell two ounces of cocaine, gifted to her by her industrious sister (after all, a dancer's salary could not support Cypress's lifestyle) to raise the money to relocate from California to the New World Found Collective for artists in New Orleans. Sassafrass encounters and falls in love with the lifestyle of Orisha worship at the collective in New Orleans, which speaks to the spiritual influence of New Orleans historically and its symbolic significance to the texts analyzed in this chapter.[27] While Sassafrass finds spiritual redemption and seeks the path to *ochá* (Lucumí initiation into priesthood) there, Mitch longs for the past and rejects the lifestyle offered by the collective. For this reason, and perhaps a few others known by the *santeros* but not revealed in the text of the book, she is told by Mama Mbewe, a priestess of Oshun, through Diloggún that "there is a man leading you away from righteousness."[28] In a similar fashion to Beyoncé's own dance (discussed below), the drums of the Bembé (a ceremonial drumming in honor of Orishas) call Sassafrass to be possessed by the goddess Oshun in order to publicly chastise Mitch, and irrevocably break the link between the two so that Sassafrass may walk her righteous path.

Seeking Healing in the Sweet Waters of Oshun

At the completion of "Pray You Catch Me," a teary-eyed Beyoncé is shot standing on the ledge of a building primed to jump, finally removing her hood, revealing her shoulder-length, wavy, and undone hair for the first time in the film. This is significant as hair, its styling, and treatment often signals major change in a woman's life in both secular and religious settings. The process of cutting off one's overprocessed and damaged hair to start over from scratch and commit to keeping it natural, now commonly referred to as "the big chop," is one example of how Black women accept and promote positive change in their lives. Additionally, the Lucumí initiation process is also marked by the cutting of hair (in most cases), which must remain untouched for no less than one month before.[29] The intertextuality between *Lemonade,* and *She's Gotta Have It* as it pertains to the centrality of the head and hair is apparent. Beyoncé's character grows her hair to her ankles, Lourdes protects the vessel through which the Orisha communicate, and even Nola is shown with her head covered at a poignant moment of personal development.

Beyoncé tumbles forward off the ledge, arms outstretched as if relinquishing herself to a force not yet known, falling quickly onto the street, which in a flash, becomes a body of water and a womb where her rebirth becomes possible. As the word "Denial" flashes onto the screen, Beyoncé removes her black clothing physically shedding the pain and weight of infidelity, cleansing herself to reveal a beautiful golden mesh frock and suddenly long and beautiful flowing hair.[30] Gold, though a secondary color, is grouped with pupa (red), and "in general, refers to the vitality that the blood-stream generates in the body," or the power to bring things into fruition.[31] This shedding and revealing marks a transition in the symbolic energy attached to those clothes. Draped in black, Beyoncé surrenders to dúdú, in this instance meaning the darkness and depth of the water. Once in it, she is able to activate the energy attached to pupa and take an active role in the changes taking place.

At the bottom of that body of water is a fully furnished bedroom, where she gazes upon herself, lightly sleeping in the same clothing and recites the detailed process by which she attempts to both reconcile the reality of infidelity, stop it, reclaim her spouse, and (re)possess herself. She begins, "Fasted for 60 days, wore white, abstained from mirrors, abstained from sex . . . I slept on a mat on a floor. I swallowed a sword. I levitated. Went to the basement to confess my sins and was baptized in a river."[32] What is noteworthy here, is that many of these same rituals are required of Lucumí initiates, called *iyawos,* or "wives" of the Orisha to which they are initiated.[33] For many decades, Lucumí and other Afro-Atlantic religions were referred to as "basement religions," in the United States partly because of the secrecy associated with their practice, particularly before religious freedom had been granted, and also because of religious persecution which necessitated the locus of practice be moved to the safety of residential homes of practitioners. Basements are most often used for both their seclusion and their practical benefits like spaciousness and separate entrances.

While there are some distinct differences between the process that Beyoncé outlines, mainly that iyawos are tasked with undergoing the rigorous process for one year and seven days (perhaps longer), and that most are required to shave their hair and not grow it down to their ankles, as Beyoncé recites, the similarities here, including the aforementioned employment of white clothing, overshadow the differences and link both the imagery and the poetry of *Lemonade* to Lucumí rituals. Although the Lucumí references are most central to this study, other rituals she mentions make clear nods to Christianity especially given the presence of the Holy Bible floating in the scene and potentially a syncretism between the two belief systems. On this, Nahum Welang writes: "Oshun can therefore be conceptualized as a mediator between indigenous African religions and Western Christian thought. Her survival in the African diaspora communities of Latin America is a result of reconciliatory efforts between African and European religious practices, and Beyoncé's decision to reincarnate as Oshun while still acknowledging the validity of the black church reveals similar reconciliatory efforts."[34] Therefore, this scene provides a moment for Beyoncé to build a bridge between her various cultural and ethnic identities and experiences as a woman of African and creole descent whose life was no doubt informed by Southern Christian culture. This balancing act between Christianity and Lucumí helps establish "the agency of indigenous African religions through the process of legitimization," for Beyoncé's fan base that may have otherwise been unaware of this Afro-Atlantic religious tradition.[35] Beyoncé's monologue taken in conjunction with the imagery can also be read that her turn toward Lucumí came following a realization that Christianity alone was ill-equipped to guide her through the challenges behind and ahead.[36] In this instance, Beyoncé establishes herself in the narrative as what Mikelle Smith Omari-Tunkara would term an *abojúèjì*, or "'someone . . . that participates in the culture for a while and goes somewhere else'—not a stranger in the sense of *alejo*, the Yorùbá term for visitor, but in the sense of having 'eyes and mind in two places'—thus facilitating visualization and understanding in a number of places."[37] Throughout the narrative Beyoncé (the character) has her eyes and mind in the ways of knowing of Southern Black Christianity and Lucumí, past and present, with an acute understanding about how the implications of both merge to better contextualize the truth of her experiences and work together to help her successfully journey through them.

Further, Beyoncé engages an interesting semioptic dynamic by pairing the words "abstained from mirrors" with the image of an attentive version of herself gazing at a sleeping version of herself in her underwater boudoir. Finding ones twinned self at the bottom of a body of water brings in Oshun's influence and her theoretical tools.[38] While Oshun uses mirrors for the purpose of vanity, to admire her own beauty, she also uses them as a tool for her children, to show them the truth, or, as Lindsay Hale claims in her article, Oshun is "in a sense, a mirror through which some Umbandistas come to see themselves."[39] Symbolically, Beyoncé asserts that without proper use, a mirror cannot truly reflect oneself or allow one to reflect on the meaning of the self. Learning proper use and practical application requires abstention from mirrors themselves, opening up the possibilities for what they can reveal when gazed into again. In this moment of the visual album, Beyoncé complicates both how and why one looks at oneself to see what the eyes cannot. Enveloped in water, Oshun's medium, and secluded, Beyoncé is tasked with looking inside of herself to find the answer to the question she posed: "Are you cheating on me?"[40] In answering herself, or rather, discovering that the answers she seeks using "Intuition," she provides her own catalyst for undertaking the journey toward healing herself and reconciliation with her partner.

After undergoing a transformation, the newly formed Beyoncé swims away from the sleeping former version of herself toward the door and emerges anew from the "liminal" underwater boudoir, draped in a flowing, tiered, goldenrod gown, presenting herself for the first time in the doorway of an unnamed building as if mounted by Oshun herself, prepared to seek retribution and restoration as water rushes past her bare feet, down the steps and on to the street below.[41] This emergence allows the underwater boudoir to visually and symbolically double as a kind of womb, and this emergence is kind of water breaking. As she leaves the safety of spiritual gestation, she is empowered to apply all that she learned in seclusion. The visual choice to emerge dressed in the garments that reference Oshun's visual repertoire is an interesting play on Lucumí ritual, performance, and spirit possession.

This emergence marks the transition in the tone and tenor of the visual album underscored by the second song on the album, "Hold Up." This moment in the film is one of the most referenced by bloggers and magazine writers to discuss the incorporation of Oshun's iconic features even though the Orisha is never mentioned by name in *Lemonade* like the other texts discussed in this chapter. New World representations of Oshun in ceremonial contexts and performances that replicate ceremonial contexts typically feature colonial-style billowing dresses, crinoline slips, and even bloomers. Beyoncé's wardrobe choice channeled not just the feminine and ornate attributes of the deity, but also the dress captured the element of water itself, rippling and waving as she walks, just as river does. The words of the song, "Can't you see there's no other man above you? What a wicked way to treat the girl that loves you / Hold up, they don't love you like I love you," both celebrate the love Beyoncé has to offer and admonishes the man for taking it for granted.[42] Twirling her way down a cityscape, taking a bat engraved with words "Hot Sauce" from a boy standing on a stoop, Beyoncé, like a woman possessed, begins smashing storefront windows, cars, and windshields, making her way to a yellow fire hydrant draped in Mardi Gras beads. In one swing, she opens it creating a water fountain for her to enjoy, which she does with a twirl, and to provide relief from the heat to the children on the street. Yellow, like gold, is categorized as a secondary pupa color and is closely associated with spiritual energy and action. It is worth noting that Beyoncé pairs her dress with red finger- and toenail polish as accents. While this dress did the symbolic work of linking this scene with Oshun, if only for the dress, it also continues to carry forth the color symbolism as red "is categorized as a catalytic and forceful color with deep symbolic associations. It is evocative of action, potency, and power, especially of the great mothers."[43] For the first time in the film, Beyoncé exhibits the potency of her own power.

Beyoncé's dance is like Oshun's ritual dance in both form and function. Like a devotee, she takes on the spirit of Oshun's movement, ease, elegance, and seduction. As George Brandon eloquently describes, "When possessing her devotees in ceremonial trance Ochun shows her happiness through the possessed person's streaming tears and her displeasure through laughter."[44]

At times, Beyoncé throws her head back in laughter playfully, a feature that is specific to Oshun's dance. This iconographic adoption is even more potent in its symbolic meaning since Beyoncé's own dance in the context of the film symbolizes not only her re-emergence, but also the first instance of retributive justice. Throughout the dance, Beyoncé vacillates between laughter and palpable rage, weaving herself through a complex web of emotions that are experienced, processed, and released to make room for the healing to come. It is important to note that even though Beyoncé takes her bat to almost everything in her path, she pays special attention to glass, reflective surfaces, and cameras. Having just emerged reborn from a water world, it is not surprising that she destroys that which might distort her newly established self-image or reflect her poorly.

In one instance, Beyoncé comes to a full stop at a surveillance camera, looks directly into, primps her hair, blows a kiss, and proceeds to destroy it with her bat.[45] This assault on cameras and reflective surfaces could also be read as a critique of the broader surveillance attached to her celebrity and serve to disrupt the constant external gaze to which Beyoncé is subject, framing her entire life as one ongoing performance. The destruction of these cameras, culminating in a frontal assault on the one filming all the action from the audience's point of view, represents the (re)possession of Beyoncé's image, freed from the limits and limitations of the external gaze of paparazzi, family, strangers, and fans to recenter her own view. Further, Beyoncé engages the Yoruba concepts of àwòrán (a representation) and awòran (beholder) simultaneously.[46] Lawal eloquently describes how the representation must also engage its beholder, writing that "[t]his illusion is most striking in àwòrán [especially in portrait], which stares back at the awòran [spectator], turning him or her [or them] into an ìran [spectacle], if not another picture [àwòrán]."[47] Beyoncé turns the attention away from herself in a moment, turning the viewer themselves into the spectacle in a moment of reversal. In an instant, the viewer is made to grapple with the àwòrán that is *Lemonade,* as an awòran and at once becomes a spectacle when Beyoncé turns herself into an awòran by gazing at the spectacle that is the viewer. Finally, she explodes the àwòrán/awòran relationship and reversal by bringing down her bat on the camera that is the vantage point of the viewer, charging the viewer with rethinking their own gaze, as she rethinks hers. Finally, following the ritual framework laid out by Brandon, Beyoncé is shown to be tearful, eyes welling up and reddened but tears not falling, toward the end of the scene.[48] Beyoncé, in the yellow dress that would indelibly mark this scene in relationship to the powerful influence of Oshun, takes her leave shortly thereafter in a monster truck, continuing to bring ruin to the cars parked on the street.

Sassafrass and Nola both turn to water as well to begin the healing process under the guidance of experienced spiritual practitioners. Sassafrass is sent to the river with five oranges and a live chicken to appeal directly to Oshun and Shango "to remove the influence of Mitch."[49] Shange, delicately addresses the "common mythic histories" between Oshun and Shango through Sassafrass's spiritual needs.[50] Reflective of the diversity of the Yoruba mythistorical archive, some mythologies place Oshun and Shango at odds, and others describe their relationship to each other as the primordial love from which the twin Orishas, Ibeji, are born.[51] Both are true and applicable. In this instance, Shango does not represent an adversary to Oshun, but an aid to their common child since they are Sassafrass's spiritual parents, this appeal to Oshun's waters is effective.[52] Though a causal relationship is not established in the text, Sassafrass being both seized by Shango when she prostrates herself to pray for a child at the Bembe celebrating his feast day, and subsequently possessed by Oshun when Mitch finally enters the ceremony, are the very interventions she asks for at the river but likely not the ones she expected.

Nola, however, turns to a submersion bath alongside a formal ritual performed by Lourdes. She is submerged in a rather small bathtub provided by the Fort Green Housing project. The tub is filled of what we can see—water, red, yellow, and pink rose petals, and a yellow pillar candle with and image of Oshun on it standing out among other smaller candles along the sides of tub—and what we cannot see—*ashe*, or Lourdes spiritual energy—to make manifest the purpose of the ritual and the wishes of her clients. It is worthwhile to note that throughout the scene, Lourdes is shown both from the perspective of the audience and in the bathroom mirror, doubling and reflecting her image as she engages in spiritual work. What is most striking about this scene, the first in a sequence following the ritual to its end, is that it opens up a glimpse into the intimate nature of ritual work that is quite authentic. While the audience doesn't get to view Nola paying for Lourdes's services in cash, it creates the correct focal point: that healing is work, and that not even the Orisha, widely known by practitioners as the benefactors of humanity, give something for nothing.

I should say something regarding how I came to see the Spike Lee's reboot of *She's Gotta Have It*, and how that introduction informs my interpretation and analysis of the show. I didn't watch the show until over a month after its debut and was refreshed by its positive take on the incorporation of Yoruba religious practices. Upon further research, I was even more refreshed that the actress portraying Lourdes, Santana Caress Benitez, is a practitioner herself. For an interview for *Okay Africa,* in an article titled "10 Things You Need to Know before Practicing Lucumí," she is quoted as saying, "For me, it didn't matter who wrote the script or who's behind the scenes. . . . I'm the face of it, and I practice, so of course for me that was a big deal because I'm not yet initiated. I wanted to make sure that everything that I did was within reason, [and] wasn't anything that was going to compromise sacred protocols or rituals that we do. It was really important to me that we only show things that could be accessible to anyone—but also done right."[53] I mirror Benitez's apprehensions, as a practitioner, and it is similarly important to me that my writing does justice to the Lucumí religion. In conjunction with Benitez's portrayal of a Nuyorican santera, an initiated priestess, Iya AkileAshe, was consulted to put together representative scenes of Lucumí in action as not just a religious system but also a healing practice.[54] Lourdes, through the spiritual gifts bestowed to her by Yemaya, guides Nola through the door to Oshun's medium, to strip away that which no longer serves her and begin again.

Sassafrass, Nola, and Beyoncé all experience ruptures that present forks in the road. Elegba (ruler of the crossroads) gives them a choice to either continue down the current path leading them toward turmoil or decide to undertake a new journey toward healing and reconciliation. While each character hangs in the balance, unsure what lies ahead, Oshun sweeps her waters over them, in one way or another, to remove the old and to wash their physical bodies and spirits clean. Following the tradition of her mythology, Oshun eventually applies the sweetness of honey to the lives of each character to allow them to begin anew with evidence that they can, and deserve, to experience the pleasure and wealth that life has to offer.

Honey, Healing, and Reconciliation: Beginning Anew

In both Sassafrass's and Nola's cases, honey is physically applied to the situation to bring about a shift toward the sweetness in life. While mounted by Oshun, Sassafrass approaches Mitch with all the vengeance of Beyoncé tearing down the street, and she reprimands him for taking both her and her daughter for granted. John Mbiti addresses the unique liminality characteristic of the state of possession, writing that it "and mediumship is one of contemporizing the past, bringing into human history the beings essentially beyond the horizon of present time."[55] Bringing to bear the actions and oversights of the past through Oshun's message in the present, a mounted Sassafrass remarks, "How dare you not recognize my beauty? . . . How dare you not make no preparations for my child who is a gift of *las potencias*, the spirits?"[56] Taking honey and applying it to onlookers as a mark of her blessing, Sassafrass closes the scene of the ceremony by shoving gobs of honey down the bell of Mitch's horn, presumably the one he assaulted her with. Viewing Mitch's horn as a site of injury, it is quite appropriate that honey was applied there as a salve. While it might seem more effective on its face to apply the salve directly onto Sassafrass, Oshun saw fit to completely dismantle the weapon brandished against her child, and the assailant, that they never do her harm again. With the help of her mother/elders in the compound, "pass[ing] chickens over her all night," as another form of a ritual cleansing, she was granted a vision of her mother "on a bed of oranges, surrounded by burning yellow candles, eating honey."[57] Heeding the vision granted to her by her spiritual mother, Oshun, Sassafrass decides that is in her best interest to return home to her natal mother, Hilda Effania.

While Shange decidedly does not write much of Sassafrass's return, save a heartfelt letter from Hilda Effania with a warm and welcoming tone, she does include a short birthing scene coached by Sassafrass's younger sister, Indigo, a midwife and spiritualist in her own right. Though the entire scene does not fill the length of a page, it is important to read it as both the start of a new generation, a physical birth, and the completion of Sassafrass's own rebirth cycle. Having made much sacrifice, and finally rid of Mitch, she is able to live out her destiny and reap the benefits of her blessing, her child. While the birth of the unnamed and ungendered child signals the end of the novel, it also signals a beginning where life is once again sweet for Sassafrass in the company of the community of women who raised and were raised with her. However clichéd, the birth of Sassafrass's child is sweet, and that sweetness is an extension of the life Oshun always envisioned for her daughter.

Turning back to Nola Darling, while talking to Mars in the bike shop/café that employs him, she admits to him out loud that her life has been "straight Murphy's Law. Everything that could go wrong has gone wrong."[58] Certainly, her life has been a roller coaster, most recently because the $10,000 check that Jamie wrote for her self-portrait, had not made it to her account because his wife caught wind of it and promptly canceled it. Though Nola, a veritable starving artist, had high hopes for paying her bills with the money from the sale, her hopes are dashed when her debit card declines while attempting to treat herself to new art supplies and the rent check she wrote to her landlord/godmother, Miss Ella, bounces. Giving her a tough ultimatum to either move out or pay her rent in two days, Nola returns to wearing herself thin with odd jobs. Relaying her woes to Mars, he reiterates to Nola in an uncharacteristically serious tone that "[y]ou should really consider Lourdes and the Yoruba cleansing."[59] He reveals to her the tattoo on Onyx's hand and urges her to remember what the previous reading cautioned her about, and she finally acquiesces. Though hesitant about the cost of the services and her shortage of funds, Mars assures her that he will persuade his sister to perform these services without payment. This is affirmed, since the audience never views Nola exchanging money with Lourdes. But Nola does not receive something for nothing. Her work and payoff all are her own.

Though much of the scene is described above, as it relates to Nola's immersion in the bath, I've saved the best part for last. Before Lourdes fills the tub and prepares it for Nola's submersion, she is shown dipping leafy green plants into a silver *palangana* (Spanish for large bowl/basin usually used in ritual settings) with blue-tinted liquid, blowing rum on the plants, then brushing Nola down with them while singing in a language that is neither clearly Spanish or Yoruba, but with a translation that appears on the screen as "Take Away Negativity. Take Away Evil. Take Away Bad Luck."[60] At the end of the brief song, she clearly says "ashe," which is translated to "Blessings" on screen as she forcefully breaks the leaves in half, to break all of the negative energy brushed away by the leaves. Again, Lourdes is wearing a white dress with gold trim around the collar for the ritual undertaking, but this time, her large Afro is exposed to the audience. She then forcefully tears away the clothes Nola wore to the ceremony, to remove the old energy. This process is not unlike the one Beyoncé undergoes when shedding the heavy black clothing associated with her own angst. While Nola is submerged in the tub, Lourdes offers her a *jicará* (coconut husk bowl) full of "the essence of Oshun," or honey.[61] Before Nola pours it on herself, Lourdes sincerely says, "May this help you realize the goddess strength that's in you . . . that surrounds you."[62] After internalizing those words, Nola drenches herself in the saccharine viscous substance, hoping to cover herself with the very abundance and inspiration that is Oshun. Importantly, Lourdes also hopes that the bath brings her the comfort of Yemaya, which further underscores Yemaya's collaborative work with Oshun through her daughter, Lourdes.

When Nola finally dresses, she is in an all-white peasant dress.[63] Lourdes carefully paints Nola's face with four white dots above each eyebrow, four down the bridge of her nose, and a vertical line from the bottom of her lower lip down to her chin, remarking that "[t]hese are the tribal markings of goddess."[64] This was artistic license on the part of Lee, as experienced priestess of Obatala and my own godmother, Iya Gheri, remarks interview: "I've seen lots of baths to Oshun that didn't end in face painting. I don't know how that priest's *ilé* [spiritual house] does things, so you know, I won't judge that, but having had 40 years of Ocha and seeing a lot of Oshun baths, most of them did not end in any face painting at all."[65] Still, similarities appear again between Beyoncé and Nola Darling, as both appear in their respective narratives with their faces painted at critical shifts, just as both are gaining momentum toward reconciling their internal and external conflicts. In Nola's case, the markings painted at the end of her ceremony punctuate the first phase of the (re)possession of herself. Scrubbed clean and ready to restart, Nola is not done working: her own contribution to breaking the cycle of negative energy derailing her life, an ẹbọ requiring her to take the torn clothes, nine pennies, and another item connecting her to the negativity to the gates of the Greenwood Cemetery to give to the "spirit of the night."[66] This spirit can easily be identified as Oya, the Orisha of the wind, who guides the dead to the afterlife, and rules over sudden and immediate change. After offering these items at the gate, she is carefully instructed by Lourdes to never look back, a sign of complete surrender of the burden to Orisha and an embrace of forward progression. Perhaps Oya opened the road for Nola, in conjunction with Oshun and Yemaya (Lourdes's own patron Orisha), so that she could make the changes necessary to continue successfully on her journey to self. The most immediate change is the return of her self-portrait, which can be read on its face as symbolic of this (re) possession. Attached to the painting is $10,000, in cash, as an apology from Jamie for the cancellation of the original check. For the moment, her material needs are met. And while she could have immediately spent the money, the episode closes with her gazing intently at the two thick wads of money, thinking carefully about what to do with it.

Oya's heavy influence toward the end of the episode, foreshadows the beginning of the next, aptly titled "#ChangeGonCome (GENTRIFICATION)," which opens with a tribute to the egun, or ancestors. It is worth noting that nine is Oya's number, and this is the ninth episode of ten. Nola opens the episode, naming those who transitioned into ancestral plane in 2016, perhaps most notably, Prince, as well as Bill "Radio Raheem" Nunn, further underscoring Oya's iconographic influence through her close connection with egun. On the way back to herself, Nola finds it important to make two pit stops at the Woodlawn and Ferncliff cemeteries, to pay homage to ancestral energies that allow her to exist and inspire her to thrive in her current physical manifestation. While the gravesites she visits do not belong to bloodline relatives, the contribution of the communal ancestors to whom she offers flowers are no less influential and gets the message across that ancestors are as important as Orisha and priests in developing and maintaining a balanced relationship with the self, mediating the spiritual world, and navigating the material world in the Lucumí tradition. After she concludes her visit with the ancestors, Nola's life takes off quickly toward resolution.

Her session with Dr. Jamison reveals that her four on-and-off lovers (three men and intermittently, one woman), are distractions from her work. Instead of being present for her work and engaging an art critic that could have given her work much-needed positive publicity, she split her energy to manage her uninvited guests. Nola realizes that all the rules that she has in place to keep her lovers under control only serve to control and exhaust herself. Before she has a chance to address that truth, her students show her that her friend, Clorinda, has attached Nola's name to her street art campaign on Instagram. Even though the post garners over fifty thousand views and gives Nola's art a platform on which to flourish, she is upset that Mars broke his vow to keep the fact that she was behind the posters by telling Clorinda, and also upset that Clorinda posted the video without her permission.

Nola channels her upset into physically reworking her notions of self through reforming her returned self-portrait into an entirely new work of art. She starts by covering the portion of the painting where her face and head wrap would be with an expensive black, velvet dress she purchased as a pick-me-up after her assault, creating a silhouette. Though the process isn't shown in the episode, the finished portrait features white, bold capital letters over the fabric, quoting Audre Lorde's edited collection of essays *Sister Outsider*. The text reads: "IF I DIDNT DEFINE MYSELF FOR MYSELF."[67] Making the portrait twice as wide, she pastes ten black-and-white copies of the top half the portrait of her face, obscuring her face below her cheekbones and mimicking the poster campaign. In the negative space between the posters, it reads "I WOULD BE CRUNCHED INTO OTHER PEOPLES FANTASIES FOR ME AND EATEN ALIVE."[68] She uses this painting to process her grievances with the many definitions of her person that don't stem from the "self," just as she used the poster campaign to process her traumatic experience with street harassment and assault. From Clorinda referring to Nola as a "street artist" in the video she posted, to each of her male lovers referring to her as some version of a "freak" or "nymphomaniac," Nola experiences her share of labeling, mislabeling, and categorization. Her remade self-portrait exclaims that Nola Darling the artist, and the woman, is committed to confounding and collapsing categorization as well manifesting as self-definition and self-possession.

Her second recommitment to herself comes in the form of returning the $10,000 to Jamie with a note enclosed. In the note, she raises two interesting points, asking the question, "Who knows why the universe brings people together? Maybe it's to share these exchanges of light . . . illumination to better see ourselves."[69] This is a shift in Nola's perspective regarding her lovers, because she initially relates to them as three objects obstructing her view of herself. Her shift in focus allows her to see that her lovers are as much mirrors as they are reflections of her own wants and desires for material stability, fun, and beauty. As if finally understanding that all these things are attainable and can be gathered from her own wealth of resources, she eloquently notes to Jamie that "if I'm going to make it, [I] need to know that the greatest lift is one I can give myself."[70] The words in her letter to Jamie not only destabilize his relationship to her as a patron, they also clearly outline her readiness to take a risk bigger than having three and a half lovers: having faith in herself. Penance paid, and the first leg of her journey back to her self completed, Nola is rewarded with Oshun's abundance and is notified by letter of her receipt of the Elizabeth Catlett Grant.[71] This serves the function of stabilizing her financially so that she can focus more acutely on her artistry, and as she hoped for in her letter to Jamie, a signal that she is on the right path.

Director Spike Lee takes care to visually capture the transformation, devoting the final four minutes of the episode to a tightly shot Nola Darling dressed in a white head wrap and button-down, collared shirt. Again, adopting the symbolism attached to white, "power to reflect, signify, and give individuality to every creation," Nola is shown reflecting on the events of her life, a much-needed moment of introspection. Scored to Meshell Ndegeocello's song "Faithful," Nola is filmed in the foreground making 360-degree turns facing to and from the camera, while her new self-portrait is proudly displayed in the background sitting squarely on the mantelpiece. She makes one and a half turns before she is pictured in the same outfit, but instead of white, she is dressed in a maroon and orange multicolored shirt and head wrap, all colors grouped with pupa. This can be read as symbolic of Nola's own action to bring forth the positive change of which she is now reaping the benefits. Similarly, the multicolored clothing could be welcoming, the change or the "something" that is happening, as both maroon and multicolored prints are also associated with Oya. The lyrics to the song are displayed on the screen as she continues to turn one and a half times, and again her clothes change to white. Prepared to release all that was holding her back from herself, she begins to cry and then finally lets out a guttural scream and becomes a large cloud of jumbled lyrics from the song emerging from her mouth onto the screen, ending with the names Jamie, Greer, and Mars in bold red letters. This final scene of the episode, though not the series, signals a conclusiveness to her journey.

And while Nola does not express any further interest in developing a relationship with Oshun, or the Lucumí religion more broadly at the end of season 1, her plea for help in the form of seeking Lourdes was answered. Her ẹbọs in the forms of the spiritual bath and coins at the gate of the cemetery allowed Yemaya, Oya, and Oshun to clear her path of obstacles, the largest one being herself, and invited Oya to enact positive change in her condition. Although it was Lee's intent to run the show for one season, as a revival of the original film, it appears that its wide viewership prompted Netflix to renew the show for a second season. News of the show's renewal was confirmed by both Lee's and DeWanda Wise's Instagram posts on January 1, 2018.[72] Lee's usage of Lucumí in the first (and second) season is sufficient evidence of the efficacy the religion has in sorting through the complexities of worldly and otherworldly existence, carefully bridging the gap between Nola and Sassafrass, just as Beyoncé, with the help of Warsan Shire, bridges the gap between herself and her own ancestral memories and experiences.

Though Beyoncé never physically applies honey to herself, or anyone else, there is a notable similarity in the ways in which both hers and Nola's narratives progress. While Nola's journey is episodic, Beyoncé breaks her visual album into ten chapters that align with stages of development—adapted from Shire's original seven—to carry the viewer through the progression of the story and the processing of her trauma, which in many places is not linear. Starting with Intuition, the narrative explores the stated themes of Anger, Apathy, Emptiness, Accountability, Reformation, Forgiveness, Resurrection, Hope, and, finally, Redemption. Like Nola, Beyoncé experiences a beginning of the end, or resurrection, that is marked by the inclusion of egun. Beyoncé is shown, gazing on at pictures of people presumed departed somewhere inside of Fort Macomb, before placing them into a wooden chest (the contents of which are obscured, except a mirror with ornate golden trim), and walking away. The visual album also devotes time to address those gone (presumably, too soon), but not forgotten. Scored by the interlude, "Forward," featuring James Blake, the visual album slows to give time to footage of mothers Gwen Carr, Sybrina Fulton, and Lesley McFadden, holding framed pictures of their murdered sons: Eric Garner, Trayvon Martin, and Michael Brown. Joining these women, are four other actresses from the visual album, also holding pictures frames with departed relatives, all males but not all men because some of them were slain in their youth. One woman notably dressed in an all-white Mardi Gras Indian costume (Queen Ya Ya Kijafa Brown of the Washitaw Nation) holds a black-and-white picture of her own but goes on to have a more significant visual role in the film.[73]

While the long history of festival or carnival in African diasporic communities is tangential to the points of analysis in this chapter, the inclusion of Queen Ya Ya is worth noting not just because of the project's anchoring in Louisiana's cultural landscape, highlighting Beyoncé's own maternal roots, but also because Mardi Gras's link to the Yoruba *egúngún* procession through masquerading. Joyce Marie Jackson refers to the procession of Mardi Gras Indians, in their ornate costumes as a cultural continuity, one that links the two traditions together.[74] This is taken even further by the masquerader's role in the film. At the conclusion of the interlude, she is tasked with shaking a tambourine over a fully set white table lit by white candles, where no one is physically seated. This action is mirrored and done over again in a room that appears to be directly across from the other. The scene itself is "so magic folks feel their own ancestors coming up out of the earth to be in the realms of their descendants," and unfortunately, the ancestors featured are mostly children who predeceased their mothers.[75] Given the context of the footage, its meaning can be interpreted as a call to the ancestors to come into the space, as they are often called with bells or percussion. As Moyo Okediji writes in *Shattered Gourd*, "[T]he spirits of the departed ancestors are always at hand to help mortals. . . . The people are thus reassured that their ancestors are not irredeemably dead are within easy reach, whenever the need arises to consult with the spirits of the other world."[76] If the scene immediately before Queen Ya Ya's intervention is taken to be as a vigil of sorts for the aforementioned slain victims, then it follows that the call was specifically for those slain victims, who left the earthly plane before their mothers, and the other ancestors featured. Queen Ya Ya's tambourine and the necessary elements, funfun, water, and fire (candlelight), allow for the ancestors to cross into the earthly plane to consult with, console, and bless their living relatives.

Since the sequence ends with a close pan of a baby, the film continues to follow the mystical framework. Death, its mourning, and its celebration are naturally followed by birth and rebirth. The infant is presumably a girl, since the following the scene is narrated by a disembodied Beyoncé saying the following: "The nail technician pushed my cuticles back . . . turns my hand over, stretches the skin on my palm and says, 'I see your daughters and their daughters.' That night in a dream, the first girl emerges from a slit in my stomach. The scar heals into a smile. The man I love pulls the stitches out with his fingernails. We leave black sutures curling on the side of the bath. I wake as the second girl crawls headfirst up my throat, a flower blossoming out of the hole in my face."[77] The camera takes the viewer on an interesting journey through what appears to be catacombs alongside the poetry. Just as "the first girl emerges," the camera's vantage point travels through a slit in a wall where bricks are missing from dilapidation, signifying a cesarean incision. A second time just as "the second girl crawls headfirst up my throat," the camera takes the viewer up through a circular hole in the ceiling, which similarly calls to mind an infant emerging from the birth canal. For a second time, Beyoncé engages the relationship between àwòrán and awòran, turning the viewer into the first and second girl. The close pan of the baby girl signaling the rebirth of Beyoncé, and the birth of a new generation unencumbered the weight of the generational trauma Beyoncé has just thrown off, moves the viewer into the next chapter, "Hope," and the emergence of sweet love. This recalls the end of *Sassafrass, Cypress & Indigo*, which marked Sassafrass's new beginning with her laboring to birth her child, the gift of "the spirits."

Beyoncé's own version of hope is rooted in a sense of freedom. The eponymous song, from which the epigraph is taken, is sung acapella through the first verse on a wooden fire-lit stage in front of the audience, which is made up of all the women who appear in the film. The mothers of the men and boys slain noticeably occupy the first row of seating. In singing soulfully, "I'ma reign, I'ma rain on this bitter love / Tell the sweet I'm new," Beyoncé acknowledges at once both her own newness and the sweetness she has welcomed back into her life, or the influence of Oshun.[78] This is taken even further in the second verse when she sings forcefully, "I'ma wade I'ma wave through your shallow love / Tell the deep I'm new."[79] Again, she recalls the fundamental element of Oshun, the river, and addresses the depths of it, where Oshun resides, taking the viewer back to the moment where Beyoncé herself occupied the depths of a body of water and was reborn.

Having explored those depths of herself, and finally understanding what it truly means to love oneself, Beyoncé is no longer willing to accept bitterness or shallowness into her life or from her relationships. The song is aptly named because although it invokes themes of social justice, the multilayered meaning of the song in the context of the album simultaneously invokes Beyoncé's freedom or liberation from external overdetermination and romantic relationships devoid of reciprocity.

Finally unified with herself, she is able and ready to afford redemption to her partner. In the chapter titled "Redemption," Beyoncé offers the viewer pieces of her past and mother-wit that guided her to this place of healing in conjunction with the various ancestral and Afro-Atlantic energies symbolically employed throughout the film. Not unlike Ntozake Shange's own inclusion of Hilda Effania's recipes, spells, and other pieces of magic, Beyoncé slowly and intentionally recites her grandmother's own lemonade recipe, which brings the viewer into a conceptual understanding regarding the title's many layers of meaning. "Take one pint of water, add a half pound of sugar, the juice of eight lemons, the zest of half a lemon. Pour the water from one jug then into the other several times. Strain through a clean napkin."[80] On its face, the colloquial meaning of turning a sour situation into a sweet one can be gleaned early in the film. However, the intergenerational implications only come into the fore after raw footage of Jay-Z's grandmother saying "I had my ups and downs, but I always find the inner strength to pull myself up. I was served lemons, but I made lemonade" at her own ninetieth birthday celebration.[81] Important here is Hattie's own acknowledgment of strength and fortitude as requisites for the transformative process, or the alchemic process of taking metaphorical and actual lemons to lemonade.

Beyoncé further underscores this process by paying homage to Hattie's sacrifices and contributions to her lineage, as well as her own maternal line that will surely benefit her daughters. An ode, which can also be read as an oríkì (praise poem), ties together the metaphysical and timeless elements of the film and grounds them in the physical bodies of the women who bore one another's pain and pleasure so that Beyoncé, the woman, and the character, might be in the present moment. It reads: "Grandmother, the alchemist, you spun gold out of this hard life, conjured beauty from the things left behind. Found healing where it did not live. Discovered the antidote in your own kit. Broke the curse with your own two hands. You passed these instructions down to your daughter who then passed it down to her daughter."[82]

Beyoncé uses language to signify and invoke the power of *àjẹ́*. Wrongly translated to mean "witch" in English, the term is laden with the burdens of specific Yoruba social constructs and categories that at once intersect time, geographic location, gender, biological sex, and marital and social status, as well as age. It is true that the term is generally and traditionally used to describe powerful women, and usually those of an advanced age (postmenopausal). The term is better translated by Diedre Badejo as powerful beings who "possess innate kinetic power to reap benefits from her actions ... who use that power both positively and negatively."[83] Beyoncé's grandmother, and Hattie both fit squarely into the ways in which àjẹ are described by Badejo. Beyoncé's description of her grandmother as both an "alchemist" and a "conjurer" does the work of locating her as a powerful being in her own right, with the ability to manifest positive outcomes for herself, despite the bitterness of social structures that sought to limit those possibilities. Perhaps more importantly Hattie's commitment to herself allowed her to equip her women children with those same tools. Teresa N. Washington addresses the heritability of àjẹ and describes the mothers' womb as "literal doorways to existence and the terrestrial origin-sites of *àjẹ́*."[84] Here Beyoncé situates herself as an immediate beneficiary of Hattie and her own grandmother's sacrifices. It is here that the viewer is brought into the awareness that Beyoncé is equipped with the necessary toolkit, gifted from her grandmother, all along, but that she needed to experience crisis and the guidance of Oshun's energy to access it and understand the tools.

Moving quickly toward reconciliation, the next monologue recited closes the chapter dedicated to "Redemption" before the final song of the narrative, "All Night Long." It reads over fire crackling: "My grandma said, 'Nothing real can be threatened.' True love brought salvation back into me. With every tear came redemption and my torturer became my remedy. So we're gonna heal. We're gonna start again. You've brought the orchestra, synchronized swimmers. You're the magician. Pull me back together again, the way you cut me in half. Make the woman in doubt disappear. Pull the sorrow from between my legs like silk. Knot after knot after knot. The audience applauds ... but we can't hear them."[85] Drawing on the wisdom of her grandmother, Beyoncé reconciles for the audience how she arrived at an outcome that resulted in self-actualization and the reconciliation of her marriage. While the line, "true love brought salvation back into me," can be read as an acknowledgment of the reconciliation, I argue that it is an acknowledgment of the achievement of self-love, arguably the truest love that can be experienced. And using that as a basis, provided solid ground on which to rebuild with her partner, or for her to practice her own alchemy and change her torturer into her remedy. Staying with the spiritually charged language, she assigns magical powers to her husband, Jay-Z, as well, referring to him as a "Magician." The following line, "pull me back together again, the way you cut me in half," indicates that both acts require great amounts of power, and that, the latter can be reversed but must be reversed by the magician who did the act. This is one of the few places in the language of the film where Jay-Z is charged with making amends for his role in the crisis. While this can be written off as another case of a man skirting accountability for infidelity, I argue that redemption is not possible before Beyoncé achieves a unified sense of self, and therefore comes it comes in sequence. It is now his turn to do the emotional and spiritual work to re-establish their marriage, and to undo all that he has done to tear it down. Last, Beyoncé returns to the broader staging of her life and their relationship by saying that "the audience applauds ... but we can't hear them," and decentering the need to perform reconciliation in lieu of the actual work of healing. She acknowledges that their celebrity is, to a large degree, beyond the scope of their control, and that fans and dissenters will attempt voyeurism despite their best and often successful efforts to keep their private lives private. The audience applauding, in this case, is made to be inconsequential as it falls on the deaf ears of two performers seeking to live out their lives, not their roles.

The final song of the visual album marks the fact that "the healing cycle had completed its trajectory from the bitter to the sweet."[86] Underscored by Beyoncé slowly but surely looking toward and then away from Fort Macomb, which has come to signify her boundedness to turmoil, she walks away from that place and toward, "sweet love."[87] The images move away from the women in the film, and Beyoncé as an individual actor, toward cameos of couples of all kinds on the street showing public affection for each other. Interwoven into this footage, are home videos of key moments of Beyoncé and Jay-Z's life together, including the moment they tattooed their wedding bands (matching roman numerals "IV" on their ring fingers), their wedding day, as well as her pregnancy with their first daughter, Blue Ivy Carter. Footage of the wedding of her mother, Tina Knowles, to her second husband, Richard Lawson, brings healing work full circle, not just for herself but also for her mother, her daughter, the twins to come, and the larger Black community anchoring her commitment to methexis. Lemonade, then, becomes both a metaphor for the physical elements required to transmute a negative experience into a positive outcome, and Oshun's intervention, which is to take the bitter and make it sweet or, to take pain, transform, and heal it. "That's the story of Oshun, it's the full circle of the bitter and the sweet, and people just want all the good, they don't want to hear about the bad. Not that she's associated with bad, don't get me wrong. It's that they don't understand that you can't just get it all good without the negative to show you a lesson. And Oshun is good for teaching lessons about happiness. She's really good at that."[88]

2

Don't Hurt Yourself

Odù Ọ̀ṣẹ́túrá as a Method for Analyzing Fault, Retribution, and Accountability

> When you hurt me, you hurt yourself / Don't hurt yourself / When you diss me, you diss yourself / Don't hurt yourself / When you love me, you love yourself / Love God herself
> —Beyoncé Knowles-Carter, "Don't Hurt Yourself"

What's in an Odù?

The Odù Ifá is a widely practiced Yoruba divination system based on sixteen primary odùs (scriptures) as well as the combination of the sixteen, resulting in 256 possible outcomes in any given divination.[1] Originally an oral corpus of scriptures, various scholars and practitioners have recorded the odùs and their corresponding verses into books, including William Bascom, Philip John Neimark, Afolabi Epega, Ochani Lele, and Awo Fategbe Fatunmbi Fasola. Though most of the odùs *and* their corresponding verses have been recorded and compiled, these books are not exhaustive, and so the orality of the Ifá tradition has been preserved, as many diviners are still tasked with memorization during their rigorous training to become *babalawos* (fathers of secrets) or *iyanifas* (mothers of Ifá). Additionally, the orality of the tradition undergirds the mutability of it. "Far from being literal and unalterable, the odus are alive. They are complex organisms, waiting to be meshed uniquely with each client's personal energy before being 'written.'"[2] The Ifá corpus is alive, and therefore expands to accommodate the needs of its adherents through time and space. As such, written compilations are reference books at best, not veritable stone tablets recording static scripture and verse from which there can be no deviation.

Diloggún, which is similar to and often thought to be derivative of Ifá, is more widely practiced in the United States, Cuba, and Brazil. Where Ifá employs kola nuts, ọpẹlẹ (divining chain), and other divinatory tools, Diloggún uses cowries exclusively.[3] Scholars differ on the reasons as to why Diloggún is more widely practiced in those places, though many agree that the predominance of women practitioners, and their lack of access to Ifá resulted in the widespread use of Diloggún as the standard method of divination alongside Obí (employing coconuts in lieu of kola nuts).[4] In both Diloggún and Ifá, each odù carries with it, hundreds of verses that elucidate plausible sources of imbalance, as well as a series of course corrective offerings known as ẹbọ and *adimu* (offering, usually food items). The odùs themselves are not solutions but are better described as allegories that aid the diviner and the client in establishing a conversation, a diagnosis, and a prescription from which solutions emerge. To initiate the process, the diviner casts either sixteen kola nuts (*ikin*), cowrie shells, or a divination chain strung with eight kola nuts (*ọpẹlẹ*), to read the combinations of shells that are either facing up (convex side visible) or down (concave side visible) and mark either a single or double mark on the divining tray (*ọpọn Ifá*) on the left or right side depending on whether the number of up-facing nuts or shells is odd or even. What the diviner and client find in the odù that emerges is the client his/herself. "Ifa divination functions both as a navigation system, helping clients locate themselves and map their lives."[5] Although each odù is different, each is complete—including conflict, supplication, and stasis or, as Vincent L. Wimbush terms it, "Flight, Formation, and Reform(ul)ation."[6] This process is captured well in Spike Lee's *She's Gotta Have It.* Nola's consultation with Lourdes is discussed at length in the previous chapter, but it is worth noting here that although Lourdes does not cite or quote a specific odù during the divination process, the consultation provides guidance to Nola that she was looking for and desperately needed.[7] Properly deployed, odùs facilitate a cartography of the self.

This chapter addresses Odù Ọ̀ṣẹ́túrá and its analytical implications as it concerns Oshun's hierarchical and social positioning among the Irunmolé (the first seventeen Orishas to descend from heaven to earth), exclusion, and social justice. Returning to *Lemonade,* I employ Odù Ọ̀ṣẹ́túrá to excavate and analyze the ways in which it operates as both and guide and method for seeking corrective measures in instances of gender-based (and nongender-based) exclusion or maltreatment. The seventeenth odù tells the tale of Oshun's own exclusion in making important decisions regarding the development of the world. The only feminine energy in the Irunmolé, according to the patakí Oshun is not consulted and consequently, the plans fail. Following the lyrics of Beyoncé's song "Don't Hurt Yourself," this chapter applies this odù to examine the ways in which hurting and excluding women and femmes, hurts everyone. Further, it argues that, as in the case of the odù, Beyoncé constructs a narrative where both accountability and amends are required for stasis to be restored. Linking the developmental stages of *Lemonade* to the conceptual understandings of fair treatment for women specifically and Black people broadly, this chapter explores the ways in which Beyoncé's narrative centers seeking retribution, holding transgressors accountable, and ensuring that they make amends so that forgiveness is conferred and stasis restored.

Ifá, Diloggún, and a Gendered Interpretation of Divination

Oshun's influence and its implications for the feminine in the Ifá corpus extends beyond the fifth odù in Ifá and her established ownership of the Diloggún. It has been established among practitioners that Oshun's relationship to her various consorts—Shango, Ogun, and Orunmila—resulted in an acquisition of one or more of their respective talents, attributes or wisdoms. Of special interest here, is Oshun's relationship to Orunmila, and how that relationship has shaped and misshaped Oshun's influence over Ifá divination, which is decidedly masculinist in its description and practice. Wande Abimbola is one of few scholars to argue that Oshun "has much more to do with the origins of Ifá divination than the babalawo (Ifá priests) are ready to admit."[8] Abimbola argues further that the Ifá system of divination originates with Oshun and then is passed to Orunmila as opposed to the reverse, and further that Diloggún precedes Ifá and it not its derivative. This is critical to the understanding of Oshun's broader influence in the Orisha pantheon, to my interpretation of Odù Ọṣẹ́túrá's meaning, and its implications for social correctives.

Abimbola's article "The Bag of Wisdom: Ọṣun and the Origins of the Ifá Divination" initiates a paradigm shift in the interpretation, scholarship, and practice of Ifá divination. While gender complementarity has been historically and contemporarily heralded as a feature of Yoruba religion and culture, Abimbola and others clearly point to cleavages between memory, theory, interpretation, and praxis. Given that Abimbola's argument is rooted in the divination verses themselves, how do practitioners and scholars come to remember and celebrate that Orunmila owns Ifá, and that Oshun owns Diloggún, but not the conditions under which that comes to be true? Abimbola recalls a story from Odù Okanransode that indicates that the wisdom Ifá was sent to earth by Olódùmarè in the form of a bag. The Orisha were tasked with searching for this bag to possess its power, and, surely enough, Oshun finds it first. An excerpt of the text reads:

> One day a house rat went to the garment
> Which Ọ̀ṣun hung up in her house.
> The rat ate up its chest pocket underneath.
> The next day, they got themselves ready
> And started to search for the bag of wisdom once again
> Then, Ọ̀ṣun found it.
> She exclaimed, 'Han-in! This is the bag of wisdom!'
> She threw it into the chest pocket of her garment.
> She started to go in a hurry.
> As she was crossing dead woods
> And scaling climbing stems,
> Suddenly the bag of wisdom dropped down
> From where the rat had eaten her garment's pocket.
> Ọ̀ṣun was calling on Ọ̀rúnmìlà,
> Saying, 'Ọ̀rúnmìlà whose other name is
> Àjànà,
> Come quickly, come quickly.
> I have seen the bag of wisdom.'
> As Ọ̀rúnmìlà was going,
> He saw the bag of wisdom on the ground.
> He then put it inside the pocket of his own garment.[9]

A feature of this story that Abimbola does not discuss at length is why this misfortune befalls Oshun in the first place. Locating the bag of wisdom required that a sacrifice (ẹbọ) be made. According to the story, however, Oshun refused to do it.[10] While I do not assert that this exclusion undermines Abimbola's argument, it does complicate it. A consistent feature in the Ifá literary corpus is the necessity of sacrifice to ensure victory or prevent misfortune. Despite the cunning for which she is known, even Oshun could not overcome the disadvantage caused by failing to make ẹbọ. In this instance, Oshun's femininity is not the cause of the transfer of power as much as her hubris. This refusal has long-reaching consequences for women though, because out of this experience of misfortune, Oshun "put *ase* into her mouth, [s]he said that from then on, no woman [m]ust wear the agbada dress" and therefore no other woman would have the misfortune of having wisdom fall out of her pocket.¹¹ Nevertheless, the texts reveals that Oshun is the first Orisha to make use of the bag of wisdom containing Ifá, informing her mastery of the Dilogún.

Proceeding from the notion that Oshun is the first to possess and operationalize the wisdom of Ifá, Abimbola further argues that Dilogún is the basis on which the larger Ifá corpus is developed. Dilogún consists of the sixteen single signs of Ifá, so therefore has fewer odùs. It stands to reason that the larger Ifá corpus expanded from the sixteen single odùs to build the 256 and "the apparent simplicity of the signs of ẹẹ́rìndìnlógún and even the short nature of some of its literature are indications of its antiquity upon which the more elaborate signs and wider frame of reference of Ifá were based."¹² Shifting the paradigm of Oshun's broad influence over divinatory practice also shifts the perception of Dilogún's efficacy in practice and works to re-establish the gender complementarity for which Yoruba religion and culture is often praised. The academic discourse generated by Abimbola's inquiry into Oshun's rightful position as at least equally responsible for the development of Ifá divination undergirds my own interpretation of Odù Ọ̀ṣẹ́túrá, as I read his inquiry as its own form of corrective social justice prescribed by Odù Ọ̀ṣẹ́túrá. The necessity of Oshun's power and influence in the creation of the world and the maintenance of balanced human relationships ought not be overlooked given the social cost described in the Ifá literary corpus, particularly in Odù Ọ̀ṣẹ́túrá. I argue that the implications of Oshun's exclusion, which find themselves apparent even in the divination systems that caution against such behavior, extend to her earthly daughters, and will be explored through the aforementioned narratives.

Odù Ọ̀ṣẹ́túrá: Exclusion and Social Justice

Contributing to the contention regarding Oshun's primacy in divinatory practice, interpretations of Odù Ọ̀ṣẹ́túrá are hotly contested because the issue of gender in Yoruba Studies is itself contentious. Senior scholars Oyèrónkẹ́ Oyewùmí, Oyeronke Olajubu, J. Lorand Matory, Rowland Abiodun, Wande Abimbola, and others have constructed an extensive discourse regarding whether gender exists and how it functions in Yoruba socioreligious construction. Translation of Odù Ọ̀ṣẹ́túrá can be considered a linchpin in the discussion, as the primary moral of the story has been up for debate. Has Oshun been excluded based on her divine femininity, based on her perceived lack of seniority among the Irunmolé, or for some other obscure reason? In her book *What Gender Is Motherhood?: Changing Yorùbá*

Ideals of Power, Procreation, and Identity in the Age of Modernity, Oyewùmí asserts that a gendered interpretation of this òdù results from poor translation from Yoruba to English, and that this reading is not fundamental to the Ifá corpus, taking Abiodun and David Ogunbile's translations as examples.[13] It is Oyewùmí's contention that the crime of the Irunmolé was excluding their elder, not a sexist exclusion of a feminine divinity. Abiodun's translation of the òdù is reproduced below and will be used due to its wide reproduction, general readability in contrast to Ogunbile's translation, as well as Oyewùmí's critique:

> It was divined for the sixteen Odù
> Who were coming from heaven to earth
> A woman was the seventeenth of them.
> When they got to earth,
> They cleared the grove for Orò,
> Oro had his own space.
> They cleared the grove for Ọpa,
> Ọpa's abode was secure.
> They prepared the grove for Eégún,
> Eégún had a home.
> But they made no provision for Ọ̀sun,
> Also known as "Ṣẹ̀ẹ̀gẹ̀sí the preeminent hair-plaiter with the coral-beaded comb."
> So, she decided to wait and see
> How they would carry out their mission successfully;
> Ọ̀sun sat quietly and watched them.
> Beginning with Èjì-Ogbè and Ọ̀yẹ̀kúméjì,
> Ìwòrí méjì, Odi méjì, Iròsùn méjì
> Ọ̀wònrín méjì, Ọ̀bàrà méjì, Ọ̀kànràn méjì,
> Ògún-dá, Òsá, Orangun méjì and so on,
> They all decided not to countenance Ọ̀sun in their mission.
> She, too, kept mute,
> And carried on her rightful duty,
> Which is hair-plaiting.
> She had a comb.
> They never knew she was an "àjẹ."
> When they were coming from heaven,
> God chose all good things;
> He also chose their keeper,

And this was a woman.
All women are àjẹ.
And because all other Odù left Ọṣun out,
Nothing they did was successful.
They went to Eégún's grove and pleaded with him,
That their mission be crowned with success.
"Eégún, it is you who straightens the four corners of the world,
Let all be straight."
They went to Àdàgbà Òjùmù
Who is called Orò
"You are the only one who frightens Death and Sickness.
Please help drive them away."
Healing failed to take place;
Instead epidemic festered.
They went to Ọ̀sé and begged him
To let the rain fall.
Rain didn't fall.
Then they went to Ọ̀ṣun
Ọ̀ṣun received them warmly,
And entertained them,
But shame would not let them confide in Ọ̀ṣun,
Whom they had ignored.
They then headed for heaven
And made straight for Olódùmarè,
Who asked why they came
They said it was about their mission on earth.
When they left heaven,
And arrived on earth
All things went well;
Then later things turned for the worse,
Nothing was successful.
And Olódùmarè asked
"How many of you are here?"
They answered, "Sixteen."
He also asked, "When you were leaving heaven, how many were you?"
They answered, "Seventeen."
And Olódùmarè said, "You are all intriguers.
That one you left behind

If you do not bring her here,
There will be no solution to your problem
If you continue this way,
You will always fail."
They then returned to Ọ̀sun,
And addressed her, "Mother, the preeminent hair-plaiter with the coral-beaded comb.
We have been to the Creator
And it was there we discovered that all Odù were derived from you [Ọ̀sun],
And that our suffering would continue
If we failed to recognize and obey you [Ọ̀sun]."
So, on their return to the earth from the Creator,
All the remaining Odù wanted to pacify and please Ọ̀sun.
But Ọ̀sun would not go out with them.
The baby she was expecting might go out with them,
But even that would depend on the gender of the baby
For she said that if the baby she was expecting
Turned out to be male,
It is that male child who would go out with them
But if the baby turned out to be female,
She [Ọ̀sun] would have nothing to do with them.
She said she knew of all they [the Odù] had eaten and enjoyed without her,
Particularly all the delicacies and he-goat they ate.
As Ọ̀sun was about to curse them all,
Ọ̀sé covered her mouth
And the remaining Odù started praying
That Ọ̀sun might deliver a male child.
They then started to beg her.
When Ọ̀sun delivered
She had a baby boy
Whom they named Ọ̀sé-Túrá.[14]

I agree with Oyewùmí that a contemporary issue emerged under what is now termed gender, and that what we contemporarily understand to be gender is not a fundamental to Ifá or to this particular odù. However, I assert that since issues of gender-based exclusion have emerged that are rooted in contemporary notion of gender, the pliability of Ifá divination lends itself to applications by men and women alike to think through and address issues of gender disparity and exclusion. Further, there is not any conceptual reason that this issue of exclusion could not cover both the issue of seniority (one that has remained pivotal in Oyewùmí's own scholarship), and the issue of women's disempowerment. Simply put, Abiodun and Oyewùmí are both right. Just as this odù can be interpreted along the lines of gender, exclusion occurs along many lines and Odù Ọ̀ṣẹ́túrá could be accurately applied to them all. Iya Gheri concurs, remarking that "the nice thing about patakís is that there are many, many, many, many conclusions that you can come to in every single patakí. Every single one. So that's just but one. I mean you could talk about it being about gender exclusion, but we can also talk about it as being, 'you didn't ask me.'"[15] As the *odù* mentions, the Irunmolé consulted, or "asked," Eégún, Orò, Ọ̀sé, and Olódùmarè before they were redirected to return to where they had not asked. While the exclusionary element of the tale is important, the negative community impact calling for broad social justice to restore balance also requires analysis.

In reference to Abiodun's translation of Odù Ọ̀ṣẹ́túrá, Oyewùmí argues that his translation is not sexist, but rather that "there is no limit to Ọ̀ṣun's domain, it extends to the whole world; there are no two domains here, let alone a gender dichotomy."[16] To Oyewùmí's point, Oshun's exclusion did not result in the othering or specific oppression of women and the feminine, it resulted in the complete unraveling of both the social and natural order. This unraveling, however, does not preclude that the imbalance is not one rooted in gender. Humans and Orisha alike suffered as a result of the arrogance exhibited by the masculine Orisha, and their exclusion of Oshun along the lines of difference regardless of the nature of that difference. For that reason, their propitiation of Oshun must be read simultaneously as an apology, accountability, and a pursuit of social justice. This odù provides a timeless lens through which to glean issues of exclusion, one in which all must and do suffer the consequences for this oversight. The communal implications are carried further by the birth of Ọ̀ṣẹ́túrá, also known as Èṣù/Elegba/Eleggua.[17]

The circumstances surrounding Elegba's introduction into the Orisha pantheon underscore the importance of his role. Though Elegba is often heralded as the primordial gatekeeper, the nature of this role is typically unassociated with his birth, which is notable considering the social significance of birth circumstance and naming in Yoruba culture.[18] His name means "Owner of power," indicating not only his own role as intermediary between the complicated relationships of humans, Orisha, and Olódùmarè, but also the fulfillment of Oshun and the Irunmolé's needs.[19] I read Elegba's ability to remove and place obstacles alongside Oshun's own circumstances during her pregnancy in the odù. Ọṣẹ́túrá is birthed with the expressed purpose of removing the obstacles preventing the world's creation and restoring balance. Also known as "the one who approves of, and bears sacrifices to the òrìṣà," Ọṣẹ́túrá is one whose birth represents his own approval of the Irunmolé's plea to Oshun. Even the literary (and perhaps actual) emphasis placed on Elegba's penchant for trickery acknowledges that the trick itself often serves as a catalyst for learning a hard lesson before the onset of positive change.[20] Accordingly, the social justice produced in the context of the odù is not the pleas and apologies of the sixteen Irunmolé; it is the birth of Elegba. At his birth, humanity and Orisha alike received a warrior, a messenger with the power to balance positive and negative energetic forces and therefore the capacity to cause complete disarray or maintain social justice, and even this gift is one bestowed by Oshun.

Until You Do Right by Me . . .

The immortal words forcefully cast by Whoopi Goldberg's rendition of Celie in *The Color Purple* (1985), "I curse you. Until you do right by me everything you think about is gonna crumble," signals not only a critical shift in Celie's own identity development as she overcomes the decades of trauma thrust upon her. It is an apt and concise description of Oshun's rebuke of the male Orisha comprising the Irunmolé in Odù Ọṣẹ́túrá.[21] The words themselves spellbind Albert to live out the very misery he imparted on Celie until accountability is undertaken.[22] In Albert's case, the spell likely ran the course of his natural life, however, *Lemonade* constructs a narrative where Beyoncé issues a warning of her own, with room for redemption and healing.[23] Calmly and simply stated, Beyoncé's admonition, "Don't hurt yourself," signals a shift in her identity development and in the narrative from her quest for seeking answers, to seeking what she is owed: sincere apology, accountability, and reconciliation.[24]

"Anger" marks the chapter of the film where Beyoncé purposefully recites the poetry adapted by Warsan Shire "If it's what you truly want . . . I can wear her skin over mine. Her hair over mine. Her hands as gloves. Her teeth as confetti. Her scalp, a cap. Her sternum, my bedazzled cane. We can pose for a photograph, all three of us. Immortalized . . . you and your perfect girl. I don't know when love became elusive. What I know is, no one I know has it. My father's arms around my mother's neck, fruit too ripe to eat. I think of lovers as trees growing to and from one another. Searching for the same light. Why can't you see me? Why can't you see me? Why can't you see me? Everyone else can."[25] The first three lines of the poem takes us down a dark and poorly lit stairwell leading into the Royal Parking Garage. They describe a grim process of incorporation of the other (woman). Figuratively cannibalizing this known but unidentified woman, Beyoncé exercises her agency in choosing that which she will appropriate to fulfill the wants of her unfaithful husband and empower herself. Here Beyoncé refuses to be rendered invisible, even if it requires the critical or strategic incorporation of her husband's mistress. Additionally, the grisly details of this woman's dissection for the purpose of becoming Beyoncé's accoutrements foreshadows the at-times chilling nature of the cinematography throughout the duration of "Anger."

In critiquing her own quest for love in her marriage by acknowledging that "no one [she] knows has it," Beyoncé maintains the intergenerational aspect of tenuous marital relationships as a focal point. She acknowledges that despite her best efforts, love is eluding her and that this is not unrelated to the frame of reference produced by her natal family, witnessing her "father's arms around [her] mother's neck."[26] Returning to herself and, perhaps to the present, she closes with an echoing question, "Why can't you see me? Why can't you see me? Why can't you see me?"[27] Staying with her meta-analysis of her own celebrity and the various gazes under which she is scrutinized, she takes her husband to task for rendering her invisible and obscuring her own view of herself, even though she is hypervisible to everyone else. The theme of visibility is further complicated by her recommendation to "pose for a photograph, all three of us. Immortalized . . . you and your perfect girl."[28] Though she acknowledges that three people will exist in the photograph, she notes that only two will be seen: her husband and his perfect girl, an amalgamation of herself and his mistress. Though she will be seen and immortalized in the photograph, Beyoncé's is only visible to her husband because of her appropriation of the other woman's body turned accessory.

At the end of the poem, the imagery of the film shifts from the haunting emptiness of the parking garage toward a gritty urbanity of the Royal Parking Garage occupied by Beyoncé, her drummer, and backup dancers to stage her direct confrontation of the viewer and her husband. Re-engaging the àwòrán/awòran dynamic, Beyoncé glares directly into the camera as she adjusts her luxurious fur coat draped over her taupe two-piece legging and midriff top and asks, "Who the fuck do you think I am?"[29] This question, like the one above, indicates that clarity and confidence are restored, and further that his answer will be rendered moot against the self-possessed nature of the lyrics to follow. She continues a list of remarks regarding her own independent status, what she brings to the relationship, and her prospects for a happy (or perhaps happier) life without the relationship in its current state. More rapping than singing the lyrics "keep a bigger smile on my face being alone / bad motherfucker / god complex / motivate your ass / call me Malcolm X," she flaunts her regained confidence, verbalizes her connection to god(dess) energy, and establishes her indispensable role in the relationship. Leaning on the words and iconographic capital of Malcolm X, Beyoncé uses this moment in the film to broaden her criticism to the plight of Black women broadly, superimposing audio of Malcolm X reciting an oft-quoted excerpt from his speech "Who Taught You to Hate Yourself?" A montage of differently aged, shaped, and complexioned women rolls as Malcolm X recites "The most disrespected woman in America is the black woman. The most unprotected woman in America is the black woman. The most neglected woman in America is the black woman."[30] Like Oshun in Odù Ọ̀ṣẹ́túrá, Beyoncé uses her own instance of maltreatment to call attention to and demand redress for and imbalance that is as communal as it is personal: the subjection of Black women by society at large as well as by men who claim to love them, maintaining methexis as a priority in her performance.

Used as the epigraph of this chapter because of its significance, the chorus of the song connects the moral of Odù Ọ̀ṣẹ́túrá and underscores its utility as an analytical tool for the visual album *Lemonade*. Beyoncé screams, "When you hurt me, you hurt yourself / Don't hurt yourself / When you diss me, you diss yourself / Don't hurt yourself / When you hurt me, you hurt yourself / Don't hurt yourself, don't hurt yourself / When you love me, you love yourself / Love God herself."[31] Taking the chorus of the song as a rallying cry for women and a cautionary tale for men, it lays out quite frankly that despite a long historical track record of society's dismissal of Black women's abuse, there are cosmic and perhaps karmic consequences for mistreating women. In a bold, subversive, and somewhat controversial move, Beyoncé's lyrics clearly express the divinity of Black womanhood and the femininity of God. This association moved Knowles to add the following text in capital, bold white letters: "GOD IS GOD AND I AM NOT."[32] Quick though it may be, such that one could miss it entirely, this visual caveat does the work of maintaining the message that Black women are of God and therefore divine, and that God's vast existence exceeds masculinist interpretations from being overshadowed by accusations of blasphemy and other claims of self-deification.[33] I would venture to speculate that such a caveat would not have been required if the lyrics maintained masculine pronouns in reference to God further highlighting the social imbalance regarding constructs of gender and religious culture, and how the lyrics themselves do justice by expanding notions of the divine feminine, and reminding the world of Beyoncé's own humanity, which I assert is a priority of the visual album. The visual aspects of this moment in the film engages funfun, dúdú, and pupa extensively. The cinematography itself jumps back and forth between full color and black and white. The staging itself is dark, as the garage is poorly lit by overhead fluorescent lights. The darkness or dúdú of the parking garage alongside the darkness of the wardrobe of the women backing up Beyoncé foreshadow the unpredictable and erratic nature of Beyoncé's behaviors.[34] The camera moves from a corn-rowed Beyoncé in a taupe high crop top and leggings under her fur to a wild-haired Beyoncé surrounded by a square of flames in a red, strapless floor-length gown and large ornate necklace. It shows her thrashing about wildly in the flames in both full color and black and white. The color shots engage pupa with the fullness of the flame and the intensity of the dress, clearly visualizing the anger indicated by the chapter title, as well as the power she harnesses to issue her warning. The same scene is almost inverted in black and white as both Beyoncé and her dress appear to be white, or funfun, although not quite inverting the meaning. The spookiness of the scene is driven home in between the chorus and second verse when the music itself stops until Beyoncé appears to levitate to her feet from a seated position. In fact, she comes across as an angry bride, engaging the irony of the white dress's traditional meaning. Her skin is also made to appear white, giving her a ghostly/ghastly appearance.

Omise'eke Natasha Tinsley suggests that Beyoncé abandons the imagery associated with Oshun in the Royal Parking Garage for that of Afro-Brazilian deity, Pomba Gira.[35] Regarding this iconographic adoption, Tinsley says that "[p]ractitioners of Afro-Brazilian religions cast Oshun and other orishas as 'spirits of the right' who are 'said to work only for good, that is, in ways that accord with dominant moral codes.'"[36] While this reading is accurate in one way in that Pomba Gira is "the Madonna/Whore complex an innocent who becomes a prostitute, but reformulated as an archetype of female strength overcoming male victimization or domination," it is not strictly true that Oshun is considered a spirit of the right among practitioners of the various religions that revere her.[37] Each Orisha has virtues and the story of *Swan Lake,* whose central themes also include, "betrayal, desire for true love, competing female roles, being trapped because of men, and symbolic opposition between black and white," which functions here visually first, and racially through the lyrical reference in "Sorry" to "Becky with the good hair" implying a phenotypical difference between Beyoncé and the alleged mistress.[54] Continuing to hold Jay-Z accountable, Beyoncé recites the poems playfully, "So what are you gonna say at my funeral, now that you've killed me? Here lies the body of the love of my life, whose heart I broke without a gun to my head. Here lies the mother of my children, both living and dead. Rest in peace, my true love, who I took for granted. Most bomb pussy who, because of me, sleep evaded. Her god was listening. Her heaven will be a love without betrayal. Ashes to ashes, dust to side chicks."[55] I interpret this poem to be about an emotional death. The woman who loved and cared for her husband despite his various trespasses has finally been killed, and her assailant was not under duress. Emphasizing that this crime was committed without "a gun to his head" continues to hold Jay-Z solely responsible for his misdeeds leaving no room for excuses and no escape from the ownership and accountability required to begin to rebuild the relationship.[56] Simultaneously eulogizing herself, Beyoncé engages another Yoruba practice of oríkì, or praise poetry. On this, Adélékè Adéẹ̀kọ́ writes that "*[o]ríkì* given at birth reflect, like common names, the circumstances of birth and family aspirations. As they grow up, individuals accumulate more epithets that remark peculiar behaviors and deeds, significant achievements, and characteristic foibles in degrees of elaboration and poetic quality that vary with the individual's degree of social eminence and the kind of artistic capabilities the celebrated status can purchase."[57] Here, Beyoncé puts the words of her own oríkì into the mouth of her husband, making him praise and confront that which he destroyed, eat her words and his actions. Accordingly, oríkì and ìtàn are interrelated. "For a Yoruba intellectual, *oríkì* as a concept and a discursive practice is inseparable from the concept and discursive practice of *ìtàn*. Indeed, it can be argued that both are members of a constellation of basic Yoruba concepts without the elucidation of which it is almost impossible to understand any aspect of Yoruba cultures."[58] The aural layering of Warsan Shire's praise poetry over Laolu Senbajo's visual orí painting in *Lemonade* provides one example of how these concepts are intrinsically linked, how they merge to create and complicate meaning, and engage diaspora.

As for Beyoncé's own oríkì, it is worth noting what emerges as praiseworthy. In this poem, her role as a mother is characterized as a "significant

Regarding Beyoncé's own iconographic adoption of Yoruba-derived body painting, Senbanjo argues in his 2017 TED talk, "The Sacred Art of the Ori," that "Beyoncé wanted to pay homage to New Orleans and my art reminded her of her creole origins."[47] Beyoncé's incorporation of Senbanjo's art underscores key intersections in New Orleans's complex history of religion and culture. Visually, these women who are all painted uniquely to capture their own orí, which Senbanjo describes as "your soul, it means your essence, it means your instincts."[48] In conjunction with capturing their orí, their presence in the video also captures the orí of New Orleans including the varied contributions of Yoruba, Dahomean, Kongo, Haitian and distinctly African American ways of knowing, seeing, and being in the world. Senbanjo accurately describes his body painting as "art in motion." Functioning semioptically here, Senbanjo's orí painting also functions as history in motion. Olabiyi Yai's work on ìtàn, a memory-based oral art form, and Moyo Okediji's interpretation of ìtàn's influence on visual art, is helpful in making sense of how Senbanjo's orí painting physically represents, "the past and the present merg[ing] to meet us here."[49] Yai writes that "[e]tymologically ìtàn is a noun derived from the verb tan. Tàn means to spread, reach, to open up, to illuminate, to shine ... In that sense it is important to observe that the Yoruba have always conceived of their history as diaspora."[50] Yai's interpretation of Yoruba history as diaspora and Okediji's understanding of visual organization, meaning, and memory elucidates Senbanjo's own inspiration: "because as orature, it is based on remembering, ìtàn resides at the crossroads between the visible present and the invisible past, bearing implications of diaspora, of the past broken from the present, of the present seeking a dim or lost past."[51] Senbanjo's own "creative instincts were actually based on [his] childhood memories and the art on [his] grandmother's skin," and similarly Beyoncé's creative instincts are rooted in her desire to bring forth a cultural past indelibly connected to the present, and both have distinct implications of diaspora and transnationality.[52] Senbanjo's inspirational inquiry, "[W]hat would it look like if we all walked around like gods and goddesses from Yoruba mythology?" calls forward his own understanding and participation in Yoruba myth, underscores his own transnationality as a Yoruba American whose artwork gained popularity in New York City, and his interconnectedness to the broader African diaspora, as his work reminds Beyoncé of herself.[53]

The poem "Apathy" is recited over Pyotr Ilyich Tchaikovsky's *Swan Lake*. This choice offers an interesting and layered textuality between *Lemonade* and failings based of the extremities of their respective archetypes. This is relevant in Oshun's case as it pertains to Tinsley's reading since Oshun has been considered a harlot and protectress of sex workers as well.[38] After all, "the orisha do not have to be 'good' to be worshipped."[39] And though reading Pomba Gira into this scene is valid, and Oshun can appear in a red gown when going to battle, I find Vodun's Erzulie-Gé-Rouge more accurate given the geographical and cultural relationship between New Orleans and Vodun, and especially since Erzulie and her multiple aspects are also syncretized with Oshun.[40] Valorie D. Thomas advances this idea, writing that "Oshun and her Haitian persona, Erzulie Gé Rouge, are evoked through the ruffled saffron gown, gold embellishments, parasols, veils, passion, sensuality, red hues, whirling fire, breaking glass, anger, protection of children, affirmations of care and kinship among women."[41] This righteous rage bears a striking resemblance to the earlier scenes of Beyoncé in her Roberto Cavalli gown with a darker inflection. Taken together, the scenes with Oshun and Erzulie-Gé-Rouge represent two sides of the same iconographic coin: day and night, light and dark, *rada* (cool and benevolent) and *petro* (hot and potentially dangerous).[42] Flipping to the dark side of the coin and imagery of the night here foreshadows later scenes where the significance of the night, the moon, sleep, and dreams are emphasized.

The spookiness of the scene is magnified by the cinematography that plays up the darkness of the background against the contrast of the white sheen cast over her body. Alternating between the fierceness of her Afro-urban apparel replete with an ankh chain and the chilling/thrilling tone of her white/red gown, the camera also takes the viewer to another floor of the parking deck where dancers intertwined by the sleeves in white liturgical dresses dance and sway under the brightness of an overhead lamp. Here the engagement with funfun does draw on the holiness associated with white. I read these women as performing a praise dance for "God herself," turning the parking deck into a sanctuary of worship. Showered in light from a single bulb, the dancers, like lovers, "grow to and from one another," extending their arms up as if they are "searching for the same light," striking on poses of adoration before moving through the pose to another.[43] The cinematography brilliantly captures the visual complexity that undergirds the lyrics and poetry in this chapter of the film: anger and wrath alongside divine femininity.

The second verse marks a transition from the arrogance of the first toward holding Jay-Z accountable. Here, the hard work she undertook to shift her perspective from being inadequate and to blame for the betrayal in her marriage is on display. The lyrics shift the blame squarely on the shortcomings of her husband. Beyoncé sings, "I am not broken / I'm not crying / I'm not crying / You ain't trying hard enough / You ain't loving hard enough / You don't love me deep enough / We not reaching feats enough / Blindly in love, I fucks with you / 'Til I realize, I'm just too much for you."[44] Moving away from the uncertainty of Intuition, Anger establishes that the feelings of inadequacy throughout the first chapter of the film have dissipated, and it is clear that he is not pulling his weight in the relationship. She emerges out of her anger prepared to demand what she deserves. Beyoncé closes the song and chapter with a self-assured statement, "This is your final warning / You know I give you life / If you try this shit again / You gonna lose your wife."[45] Like Odù Ọ̀ṣẹ́túrá, Beyoncé delivers a final admonition that both chastises her husband for past transgressions and demands corrective behavior as a requirement for balance to be restored, while maintaining that dissolution of the relationship is pending following Olodumare's warning to the Irunmolé in the divination verse, "If you continue this way, you will always fail."[46] The onus of reconciliation has rightfully been placed on the transgressor. Placing the viewer into the role of the transgressor, Beyoncé throws a ring removed from her left ring finger directly into the camera. The removal of the wedding ring underscores the seriousness of her statement and centers her husband's own carelessness with his commitment to the marriage. The discarding of the ring provides an excellent transition to the next chapter, which is "Apathy." Jay-Z's lack of interest is met with Beyoncé's own divestment of energy and resources which are redirected toward the self. "Apathy" is visually marked by flippancy and unapologetic posturing staged by the song "Sorry."

The song, chapter, and stage of development each celebrate Beyoncé's refusal to feel bad for feeling good while acknowledging the death of her former self. The poetry that opens the chapter is recited as she is on a school bus filled with women covered in sacred *orí* paint by Laolu Senbanjo and ornately braided, coiffed hair. Like the iconic yellow dress scene from the "Hold Up" video, this is another key moment in the film that highlights Beyoncé critical iconographic adoptions of Yoruba cultural features. This moment recalls Lourdes painting Nola's face after her Oshun bath. And though face painting doesn't generally occur after a spiritual bath in the Lucumí tradition, there are key moments in the initiation process where painting and otherwise adorning the body, face, and head serves critical sacred, ceremonial, and iconographic purposes.

achievement" against the backdrop of the difficulty she endured to become a mother. In her 2013 documentary, *Beyoncé: Life Is But a Dream,* she revealed her difficulty conceiving and that she experienced a miscarriage in the process.[59] In an interview shortly before the release of that film with Oprah Winfrey, Beyoncé remarks that having a miscarriage "was a big part of my story. It was one of the hardest things I've been through. . . . And in the end I have my daughter and there is hope."[60] The line, "here lies the mother of my children both living and dead," in conjunction with Beyoncé's interview can be further explicated in Yoruba spiritual context through the concept of *àbíkú,* or a child that is born to die. Babatunde Lawal writes that "[t]he Yoruba believe that a woman who has lost several successive children is being troubled by *Ẹ̀gbẹ́run* [spirit partners of children] or *Arágbó* [forest-dwelling spirit children], and that the spirit or soul (*ẹ̀mí*) of the same child has been dying and returning to the same woman."[61] While this offers some context to this vulnerable moment in Beyoncé's personal life, Beyoncé's public iconographic and actual engagement with àbíkú and one ceremonial intervention for the phenomenon, Gẹ̀lẹ̀dẹ́ continues and is discussed at length in chapter 4. The line also gives praise to her status as a mother as well as her characteristic perseverance, and orientation toward hope, which appears as the title of a chapter later in the film. Telling the viewer what else she has to hope for, "Her God was listening. Her heaven will be a love without betrayal," the physical, spiritual, and actual work of the film are undertaken with the hope for heaven, which for Beyoncé is "a love without betrayal."[62]

Moving toward the lyrics of the song "Sorry," and back to Odù Ọ̀ṣẹ́túrá, both engage with apathy and its place in the reconciliation process. In both cases, apathy describes inaction in one direction and action in another, where doing nothing is doing something. In Odù Ọ̀ṣẹ́túrá, Oshun takes the following course of (in)action:

> So, she decided to wait and see
> How they would carry out their mission successfully;
> Ọ̀ṣun sat quietly and watched them.
> They all decided not to countenance Ọ̀ṣun in their mission.
> She, too, kept mute,
> And carried on her rightful duty,
> Which is hair-plaiting.[63]

Where Oshun could have interceded on her own behalf to demand acknowledgment, she waited for the Irunmolé to discover the error of their ways of their own accord. And, further, Oshun carries on with her own work so as not to create imbalance in her own life waiting for the Irunmolé to restore balance to theirs. In this way Beyoncé is like Oshun as the lyrics describe the physical and emotional distance Beyoncé creates for herself while leaving room for her husband to make the critical realizations and decisions quite literally on his own.

Opening the song with the chorus, "Sorry, I ain't sorry / Sorry, I ain't sorry / I ain't sorry, nigga, nah," she is unapologetic about taking time and space away from her husband and with herself.[64] Taking that further, the first verse details apathy at work. "He trying to roll me up / I ain't picking up / Headed to the club, I ain't thinking 'bout you."[65] Here she details that apathy is work, requiring phone calls to be ignored and a good time to be had. The second verse indicates that apathy does work, changing the power dynamic between the two. "Now you want to say you're sorry / Now you want to call me crying / Now you gotta see me wilding / Now I'm the one that's lying / And I don't feel bad about it / It's exactly what you get / Stop interrupting my grinding."[66] After waiting with bated breath in "Pray You Catch Me," this verse illustrates a complete turn of events wherein the relationship is on Beyoncé's terms and Jay-Z is at Beyoncé's whim for the first time in the film. Further, this reversal is characterized as "just desserts" allowing themes of retribution and justice to emerge. Like Oshun, Beyoncé also uses this time to return to her craft, or to carry on "with her rightful duty."[67] At the end of the second verse, she commands Jay-Z to "stop interrupting my grinding," acknowledging that his belated sense of urgency is a mere inconvenience to her and will be treated as such.

The following and fifth chapter is "Emptiness." The poetry of this chapter draws on the theme of emptiness in two ways: a physical emptiness of the womb during menstruation, and a grieving separation of two lovers. Spoken over the same underwater that opens the film while the camera pans from underneath a floodlight in the rain back into the emptiness of the parking garage, Beyoncé's voice is disembodied as we view her again in the red gown surrounded by fire, this time donning an ornate horned headpiece. "She sleeps all day. Dreams of you in both worlds. Tills the blood, in and out of uterus. Wakes up smelling of zinc, grief sedated by orgasm, orgasm heightened by grief. God was in the room when the man said to the woman, 'I love you so much. Wrap your legs around me. Pull me in, pull me in, pull me in.' Sometimes when he'd have her nipple in his mouth, she'd whisper, 'Oh, my God.' That, too, is a form of worship. Her hips grind, pestle and mortar, cinnamon and cloves. Whenever he pulls out . . . loss.

Dear moon, we blame you for floods . . . for the flush of blood . . . for men who are also wolves. We blame for the night for the dark, for the ghosts."[68] Sleeping is subordinated by the importance of dreaming, long considered to be a means to access otherworldly information. The mysticism associated with dreaming is heightened by the emphasis on menstruation. In many cultures, but specifically Yoruba, menstruation is a both a source of great power and fear. "The ability to pray effectively is called ọfọ aṣẹ. Ifá scripture suggests that women have ọfọ aṣẹ as a consequence of menstruation. Men receive ọfọ aṣẹ as a consequence of initiation. Because the power of the word is a natural birthright of women, this power has been erroneously associated with 'witchcraft' by those who have tried to give it a negative connotation."[69] Placing God in the room shifts the perspective of sex from a carnal experience to a religious one, and exercising the "power of the word" during a moment of coital bliss being defined as worship draws back to the divinity of the Black womanhood established earlier in the film. The poem explores reproductive power at the intersection of menstruation and sex, both intimately related to prayer and worship. Here both are mediating Beyoncé's acknowledgment of "Loss," the following chapter, as well as her grieving process. The poem speaks not just of emptiness, but also that emptiness is the result of loss—of blood, of a connection, and of a partner. The incorporation of lunar cycles and their causal relationship with "the flush of blood" alongside "men who are also wolves" continues the intimate relationship between menstruation, the moon, night, and magic/witchcraft. The same entity that imbues women with power gives the cover of night to predators and spirits benevolent and malevolent alike. For the first time in the film, Beyoncé verbalizes the visual contrast between dúdú and pupa, between the vitality and redness of blood, and the uncertainty and darkness of night, as the camera takes the viewer down a narrow hallway lit by hanging red light bulbs that leads to a door with a small window, also beaming with red light.

Before the viewer is invited into the doorway, the scene changes again to Beyoncé in the backseat of a limousine. Carrying over the charged pupa energy from the previous poem, this transition serves as a bridge between "Emptiness" and the next chapter, "Loss," scored to her song "6 Inch." The Weeknd's featured verse (one of few male voices featured in the film) is disrupted by another male voice saying "yeah" over quick clip of a man's mouth smiling to reveal his gold teeth.[70] The camera takes the viewer on yet another journey up a short stairwell, lit by red light to reveal a room where Beyoncé is standing still but twirling a red lightbulb above her head. Wearing a long-sleeved dress covered in black sequined appliqués, she twirls in the center of the room where other women are seated stoically as her voice recites "Every fear . . . every nightmare . . . anyone has ever had."[71] Taking this short poem to be her definition of "Loss," which flashes quickly onto the screen at the conclusion the first verse that resumes at the end of the poem, it explains the emphasis of red and black, pupa and dúdú, capturing both the uncertainty of confronting loss, fears, and nightmares, as well as her power to overcome them.

The song is self-congratulatory as well as a glimpse into how Beyoncé processes "Loss" by working. Previously, she referred to Jay-Z's hounding as an interruption to her rightful duty: performing and making music. Staying with that sentiment, the song dives into the ins and outs of her work ethics, morals, and financial prowess. The post-chorus highlights her need to situate her wealth as earnings: "She works for the money / She work for the money / From the start to the finish / And she worth every dollar / She worth every dollar / And she worth every minute."[72]

Beyoncé emphasizes her labor in producing music, constructing a brand, and building positive equity in that brand. Establishing a track record for showing up and showing out, Beyoncé reinforces her self-worth personally and professionally. Ending the second verse, "She don't gotta give it up cause she professional," Beyoncé makes clear that she values herself enough to avoid sexual exploitation in an industry that is predicated on the "thingification" of Black women and girls, and that she is ethically concerned about her career, image, and legacy.[73]

While verses and chorus focus on her ability to amass wealth, as well as her professional value, the bridge explores the motivating force behind Beyoncé's tireless labor. "She fights and she sweats those sleepless nights / But she don't mind, she loves the grind / She grinds from Monday to Friday / Works from Friday to Sunday."[74] Here, the film and song make apparent that the overproduction Beyoncé is famous for is not unassociated with her state of mind. Experiencing loss keeps her up at night, yet she turns insomnia into productivity. Work and overworking are characterized as coping mechanisms and tactics of avoidance. During the bridge of song, the film stages Beyoncé as pensive. The room is still tinted in red, and though her lacey leotard and overcoat are white, they, too, are cast in a red glow. Above the bed is a large mirror that gives the viewer the first glimpse of Beyoncé laying on her back and is reminiscent of the first boudoir scene where she mirrors herself. The camera switches between shots of her gazing out of the window on to the nightlife of New Orleans and the bedroom where she is clutching a pillow close to her chest and laying in a bed where she often lies but seldom sleeps.

At the conclusion of the song, Beyoncé is seen walking down the same hallway that led us into the building with the door behind her engulfed in flames. She sings "[N]ow you know / I'll make you feel / You'll always come back to me," which taken with the flames presents an interesting transition from loss toward accountability.[75] Beyoncé burns down the room, the site of her sleeplessness and where she processes her loss. These flames represent a finite end to this chapter in the film as well as her openness to repairing her relationship. She sings "come back" six times after the above lyrics, the last of which coincides with a tight shot of Beyoncé standing in front of the flaming building.[76] The camera pans out to reveal the women seated with her earlier in the film standing to the left and right of her under flashing red lights like those of an emergency response vehicle parked off-screen. Glaring into the camera, she is intent on leaving "Loss" behind, and perhaps pleading with Jay-Z to come back, but to come back to her differently than when she decided to leave, ready to embrace accountability.

Doing Right: Restoring Balance

The cinematic transition between Loss and Accountability takes the viewer through a bayou at night to get to the Madewood Plantation House in the light of day. The setting is apropos given Beyoncé's preoccupation with the generational implications of a tenuous filial relationships. It opens with little girls at play with one another and with dolls in a neatly organized bedroom inside the house. Beyoncé's occupation of the plantation, alongside the other women and girls in the film visually captures the past and present collapsing time and space as well as the necessity to address issues old and new in seeking to restore damaged relationships.

> You find the black tube inside her beauty case where she keeps your father's old prison letters. You desperately want to look like her. You look nothing like your mother. You look everything like your mother. Film star beauty. How to wear your mother's lipstick. You go to the bathroom to apply your mother's lipstick. Somewhere no one can find you. You must wear it like she wears disappointment on her face. Your mother is a woman and women like her cannot be contained. Mother dearest, let me inherit the earth. Teach me how to make him beg. Let me make up for the years he made you wait. Did he bend

your reflection? Did he make you forget your own name? Did he convince you he was a god? Did you get on your knees daily? Do his eyes close like doors? Are you a slave to the back of his head? Am I talking about your husband or your father?[77]

Here, Beyoncé engages the ways in which trauma and disappointment are passed down from generation to generation consciously and unconsciously. Focusing attention on a physical item, lipstick, which is often indicative of adultness, particularly womanhood, the poem identifies how girl children operationalize the tools of their mothers while coming of age and traversing similar and different terrain. While one may look nothing like their mother physically, the poem suggests that at any given time, a predicament might emerge that causes situational resemblance, including but not limited to disappointment.

The film creates separation between the first and second halves of the poem with footage of men talking to one another regarding the nihilism that is often associated with being Black and male in the underserved urban centers of the United States, like New Orleans. On a raining car ride, the driver says to an obscured passenger, "I even met the president one time man. I ain't tell you that? Yeah, I met the president, you know? Before I met him, you dig, I ain't really see myself going nowhere. I didn't really—I didn't really care if I lived or died. Now I feel like I got to live, man, for my kids and stuff, you know. He from the hood just like me. From Chiraq, you know? I'm from New Orleans. You know, that give me inspiration on I can be whatever I want to be, like, you know, whatever I want to be. You know, I'm probably gonna be the next Spike Lee in this shit or something. Understand what I'm saying?"[78] Oddly fixed between the two halves of the poem, the disruption it causes visually and aurally tells two sides of the same story: his story as well as those of the women who suffered alongside this unnamed man before he decided that he ought to live for his children. That line is meaningfully placed over footage of him gently placing his hand over the shoulder of a seated pregnant woman, likely the mother of his children, who are also in the frame. Switching between puddles of rainwater on the street and decidedly grainy footage of people on the street and families in their homes, the lines, "[t]each me how to make him beg. Let me make up for the years he made you wait," take on more nuance considering what waiting may have looked like to wait on a partner who was not motivated to live.[79] Giving nuance to the Black male characters under criticism, the footage allows a glimpse into the perspective of the men that the women central to the narrative often love. While Beyoncé continues to center herself and other women by asking her mother to teach her how to make up for the time she was made to wait, the male monologue adds depth without decentering women who suffer with men who are suffering.

The poem also draws back to the beginning of the film, where Beyoncé herself abstained from mirrors, perhaps because her own reflection was distorted. Collapsing time and space again, Beyoncé asks a critical question: "Am I talking about your husband or your father?"[80] Simultaneously telling her mother's story and her own, Beyoncé takes to task her father (as her father and as her mother's husband) and her husband (and as her daughter's father). The lone country song on the album, "Daddy Lessons," complicates what it means to be successful as a parent and unsuccessful as a spouse alongside accountability. Going back to her Southern country roots visually and sonically, Beyoncé takes the viewer on a journey through her youth, drawing on home videos with her father, Matthew Knowles, alongside raw footage of New Orleans: including men on horns, a second line funeral (a New Orleanian tradition that involves jazz music and a parade following the casket of the deceased), as well as a father and daughter on horseback riding through the street. As the song opens, the camera zooms in through a tunnel at Fort Macomb, where Beyoncé is dressed in an Ankara print dress that merges colonial, Victorian, and contemporary African styles as well as rubber goulashes. In the tunnel, she stands proudly next to a seated Little Freddie King, a world-renowned Blues guitarist with his own New Orleans roots. Saying "Texas" before the song begins, Beyoncé mentions her Texan rearing for the first time in the film, even as she continues to ground the film as a squarely New Orleanian visual project that pays homage to her maternal lineage. Both verses of the song take the viewer through activities Beyoncé and her father share together, but of major significance here are the chorus and the bridge. Both are far more directed at the issues at hand. "He held me in his arms / And he taught me to be strong / He told me when he's gone / Here's what you do / When trouble comes to town / And men like me come around / Oh, my daddy said shoot."[81] Beyond the scope of this album, Beyoncé has expressed a long-standing public adoration for her father, including a song in his honor on her debut album, "Daddy."[82] Matthew Knowles managed her career from her time as the front woman of Destiny's Child until she fired him in 2011, after her parent's highly publicized divorce, which included speculations that Matthew fathered at least two children outside the marriage to her mother, Tina.[83] It is worth noting that the lyrics to the chorus of the first song about her father, "I want / My unborn son / To be like my daddy / I want my husband to be like my daddy / There is no one else like my daddy," suggests a desire for her romantic interests to mirror the desirable aspects of her father.[84] In a turn of events, the opening poem of *Lemonade*, "Denial," reflects that her husband takes on the worst aspects of her father, "You remind me of my father, a magician ... able to exist in two places at once. In the tradition of men in my blood, you come home at 3 a.m. and lie to me."[85]

In the chorus of "Daddy Lessons," released thirteen years after the release of "Daddy," the reversal is apparent, as it is revealed that her own preparation for mistreatment from men was taught to her by her father, not just in language but in actions as well. These lyrics add an interesting dynamic to the chapter, "Accountability," because, for the lesson to have any salience, Beyoncé's father must admit that she should be vigilant against men who are like him, taking accountability for his own failures as a man, a husband, and a father. The bridge of the song turns the critique back to her own husband: "My daddy warned me about men like you / He said baby girl he's playing you / He's playing you."[86] The song shifts from her father warning her about men like him to Beyoncé herself acknowledging that in warning her against men like himself, he was actually warning her against men like her husband. She addresses him directly, reflecting on the utility of these lessons and perhaps, her own naivete by ignoring the undesirable similarities between her husband and her father in the narrative she constructed until now. Despite the apparent critique of her father's failings, visually, it is clear that she still has great admiration and love for him, including the footage of her younger self exchanging "I love yous" and kisses on a couch, as well as footage of her daughter, Blue Ivy Carter, playing happily with him in a hotel room. This visual gesture informs the viewer that accountability is ultimately a tool of healing and reconciliation, not of severing ties. Accountability, then, serves as a bridge over troubled water, where both injurer and injured may start the journey back toward corrective action and a relationship where balance can be restored. Like Odù Ọ̀ṣẹ́túrá, *Lemonade* situates accountability and corrective action before forgiveness is conferred. In the visual album, the chapter "Reformation" serves as the "ground zero" for the work of rebuilding the relationship to take place.

As a rule of thumb, the film transports the viewer through time and space by shifting the setting of the film from rural to urban. This is true of the transition from "Accountability" to "Reformation," as the camera takes the viewer from the catacombs of Fort Macomb through the Royal Parking Garage to arrive at the field of the Mercedes-Benz Superdome. Women in

Victorian dresses are positioned around the stands looking on to the field where Beyoncé, wearing a white dress, lays on her side with hand on her stomach while crying at the fifty-yard line. The poem begins just as the film itself starts to rewind through the other chapters. "Reformation" appears on the screen for a brief moment backgrounded by a young woman looking away from the camera as she stands on the porch of the Destrehan Plantation at night. Beyoncé narrates the film's action, which has returned to black and white, "He bathes me until I forget their names and faces. I ask him to look me in the eye when I come home. Why do you deny yourself heaven? Why do you consider yourself undeserving? Why are you afraid of love? You think it's not possible for someone like you. But you are the love of my life. You are the love of my life. You are the love of my life."[87] Notably, "Reformation" is a rather short chapter of the film that only includes the first verse and chorus of the song "Love Drought." The poem opens with an indication of action on behalf of her estranged husband, where he bathes her to wash away the presence of the "unknown women [who] wander the hallways at night."[88] Water, Oshun's element, appears again in the poem and in the film, as a critical element in the process of healing. The setting changes again from the plantation to the Mercedes-Benz Superdome, to a beach which is quite likely the shores of Lake Pontchartrain based on its proximity to Fort Macomb and its notable relationship to the city of New Orleans. This poem humanizes Jay-Z by asking critical questions regarding his inability to access, give, and receive love, but does not center his pain or use it as an excuse for his behavior.

"Reformation" sets the stage for "Forgiveness" with the song "Love Drought," which acknowledges that the love has gone out of the relationship but that together, the drought can be ended as indicated by the first verse. "Are you aware / You're my lifeline, are you tryna kill me? / If I wasn't me, would you still feel me? / Like on my worst day? / Or am I not thirsty, enough? / I don't care about the lights or the beams / Spend my life in the dark for the sake of you and me."[89] The verse walks the viewer through the tenuous nature of the relationship even as both parties are attempting to put it back together. Though the verse mentions an effort on Jay-Z's part, it still focuses squarely on Beyoncé's perspective as well as what she is willing to sacrifice to get back on track—namely, her celebrity. Here, Beyoncé returns to the problem of hypervisibility and treats it as an obstacle in two ways. First, she questions whether her husband would be willing or able to empathize with her if she wasn't Beyoncé, and second, Beyoncé, being who she is, draws a constant external gaze from fans and paparazzi alike, which makes maintaining her privacy a continual challenge. Further, it is clear by her willingness to spend her life in the dark that she is uninterested in performing and staging a loving relationship that is fundamentally unstable but would rather do the work in the dark to mend fences and create an actual healthy relationship for herself, regardless of how it will be consumed publicly. She acknowledges that she and J-Zay have both bottomed out, which as uncomfortable as that may be, is a good place for the mutual work to begin as indicated by the chorus, "You, you, you, you and me could make it rain now / You, you, you, you and me could stop this love drought."[90] The chorus highlights a mutual effort in attempts to reconcile, as well as Beyoncé's desire to rebuild a relationship now that she has processed her emotions and grieved the old one. This song shifts the tone of the film from her apathy, squarely placing the onus on Jay-Z to right his wrongs, to her recognition of the necessity of a joint effort if the relationship is truly going to be reformed.

The song stops abruptly at the end of the chorus and is interrupted by percussive music and a tight shot of Beyoncé's face, painted with five white dots over each brow, one in between both brows, as well as five dots under each eye, two of which are dragged down into lines over her cheeks, very similar to Nola Darling's paint after her Oshun bath. The shot of Beyoncé's face takes one full clockwise turn before zooming out to reveal her, now adorned with large circular earrings and two large gold necklaces encircled by women with their arms outstretched toward her, not touching her but seemingly directing their energy into her. I read this abrupt scene as a visual tribute to the cycles of individual growth Beyoncé endures in the film up until this point, as well as the aid she receives in community with women throughout. It reads as a final rite of passage out of her suffering and on to solid ground, on which she may choose to rebuild her relationship with her husband. The entire scene is very quick and accompanied by a high-pitched screeching, making the viewer feel as if they have stumbled upon something they should not be seeing, so they are only afforded a glimpse before the camera zooms out and away to trees, finally landing on the hem of Beyoncé's flowing satin dress as she stands on a branch being lightly lapped by waves. The camera pans up, barely reaching her hips before switching to a wide shot of the lake where the word "Forgiveness" finally appears on screen.

Staying on the shore, the poem that opens the chapter "Forgiveness," is also accompanied by water. "Baptize me . . . now that reconciliation is possible. If we're gonna heal, let it be glorious. 1,000 girls raise their arms.

Do you remember being born? Are you thankful for the hips that cracked? The deep velvet of your mother and her mother and her mother? There is a curse that will be broken."[91] Shifting from an artistic shot of two nude women and their shadows reclining on their elbows in the sand, the camera moves slowly along the shoreline starting at Beyoncé's feet being lapped by the light waves, then to trees, and then again to multiple women alongside Beyoncé standing calf-deep in the lake, holding hands with other women and all of their arms raised. Finally, the camera reveals Beyoncé wrapped in tulle at the shoreline gazing at the waves coming toward her, and then slowly turning her head to look directly into the camera and then past it. The film shows the viewer both her proverbial baptism as well as the unity of 1,000 girls raising their arms, though the women featured do not number in the thousands. The poem and the film do the work of contextualizing Beyoncé's forgiveness as bigger than her and her husband, as a central piece of a puzzle that comes together for the purpose of justice, not just for her, but also for the many women who came before her, and the ones who will come after. The poem's allusions to birth connect the film's quest for reconciliation and social justice back to Odù Ọ̀ṣẹ́túrá and Oshun's own quest for social justice. Oshun's relationship to the Irunmolé is reconciled and her curse broken by her birth of her son, Elegba. Beyoncé's own inquiry into the gratitude of her husband to the women who bore children that he may be born, alongside her insistence that a curse be broken, dives right into the heart of Oshun's final actions in Odù Ọ̀ṣẹ́túrá. For Oshun's curse to be broken and for stasis to be restored, the Irunmolé had to shower the primordial mother with gratitude for her pregnancy and pray that she delivers a male child to aid them in their endeavors. While Beyoncé refers clearly to a generational curse linking her and her husband to the dysfunction of their forbears, I read her inquiry as an acknowledgment of Jay-Z's lack of gratitude for the sacrifice of the women who made his life possible, including Hattie, and that his lack of gratitude informs his behavior toward her, and ultimately keeps the generational curse from being broken, just as the Irunmolé's ingratitude toward Oshun's contributions kept their plans stagnant and the earth suffering.

The second half of the poem takes the viewer into the fireplace of a house, where Nina Simone's "The Look of Love" plays softly. The camera pans to Beyoncé's feet walking deliberately on the concrete of the hallway, and then to items around the home including a black ceramic bowl with gold lines associated with *kintsugi* (the Japanese art of repair), old photographs of a man and woman, as well as the record player playing the Nina Simone album *Silk & Soul* (1967), the cover to which is prominently displayed beside it. At the conclusion of the poem, the camera pans slowly down to reveal Beyoncé seated on the floor in front of a keyboard, laptop, microphone, and filter, wearing headphones and playing the song "Sandcastles."[92] The song serves as a metaphor for the instability of the relationship that they previously built: sandcastles look nice, as they often do, but they can be easily dismantled, as sandcastles inevitably are. This chapter of the film is marked by intimacy, from a comfortably dressed Beyoncé working on the song being sung in her makeshift home studio, to shots of their daughter's arts and crafts sprawled about and the moments of embrace captured in the first scenes of the film that Jay-Z is visually featured. The song is notably without a chorus and is sung in its entirety uninterrupted, unlike many of the other songs in the film. The song outlines that, despite her best efforts and intentions to dissolve the marriage, Beyoncé's love for Jay-Z was stronger than the hurt he caused her: "Dishes smashed on my counter from our last encounter / Pictures snatched out the frame / Bitch, I scratched out your name and your face / What is it about you that I can't erase, baby? / When every promise don't work out that way, no no, babe."[93] The song is both a recap of the intense emotional roller coaster that the film has been up to this point and a marker of their first encounter after they have both gotten off the ride. For the first time, the viewer is offered a glimpse into the emotional world of Jay-Z and how he is affected by Beyoncé's actions as told by the visual album. Just as "Apathy" marks Beyoncé clear departure from the relationship that was, "Sandcastles," offers the viewer a retrospective on where Beyoncé's apathetic departure left Jay-Z, which is tearful and heartbroken. Despite the second verse's allusion to violent exchanges between the two, the third finally outlines the parameters under which Beyoncé is willing to stay, which all boil down to vulnerability. Revealing the ways in which he hurt himself by hurting her is Jay-Z's penance, calling back to her initial warning and bringing the narrative full circle.

Though "Forgiveness" is not the final chapter of the film, it marks the end of Beyoncé's quest for retribution, accountability, and corrective action on behalf of the transgressors in the film. The chapters beyond "Forgiveness," "Resurrection," "Hope," and "Redemption," can be read as the afterlife of forgiveness, the work that can be done as well as the love and healing that becomes available to future and past generations now that the curse has been broken. Regardless of the ways in which Oshun may appear as wrathful in Odù Ọṣẹ́túrá and in other patakís where she goes to battle to defend and protect her children, Oshun is ultimately about healing and restoration.

As wrathful and angry as Beyoncé presents herself to the viewer in the film, the chapters "Anger," "Apathy," "Emptiness," "Loss," and "Accountability" are necessary parts of the grieving process and must be endured if healing and reconciliation are to ever be possible. In Odù Ọ̀ṣẹ́túrá, Oshun teaches the Irunmolé as well as the readers many lessons, perhaps most vividly that there are consequences for mistreating her, and by extension her children. What hides under the grandeur of her gestures to bring the Irunmolé to the realization of their error is that there is always a way back via corrective action. In *Lemonade,* too, Beyoncé ensures the viewer that there is a way back, not only to herself, but also to love, and that the journey back is rigorous but worth the sacrifice for all parties involved.

3

Water Always Returns to Its Source

Oshun's Medium as Guiding Principle in Narratives of Healing

Golly, look at that water, boy
—Unnamed man, *Lemonade* (2016) (Film)

Now you wouldn't think they'd get very far seeing as it was water they were walking on. . . . They just kept walking, like the water was solid ground
—Eula Peazant, *Daughters of the Dust* (1991)

Water Is a Solid Foundation

The attributes of water, and of Oshun, have been addressed in terms of fluidity, depth, and mystery. While it is true that water is liquid and does not have a solid surface, I assert that in the narratives discussed below, water provides a solid foundation on which to construct a narrative visually, textually, and sonically. The many ways in which Oshun spiritually intervenes in the lives of the characters in chapters 1 and 2 remains relevant, yet the third divination verse of the Odù Ògúndá Ìwòrì provides an interesting example of how Oshun, after a physical intervention, takes the form of water and guides her followers to safety. Wande Abimbola writes that it "tells us how Ọ̀ṣun Àpara (otherwise known as Yemesé) delivered the people of Ìdó when their town was conquered and the people were being taken away as slaves. She beheaded their enemies and freed the people of Ìdó. When her people said that they did not know the way back to Ìdó, she fell down on the spot, became a river, and flowed back to Ìdó carrying her people along with her."[1] The place-name "Ìdó" literally translates to mean, "place of founding," indicating the necessity of water, or Oshun, in the establishment of the city, and the safe return of its residents. Another patakí refers to the founding of Ọṣogbo, where Oshun is celebrated annually with a two-week festival in her honor each August. An excerpt of the story recounts:

> One day, King Laro, followed by all his subjects arrived at a river named Oshún. "Is this the place?" asked his subjects. "I do not know yet," said the king. "I must consult the oracles. But it is a good place to rest." . . . King Laro's daughters came to him and asked, "Father, we are hot and dusty. May we bathe in this beautiful river?" "Yes, you may," said the king. "Be careful and do not go too far from the shore." "We will be careful, father," said the daughters, and they ran to the river. . . . King Laro was preparing the board and necklaces needed to consult the oracle when his warriors rushed into the camp. "Oh king," said the warriors. "Your daughters dove into the river and they have not come up!" King Laro and all his people ran to the river bank. His daughters were gone. They searched the shore looking for the girl's [sic] bodies. There was no trace of them. The king and his people began to cry and smear ashes on their heads. Suddenly, one of the warriors pointed and shouted, "Look, over there! The waters are opening." King Laro's daughters walked out of the bosom of the river. When they were closer all the people could see that their bodies were dry. "It is a miracle," they shouted. The king hugged and kissed his daughter. His eyes were filled with tears. "What happened to you?" he asked them, "We thought the river had taken you." "Oshún, the river Orishá, took us to her home," said the girls. "She gave us presents and said we were very beautiful." "Oh my people," said the grateful king, "we must take a fitting sacrifice to this powerful Orishá. . . ." The king addressed the river, "Great Orishá, great Oshún, we are grateful for the return of my daughters. Please accept our offering to you. . . ." "Oshún's messengers have accepted the offering," said the king. Then, a very large fish, the largest fish any of these people had ever seen, swam to the king. It held a pumpkin in its mouth, which it laid on the river's edge, right at the king's feet. . . . Very gravely, the king picked up the pumpkin and said to his subjects, "This is proof that the Orishá wishes to make treaty with me. To honor this moment, I change my name to Ataoja." . . . "Oshún Gbó, Oshún is mature, her abundant waters will never fail us. I name this place Oshogbó. Here we will settle." And so it was that, in that place protected by Oshún, the city of Oshogbó was founded.[2]

Here again, Oshun's river is a foundation for a settlement to flourish. This time, however, submersion is a key feature of establishing a relationship with Oshun's energy. Although the king intended to consult the oracles (which I am interpreting as Ifá), the bath (which became spiritual in nature despite its practical intent) of King Laro's daughters eliminates the need for the consultation and confirms Oshun's willingness to support the burgeoning settlement, perhaps to develop a cult of devotees. Written as though by complete happenstance, the daughters' need to bathe allows for Oshun's blessing to be conferred, and ẹbọ of gratitude to be made by the king, and a long-standing relationship of adoration for Oshun from the people of Ọṣogbo to begin.

King Laro's daughters' description of their experience at the bottom of the river, reflects Jamaica Kincaid's own description in "At the Bottom of the River." King Laro's daughters insist that their time submerged in the river was spent at Oshun's underwater abode, and about a similar experience Kincaid writes in her short story that "I walked to the mouth of the river, and it was then still in the old place near the lite-tree grove. The water was clear and still. I looked in, and at the bottom of the river I could see a house, and it was a house of only one room, with and A-shaped roof.... All around the house was a wide stretch of green—green grass freshly mowed a uniform length.... Then, at the line where the grass ended and the pebbles began, there were flowers: yellow and blue irises, red poppies, daffodils, marigolds."³ It is possible that Kincaid's description from the perspective of the unnamed protagonist is one that can be applied to Oshun's home. This parallel is further underscored by her description of the woman who lives there, from the protagonist's vantage point on the shore. "She wore no clothes. Her hair was long, and so very black, and it stood out in a straight line away from her head, as if she commanded it to be that way. I could not see her face. I could see her feet, and I saw that her insteps were high, as if she had been used to climbing high mountains. Her skin was the color of brown clay, and she looked like a statue, liquid and gleaming, just before it is to be put in a kiln."⁴ It is not uncommon that Orisha's faces are obscured. Particularly in Brazil, statues as well as practitioners who are dressed as or mounted by Orisha are veiled, typically with elegant beading connected to a crown, which itself has roots in Yoruba aesthetic practices, as hanging fringed beads over a wearers face indicates sovereignty.⁵ Neither in the pataki above nor in Kincaid's short story is Oshun's face described. I would assert that this is in part because Oshun takes on many faces. Also, there is a lack of emphasis placed on the physical description of Orisha's physical attributes aside from skin color, height, and general size, and perhaps hair type, texture, and length, or other elements that take on ritual and practical significance. It is generally understood from Oshun's lore that she is beautiful, but few if any patakís include a description of her face to indicate what makes her beauty so. In one way, this allows Oshun's followers, as well as readers of her lore, to expand their notions of beauty and vanity, in another, it asserts that Oshun is beauty itself manifested and therefore her physical appearance is of no consequence. Either way, Kincaid's physical description of the woman at the bottom of the river, is congruent with general understandings of Oshun's appearance including long hair and brown (though not very dark) skin.

These patakís, taken together, reflect an aspect of Oshun that is often understated—her indispensability in social organization and development. Her necessity in these matters is reflected in Odù Ọ̀ṣẹ́túrá, which is discussed at length in chapter 2. Without her aid, creation is rendered impossible and according to the odù, Oshun is the foundation on which the world itself is established and allowed to continue to flourish. Quite literally, societies cannot flourish without a potable water source, but culturally, Oshun's material influence remains alive in Ọṣogbo beyond the Oshun River, as the official title of the sovereign of Ọṣogbo remains Àtaója, the name King Laro adopted in honor of Oshun at the end of the pataki. The name is believed to be an amalgamation of the phrase, atẹ́wọ́gbẹja—that is, "one who stretches the hand to receive fish."[6] The very name of the sovereign of Ọṣogbo, is in deference to the abundance that Oshun bestows upon her children, out of the wealth of her river. Through Oshun's generosity, water becomes a solid foundation on which to build a society, or in this case, construct and guide a narrative.

This chapter draws on water as a foundational element to analyze the imagery of *Lemonade* and Julie Dash's seminal film *Daughters of the Dust* alongside Jamaica Kincaid's short story, "At the Bottom of the River." Though water baptism, ritual cleaning, or initiation is not exclusive to the Lucumí system, water being Oshun's primary element carries specific weight as it pertains to the structure of the respective narratives. I assert that the protagonists' respective quests for personal, generational, and even social healing, are not only based on submersion in water but also guided and punctuated by water. This chapter examines how integral a role water plays in the rebirth of women characters after the experience of trauma. Using the creative work of Kincaid alongside the analysis of Beyoncé, Yellow Mary, and Eula Peazant's characters, I argue that not only is pain and suffering washed away in Oshun's waters, but also that the appearance of water in each narrative signifies beginnings, significant transitions, and ends, and therefore represents both a departure and a return: a departure from turmoil and a return to the self. This cycle is evidenced by the visual and sonic structure of *Lemonade*, as the visual album itself begins and ends centrally focused on the sight and sound of water. Maintaining *Lemonade* as the central focus of the chapter, "At the Bottom of the River" and *Daughters of the Dust* provide intertextual examples of how water can frame a narrative, and more specifically, how Oshun's energy is symbolized through water, guiding the viewer/reader along the journey, just as Oshun guides her people back to Ìdó. Finally, I assert that Oshun can be found at varying locations in the river, including most prominently the bottom, but also that the weight associated with strife can be found and must be left at the bottom of the river for the characters to become light enough to float, or return to the surface leaving their burden behind.[7]

Going with the Flow

At the outset, it is important to note that to date, many comparisons have been made between *Daughters of the Dust* and *Lemonade*. While there are some clear similarities between the two films, including costuming (primarily Victorian and white color schemes, or funfun), staging, and outright scene adoptions (including Blue Ivy Carter walking sassily with her hands on her hips in the same way as a young girl on the beach in *Daughters*), many others that have been asserted regarding the films' respective narratives are tenuous at best.[8] The striking visual similarities between the two films, and *Lemonade*'s 2016, timely release in the same year as the twenty-fifth anniversary of *Daughters of the Dust* (1991) served to further connect the two films, as Julie Dash herself credits Beyoncé and *Lemonade* for drawing attention to the film and contributing to its rerelease.[9] My focus, is the ways in which both films treat water, such that Ibo Landing in *Daughters of the Dust*, and Lake Pontchartrain in *Lemonade*, become characters all their own, contributing to the plot, progress (ẹ̀tọ̀) of the protagonists and punctuating the beginning and the ends of the narratives, which I would assert are often one and the same. Anissa Janine Wardi addresses why this might be, writing that "[i]n African American cultural history, bodies of water are lieux de memoire, embodied sites where memory and history converge."[10] Past, present, and future converge to meet the characters in *Lemonade* and *Daughters of the Dust* at these significant sites where their representations can be interpreted as both "individual, as in they hold personal memories and experiences [which is certainly true for Beyoncé and Lake Pontchartrain], and communal, as waterways may be sites of significant national—or global—historical moments," which is certainly true in the case of Ibo Landing and the Atlantic Ocean for African American descendants of enslavement.[11]

In *Lemonade,* though the first images are Beyoncé in a decidedly urban setting, the Royal Parking Garage, the first audio is what the closed caption refers to as, "underwater thumping."[12] The source of the thumping is off-screen, and it is never revealed to the viewer. The source of the sound is not as significant as the fact that it opens the film, indicating an attention to submersion, the centrality of water to the entirety of the narrative, and the ways in which water reinforces the nonlinear construction of time. Though *Lemonade* concerns itself with a forward-moving trajectory, or progress, chronology is consistently challenged, through both the narration and the action of the plot. I argue that water and its sounds mark the instances that the narrative simultaneously begin and end or mark meaningful transition. The thumping that marks the opening of the film returns in during the fifth section of the film, "Emptiness." This is especially significant given that five is the number associated with Oshun in divinatory and ritual contexts. I interpret the sonic reoccurrence of this underwater thumping as a signal of the reappearance of Oshun's energy as Beyoncé transitions through the experience of "Emptiness," as constructed by the narrative and reflected by Warsan Shire's poetry.

Following my analysis of "Emptiness" in chapter 2, regarding the significance of pupa, or vitality as indicated by the redness of the section, I assert further that before Beyoncé sets the fire that consumes room that she occupies, the underwater thumping signals the end and new beginning that emerge from the section. The visual elements of the "Emptiness" section recall the pataki where Oshun appears in a red gown to go to battle for a child that had been kidnapped from his home.[13] Not only does Oshun provide a definitive end to the child's suffering by destroying his enemies (which are also hers by extension), she sets him on the path toward home and safety, guiding him along the way.[14] "Emptiness" as one poignant section of the film follows water's flow (sonically and visually) toward healing and is similar to this pataki in form and function. First, the sonic presence of water sets the stage for the visual and narrative developments to come, a beginning of an end. Second, Beyoncé actively sets the fire that ultimately lays waste to a physical structure that represents a physical space occupied by the "Emptiness" she describes. This indicates a decisive move toward a finite end to the part of her emotional journey that is marked by suffering. Finally, Beyoncé is positioned in front of the building while it is fully ablaze, glaring directly into the camera. Here, she stands firmly as an arsonist, but also her willingness and ability to take the first step forward from that place.

To begin at yet another end, "Formation" acts as coda to the *Lemonade* film, although it was the first section of the visual to be released to the public, which is another example of the temporal complexities in and beyond the visual album. The single and accompanying video were both made available to the public on February 6, 2016, one day before the Super Bowl L, where Beyoncé performed the song for the first time. The halftime performance received quite the backlash regarding its allusions to Black Power politics, given that the costumes consisted of black leather and berets.[15] Released roughly three months before the complete visual album debuted on HBO, "Formation" serves simultaneously as an introduction and conclusion to *Lemonade*. The song is a confrontational and self-congratulatory anthem, while the video, like the rest of the film, is a tribute to the diversity of New Orleans's Southern urbanity—poverty, wealth, Mardi Gras masquerade culture, Moorish culture,[16] the Black church, and prominent incorporation of modernized Victorian wardrobes. In accordance with the rest of the narrative, the video opens with a wide shot of Beyoncé squatting casually atop a partially submerged New Orleans Police cruiser in a red and white dress. The police car is not the only thing under water, as the scene is backgrounded by a row of homes that are also partially submerged, calling back to the tragedy of Hurricane Katrina in 2005. It should be noted that there are marked differences between the video released with the single, and the video included at the end of the *Lemonade* film. The former opens with Beyoncé atop the police cruiser, whereas the latter opens with diverse footage of New Orleans and its Black residents, before a tight shot of Beyoncé singing the first few words of the first verse while seated on her side as opposed to squatting on top of the cruiser. Acknowledging the discrepancies in the two versions, water remains a focal point in both, and this chapter is primarily concerned with the version released with the film. I assert that like the patakís referenced above, water is operating as foundational to the narrative of the video as well as to the story of trial, triumph, and resilience that is still ongoing for many people affected by Hurricane Katrina. Beyoncé, under the direction of Melina Matsoukas, creates a video where past is prologue, developing an opportunity for the many narratives written about Katrina, its victims, and survivors, to be signified upon and incorporated into the narrative that Beyoncé creates for herself.

Hence, water is situated in the video where injustice is in the video, driving home the healing capacity of Oshun's medium. The injustices following the tragedy of Hurricane Katrina serves as just one example, but the other prominent example featured in the video is police brutality. Beyoncé seems to engage these issues simultaneously: centering the police cruiser in the foreground situates violent overpolicing as a contemporary issue that is intrinsically linked to the many literal and figurative ways that Black communities in New Orleans were left to drown by the Federal Emergency Management Agency (FEMA), and nongovernmental agencies enlisted to provide aid. Thus, Beyoncé's ultimate drowning of the police cruiser at the end of the video symbolizes a retributive element of justice associated with Oshun that is discussed in the second chapter and recalls her tribute to the mothers who lost their children to police violence.

In conjunction with water operating as the guiding principle, Beyoncé engages more of the energetic signature of pupa in the imagery of this video. Including the red and white dress, this video also incorporates red carpeting and wallpaper in the Victorian home that serves as a backdrop for some of the choreography alongside maroon leotards worn by Beyoncé and her dancers, and this time around, a young man dressed in a red Mardi Gras Indian costume. While the video's color palette is diverse (especially in contrast to the red monochromacy of "Emptiness," for example), red maintains a similar consistency and narrative import as the body of water guiding the narrative of the video. Here I assert that alongside Oshun's influence, Shango's presence can also be detected. One of the three consorts of Oshun, Shango is primarily known for his fiery disposition, swift sense of justice, thunder, and lightning.[17] The "Formation" video provides a stage for Oshun and Shango's energy to work in tandem. It should be noted that there are instances in her lore where Oshun appears in red, as opposed to yellow or white, particularly when she is going to battle.[18] My decision to read the redness of the video as a symbolic reference and iconographic adoption of Shango's energy is predicated on the occurrence of thunder and lightning at the climax of the video coupled with the critique of criminal (in)justice rooted in the submersion of the police cruiser.

Just as Beyoncé's weight begins to drown the police car, thunder and lightning are heard audibly in the background as an unidentified man says emphatically, "Golly, look at that water, boy."[19] Beyond the clear allusions to a gathering storm (which can also be read as a reference to Oya and the sudden change associated with the goddess's intervention), perhaps a storm of social action, the thunder and lightning indicate that Beyoncé's own act of sinking the police cruiser is just the beginning, just as thunder is a harbinger of a storm to come. Again, Beyoncé, through "Formation," which is an extension of *Lemonade,* toys with temporality where the end of the video signals a beginning of something beyond the scope of the visual album itself. This temporal complexity is further underscored by the places in the video, where children are present in lieu of adults. While the Black Lives Matter movement is addressed in the broader film through the spotlight on the mothers of the boys and men slain by police, "Formation" puts the attention on the streets themselves that often become deadly for youth that are simply existing while Black. By contrast, "Formation" centers a young Black boy, instead of an adult man or even a teenager, wearing a black hoodie with the hood over his head dancing in front of and taunting police officers who are standing shoulder to shoulder in riot gear. The juxtaposition presented to the viewer by a squad of police officers standing off with an individual Black child critiques the nature of overpolicing in Black communities as well as the hypervisibility and surveillance of Black bodies in white neighborhoods and other places that are deemed suspicious for a Black person to occupy. When the boy finished his performance, he stretches his arms up and out, causing the police to put their hands up, clear reference to the Black Lives Matter chant, "Hands up, don't shoot." After this exchange, which engages an interesting power reversal, the camera pans to the off-white wall behind the boy, which is spray-painted in black paint to read "Stop Shooting Us."[20] I read the boy's participation in this police-interaction in lieu of an adult man, or even a teenager in this subversive act as a symbolic gesture toward the active potential of the Black Lives Matter movement specifically, and the future of the Black community broadly. Taken together with Beyoncé's submersion of the police car, which is the final scene of the video save a quick shot of her seated elegantly in a white lace leotard holding a small white parasol, these two scenes solidify the police as a site of communal injury, and the water as a location to sink that which no longer serves the community, signal hope for an end to the violence that characterizes policing, and beckon toward a new beginning where the killings have stopped.

With submersion as a thematic guide, the bottom of the river includes not just of the beauty of Oshun's domicile but also the ugliness of suffering drowned by her children to regain buoyancy and remain afloat. Though

Beyoncé sinks the police car at the end of the video, the very last scene is her sitting elegantly in a parlor wearing a white lacy leotard and holding a small parasol, which I read as an indication of her ability to float or resurface after sinking the police cruiser and perhaps some burdens of her own. This dynamic is also engaged by the music group, Ibeyi, in their song dedicated to Oshun, "River."[21] The second single on their self-titled album, the first being "Oya," Ibeyi incorporates explicit references to Oshun, and other Orisha, in their music a year before *Lemonade*'s 2016 release.[22] The duo are twin sisters (as indicated by their name) Lisa-Kaindé and Naomi Diaz. Their French-Cuban origin is accentuated by the ease with which they transition from English, French, Spanish, and Yoruba in their music. Their significance here occurs on multiple levels as their name, Ibeyi, is spanglicized Yoruba for twins (more commonly seen as Ibeji) but is clearly influenced by their Cuban roots, replacing a "j" with a "y." Further, the twin Orishas that are known as Ibeji, are born of Oshun and Shango. Lisa-Kaindé, the older of the two sisters, as indicated by her name (more commonly seen as Kehinde), further underscores the Yoruba cultural influence. The sisters are featured in *Lemonade* and they import their own relationship to Lucumí-informed cultural practices directly into the visual album, but it isn't their first appearance with Beyoncé. Ibeyi "accompanied the photo shoot for [Beyoncé's] September 2015 *Vogue* cover," just seven months before the debut of *Lemonade*, perhaps foreshadowing not just their involvement in the visual album but also Beyoncé's plans to include Lucumí iconography in the project.[23] And, notably, Lisa-Kaindé is the first woman whose face is shown to the camera after Beyoncé herself in the first chapter of the visual album, "Intuition," prominently displaying her own elekes representing an immediate and direct iconographic adoption of Yoruba religious iconography.

Though tangential, it is worth noting that the older of twins is traditionally named Kehinde, and the younger of the two is named Taiwo, regardless of anatomical sex or gender assignment. These names are rooted in Yoruba cultural values and indicate a nonlinear understanding and construction of time as it plays out in the lives of cultural participants. In Western linear constructs of time, those who are older are those who come before, i.e., the twin who is born first. To be sure, in most cases, eldership in Yoruba cultural contexts does follow chronological time, but in the special case of twins, this is not so. Kehinde is considered the senior sibling (ẹgbọ́n) although they are the child that comes second because they have the wisdom to send the child that comes first, Taiwo, in this case the junior sibling (àburò), first to explore that which is uncertain and ensure that the world is safe.[24] Here Yoruba conceptions of time's relativity emerge, where older does not always mean senior. This can also be observed in marital practices, where all parties in the natal family (ìdílé) of the groom (ọkọ̀), are more senior than the new bride(s) (iyawó or ọmọ-[i]lé), including children.[25] These are just a few of the ways in which the iconography and cultural symbolism is carried on through, Ibeyi.

As for water, Ibeyi's song "River" is expressly a plea for Oshun to intervene in their lives. Coupled with the songs video, the two work in tandem to explore the healing capacity of Oshun as well as the efficacy of water as a medium to commune with her. The chorus, "Come to you river / I will come to your river,"[26] indicates a need on behalf of the subject, but also the requisite effort required for anyone asking for help from an Orisha, seeking them out. In this case, seeking out Oshun means coming in direct contact with a river, any river, because they are all hers, or rather as the song suggests, they are all her. Recalling King Laro's daughters' desire to bathe themselves to remove the dust accumulated from their travel in Oshun's river and unwittingly encountering her, the chorus reflects a desire to remove the spiritual or energetic dust accumulated from the difficulty of life's journey, as well as Oshun's ability to remove it. The verses, which are similar, save a few words that do not change the general meaning. The first verse is as follows: "Carry away my dead leaves / Let me baptize my soul with the help of your waters / Sink my pains and complains / Let the river take them, river drown them."[27] A consistent theme is that washing away pain, suffering, or that which no longer serves the subject including previous version of themselves means that those things will no longer present a heavy burden for the subject to carry, as they move forward in life and on their spiritual journey. It stands to reason that those drowned things, including Beyoncé's police cruiser, remain at the bottom of the river with Oshun, and the difference is her capacity to carry those things when her children cannot, and perhaps even to convert them into the beautiful things that surround her abode, or "turn lemons into lemonade" on behalf of her devotees. The singers focus squarely on submersion, or baptism in the video as well. The beauty of the music video is in its simplicity. Both sisters are dressed in white, engaging funfun like the *Lemonade*, and laying in in a shallow pool of water. Each has a hand tightly gripping their garments in the front and gently supporting their heads in the back. It is these hands that facilitate their submersion throughout the course of the video. There are no scene changes in the video, only one sister and then the other being brought above the water just enough so that the surface of the water touches their ears and can sing the chorus and the verses. The video's aesthetics are not altogether different from those of Beyoncé's "Formation," when she sinks the police cruiser. They both share a sense of serenity alongside a sense of surrender to the forces of the water, as well as a faith that their resurfacing will result in improved outcomes for themselves or their communities.

Submersion marks critical shifts in other places in *Lemonade* which are addressed briefly in chapter 2. It bears repeating that Beyoncé's first steps toward undertaking the journey outlined in the narrative are quite literally steps toward water, into which she dives to begin the shedding process. These steps toward Oshun move the narrative from "Intuition" to "Denial," mirroring Ibeyi's own interpretation of the need to go to Oshun, or "come to you River," in order to initiate the intervention they desire.[28] Among practitioners of Lucumí, there is a belief that in many cases, "the ẹbọ is in the travel," meaning that the true sacrifice is not the item(s) one brings to Orisha, but the time and dedication spent collecting items and carefully preparing them for presentation. The emphasis Ibeyi places on going to the Oshun (in the form of a river) in their lyrics as opposed to Oshun coming to them is in line with the practical understandings of human-Orisha relationships.

Additionally, the bottom of the body of water presented in *Lemonade* follows the framework established by Kincaid's short story "At the Bottom of the River," as it is also constructed as a livable home, where the lack of oxygen presents no problem for its inhabitants, just as it did not present a problem for King Laro's daughters. This is further underscored by the duration of Beyoncé's stay in the subaqueous bedroom, as well as her ability to sleep comfortably on the bed without floating or drowning. Both her submersion and her emergence from the bottom of what I conceptually describe here as a river, although that is not presented in the film, are decidedly gold and yellow, which inform my analysis of water's (read Oshun's) narrative import as a catalytic force. This motivating force appears again in chapters 8 and 9, "Reformation," and "Forgiveness" respectively. While she decisively walks through the water in the former, Beyoncé is also gently lapped by water on the shore in the latter.[29]

Taking on the task of "Reformation," Beyoncé quite literally wades through the water, leading a procession of women behind her in matching robes. The scene bears a striking similarity to the baptism procession featured in *Daughters of the Dust*, including the ostensive Christian imagery. The visual similarity between the two films is especially present regarding the two processions and their raised arms in awe of and in deference to the spiritual potency of the water in context of the ritual. While baptisms practiced in Christianity and Lucumí have contextual specificity, the general understanding that purity and rebirth accompany the ritual, and that in many cases, the two are not mutually exclusive further anchors my analysis of the symbolic and narrative import of water and Oshun's accessibility through that medium. Though not fully submerged, Beyoncé's position in proximity to the water as she seeks rebirth and is tasked with conferring forgiveness to her estranged husband (and perhaps to unnamed generational transgressors) follows the established narrative pattern of incorporating the sight or sounds of water to signal progression through critical developmental stages as indicated by the chapters of the film.

This is especially true for "Forgiveness" since the sight and sounds of water are working in tandem with the poetry. Addressed in a different context in chapter 2, the choice to couple the poetry, "Baptize me . . . now that reconciliation is possible," with the presence of water gently washing over Beyoncé makes apparent more similarities between *Lemonade* and the "River" video, which begs the question, To whom is the demand directed?[30] I assert that this demand is spoken directly to the water with the acknowledgment that is has the capacity to wash the both the body, and as Ibeyi mentions, the soul. "Forgiveness," then, alongside its watery imagery, simultaneously marks an end to Beyoncé's individual burden of processing trauma, and the beginning of a fresh start for her marriage. To reiterate, Beyoncé is submerged in the beginning of the narrative, "Denial," as well as in the end, "Formation," using water as a symbolic gesture to punctuate beginnings. Water visually and aurally reinforces the narrative's nonlinear construction of time regardless of its commitment to forward progression, as indicated by eponymous interlude carefully positioned after "Forgiveness."

A chillingly beautiful duet sung by Beyoncé and featuring British vocalist James Blake, "Forward," acts as a bridge between the chapters "Forgiveness" and "Resurrection." The song is particularly haunting since it scores the montage of mothers whose sons were recently slain by police. Taking a moment to acknowledge the multiple symbolic layers upon which resurrection functions, the scene visually invokes the spirit of egun who are dead but not gone. In this sense, the song can be interpreted as a lament as well as encouragement for the living victims of loss to hold on to the memories of their loved ones, but to leave the pain of loss behind. It also engages the developmental stage in the narrative where the foundation of the relationship between Beyoncé and her husband is stable enough to be rebuilt and resurrected. The lyrics to the interlude, "Forward / Best foot first just in case / When we made our way 'til now / It's time to listen, it's time to fight / Forward,"[31] indicate a departure from shaky ground as well as an acknowledgment of the uncertainty of the future by emphasizing the need to put the "best foot first," but a departure, nevertheless. "Resurrection" implies that the old relationship, and perhaps the old Beyoncé are dead, or at the very least, have been washed away as indicated by the eighth song on the visual album, "Sandcastles," which itself engages the purifying nature of water, albeit the ocean.[32]

The Waters of Ibo Landing: A Catalyst for Catharsis and Healing

This is similarly true for *Daughters of the Dust*. The trajectory of the narrative is centered around Ibo Landing, as a beginning from before the film starts, as well as an end that signals a new beginning when the Peazants (except for Nana [Cora Lee Day], Eli [Adisa Anderson], Eula [Alva Rogers], Yellow Mary [Barbara O.], and Iona [Bahni Turpin]) depart from the Sea Islands for the mainland. Scored to wonderfully rhythmic music, the opening scenes of *Daughters of Dust* pan over the beautiful landscape and lingers meaningfully on Ibo Landing and the wooden statue of a fettered man submerged and yet floating in the river. The riverbank and the river itself consistently underscore milestones in the larger narrative, but particularly for Eula and her husband, Eli. Broadening the bodies of water to include the Atlantic Ocean, though largely associated with Oshun's sister, Yemaya, water again provides the backdrop to the majority of the action in the film, but most importantly the climactic catharsis that allows the Peazant family to confront and address the intergenerational trauma, largely inhabiting the bodies of the women in the family, threatening to separate them and remain connected as they set out on a journey toward the future away from their ancestral homeland. Like the introductory patakís suggest, Oshun in the form of the river that bears her name both provides a sturdy foundation on which to build a narrative (or a township like Oşogbo), as well as guide back (or to a new) home, or an end which is usually also a beginning.

In conjunction with the beautiful scenery that opens the film, there is also poem that is recited by the disembodied voice of Nana Peazant that is as follows: "I am the first and the last. I am the honored one and the scorned one. I am the whore and the holy one. I am the wife and the virgin. I am the barren one and many are my daughters. I am the silence that you cannot understand. I am the utterance of my name."[33] The poem is an adaptation of "The Thunder, Perfect Mind," which originally appears among the Gnostic manuscripts discovered at Nag Hammadi in Egypt. The poem, though paradoxical, describes a feminine divinity that encompasses all that is thrusted onto feminine bodies. Aside from the abbreviation, one interesting adaptation made to the poem is that many translations read "many are my sons," and here, Dash replaces "sons" for "daughters."[34] Though the scholarship on the Nag Hammadi manuscripts suggest that the verses could likely be in reference to Isis based on the location of the discovery and the approximate time of its composition, I assert that these paradoxes are also apt descriptions of Oshun based on the complexity and at times contradictions of her lore.[35] Additionally, this poem, taken with the other sonic tributes to Oshun throughout the *Daughters of the Dust* in the form of her praise songs seem to conceptually anchor my reading.

Regarding Oshun being both the first and the last, she is the last of the Irunmolé to be sent from heaven to earth, but the first of the feminine Orisha. Discussed at length in chapter 2, Oshun's relationship to the other Orisha comprising the Irunmolé is one of both honor and scorn, given her exclusion and subsequent propitiation. Oshun's proximity to sex and sexuality causes much debate regarding mother/whore dichotomies among practitioners and scholars alike. This is particularly true given that Oshun is syncretized with the Virgen de la Caridad del Cobre (the Virgin of Charity of Copper), encompassing the sacred and sexual aspects of both "the whore and the holy one."[36] On this, Lindsay Hale describes this paradox, writing that "[a]t both ends of the spectrum, Oxum is still the perfect mother, patient, calm, and generous; and she is in both the embodiment of fertility and sexual appeal, albeit within very different aesthetic and moral systems."[37] Oshun is generally considered the Orisha of fertility, who is especially considerate of women with problems bearing children. Though she is seen as fertile herself, she is quite literally "the barren one," with many children, as she herself had to ẹbọ for herself because of her own trouble conceiving. "Òrúnmìlà divorced Ọṣun because she was barren. She married Ṣàngó, the Yorùbá divinity of thunder and lightning." After some ritual offerings prescribed through divination, Ọṣun was led to the abode of children.[38] I would assert that Oshun's empathy for barren women emerges from her own problems with fertility and is the catalyst for her generosity when gifting them to women who seek her out. Many are her daughters (and sons) in both biological (according to her lore) and ritual contexts (including her many devotees). She is described as having "so many children that she did not have any more space to sit down in her own house. Since her children had taken up all available space, Ọṣun was always found standing up."[39]

Though Oshun is not particularly known for her silence, there are times that she weaponizes it against her enemies, as she is known for her stealth in battle. Even in her conflict with the Irunmolé, Oshun maintains her silence as they carry on without her, contributing to their inability to understand why their efforts are failing. Practitioners describe Oshun as impossible to understand because of her dynamism, but (in most cases) she is a pleasure to experience.[40] Miguel W. Ramos writes about this phenomenon, stating that "[t]his orisha's own *omós* [children], it is said, have a hard time understanding her. Oshún can be variable, unpredictable, impulsive, cynical, cunning, deceptive, all the while still managing to be kind, motherly, tender, caring, beautiful, attractive, seductive, and utterly irresistible. Enigmatic is possibly the most appropriate descriptor."[41] Like all Orisha, Oshun is evoked by her name in praise and in prayer, and is therefore, "the utterance."

Oshun is invoked by the utterance of her name in the film as well. Though visually the film commits itself to Ki-Kongo iconographic adoptions, including bottle trees, *minkisi* (small containers or sachets that hold spiritual substances), and even the Ki-Kongo cosmogram. Sonically, however, Julie Dash incorporates many different Orisha, calling them by name and by their praise songs as well. Aganju, who is associated with magma and volcanic eruptions, is the first to be engaged in this way, as his song scores Yellow Mary's entrance to the beach to join her family in reunion. The song opens, "Ẹlẹekò e / Ẹlẹekò e/Aganjù ẹlẹekò pè'láyé," which translates to "owner of vigour, owner of vigour wilderness owner of vigour we cry out greetings to you chief."[42] A pataki suggests that Oshun and Aganju's relationship also began at a river, solidifying their ritual connection.[43] The song continues, "Má má má sọ rọ́ sọ̀ ayé / Aganjù sọ rọ́ sọ̀," meaning, "[t]he wilderness shoots up to drop with a crash."[44] I assert that the song's placement there marks Yellow Mary's own emergence from the wilderness as she is greeted by the familiarity of the Peazants, if resentment, and the island itself. This especially true given that the line that announces her arrival is, "Old Man Peazant's granddaughter done come home."[45] Though home is not especially "civilized" by the standards of the Peazants seeking to leave for the mainland, I assert that the wilderness operates in reversal here, underscoring not only the wildness of the cities she's occupied in her absence, but also the wildness of her behavior and lifestyle which is generally frowned upon among the Peazants, and is verbally addressed quickly after the announcement of her arrival. Additionally, Aganju's incorporation may also be connected with Yellow Mary's Saint Christopher charm that she says to Nana Peazant's inquiry is, "for travelers on a journey."[46] Since

Saint Christopher is Aganju's Catholic parallel, the work that they both do regarding ferrying passengers establishes a connection to the river outside his/their relationship to Oshun.[47] In response to Yellow Mary's declaration of her charm's purpose, Nana Peazant asks, "What kind of belief that is? He protect you?"[48] Though Yellow Mary does not verbally respond, she and Nana Peazant share a tender moment face-to-face that confirms both Yellow Mary's need for protection, and an affirmative answer.

Though Yellow Mary is placed in aesthetic proximity to Oshun based on her name and complexion, it is important to address that it was Julie Dash's intent to center Yemaya as Yellow Mary's spiritual mother.[49] While Yemaya's iconographic and spiritual influences are present in the setting of the film, and Dash's own intentions for her film must be considered, I read Yellow Mary's representation in the film as more closely associated with Oshun's visual and textual archive, since Yellow Mary is (out)cast as a harlot and Yemaya's lore does not account for her being characterized that way, but Oshun's does. To be clear, Dash does not express an interest in representing Yemaya through the behavior and characterizations of Yemaya, but rather creates a spiritual relationship between the two, which is an important nuance, however, for my own analytical purposes, as Oshun's visual and sonic influence eclipses that intention. Consequently, I read Yemaya's influence (and its relationship to Oshun's) as more readily read into the Peazant family's proximity to the Atlantic Ocean as well as their impending journey to the mainland where Yemaya will hopefully help them safely traverse the sea with their traditions intact.

The next time Orisha music is featured, it is Oshun's, and it scores women young and old running along the shore of the beach laughing, and enjoying one another's company, while men seriously playing hand games of their own as well as mancala. The song's lyrics are "Ìyá mi ilé orò / Gbogbo àṣẹ / Ìṣe mi sàráà máā wọ́ ẹ," which translates to mean, "My mother house of tradition / All powerful / my deeds of charity habitually pull you."[50] This is significant given Viola Peazant's (Cheryl Lynn Bruce) role in the activities among the women. Though there is no dialogue, Viola, the eldest of the group, serves an instructional role, passing down traditions by way of what appears to be an impromptu etiquette class on the beach for the younger women in preparation for their entry into the mainland, and mainstream society. The song plays long enough to score Iona sitting improperly to tease Viola and for Nana to rise from her seat to witness it. Oshun's relationship with tradition underscores the very root of the film as the departing Peazants grapple with which tradition to take with them, and which to leave behind. This song also describes Nana Peazant's crucial role as a receptacle for tradition, where tradition is held, and where it can be accessed, particularly regarding the tin can that she herself carries around containing ingredients to her own magic, including notably a lock of hair from her mother. As Bilal Muhammad (Umar Abdurrahamn) aptly describes, "We Peazants, we come from a long, long line of creation and hope begun by those first-captured Africans. And Nana, Nana she carried them with her, four generations of Peazants. And we, we must carry them with us, wherever we go."[51] The song perfectly punctuates the intergenerational exchange taking place in this moment of the film, as well as in the broader plot. Maintaining water as a centralized theme, the song continues, "Omi yọ̀ wẹrẹ wẹrẹ/ omi o," which means, "water slithers gently rippling / water."[52] Though it is not featured in the film, the line following is "ṣẹ kúū ṣẹ," meaning, "I hope your work proceeds smoothly." I interpret the inclusion of the first line as a plea for the work of tradition and transfer to proceed as smoothly as water slithering gently.[53]

Later in the film, Viola explains the importance of naming to Mr. Snead (Tommy Redmond Hicks) and includes a series of nicknames given to children based on the circumstances surrounding their birth or characteristics of the child. In the list are the following: Shango, Obatala, Oya-yansa, Yemoja, and Eshu Elegba.[54] Though the list begins with names unassociated with Orishas, as it transitions to them, the camera pans to Eli stumbling through the Peazants ancestral burial ground and eventually falling to his knees, placing his head at the base of a specific plot. Orisha music enters again, this time paying tribute to Ogun, the warrior blacksmith. The tempo of the song is notably quicker marking the approach of the film's climax and the immediacy of Eli and Eula's conflict.[55] The song, "à Ògún méje / à méje méje," translates to mean "Ah, Seven Ògúns! Ah, Seven by seven!"[56] Because of his warrior status, practitioners call on Ogun in times of trouble to clear their path with his cutlass. Eli's troubled and hurried trip to the burial ground indicates his own preparedness to do battle, with the unknown transgressor but also with himself. The song not only scores Eli's consultation with egun, but also Eula's own experience in the burial ground where she is shown slowly flapping her arms like wings freely and happily. Though Eli and Eula are connected by the trauma of her rape and the uncertainty regarding the paternity of the baby she is carrying, their experiences are discrete in many ways, and it is visually explored here. Eli is clearly suffering through the turmoil of his wife's violation based on his own sense that his right of possession, or "exclusive sexual rights" over her have been violated and is staged as desperate for relief from the turmoil plot.[57] Eli's frustration with ownership is elucidated earlier in the film in a dialogue with Nana, which also takes place in the burial ground. On this issue, Nana redirects Eli stating firmly, "You can't get back what you never owned. Eula never belong to you, she married you."[58] Conversely, Eula's spirituality takes center stage as she seems not only at home in the burial ground among the "old spirits," but truly liberated from her burden of what the Peazant family refers to as "ruin." Though Eula believes throughout the entire film that her unborn child was sent to her from the ancestors, it seems that her fidelity to faith is confirmed as the ghost of the unborn child runs into her while her arms are outstretched to receive her as if for a hug. Eula's confirmed feeling of resolve regarding the conditions surrounding their child's conception transferred to her husband to offer him peace of mind after he finally reaches out to egun for help.

It is worth mentioning that the visual break between Eli and Eula's experience is a slow pan of Ibo Landing. The focal point is a wooden statue of a fettered man floating in the water, bringing in Oshun's influence alongside Ogun's. Regarding the lore of Ibo Landing, despite the heaviness of the shackles somehow the men, women, and children were able to float or fly away. On this, Bilal says to Mr. Snead, "But mister I was there. Those Ibo men, women and children, a hundred or more, shackled in iron, when they go down in that water, they never came back up. Ain't nobody can walk on water."[59] Here is another convergence of Ogun and Oshun through their elements. Iron is squarely the domain of Ogun, the blacksmith, which is used in this case is being employed to the detriment of the Ibo people. Oshun is known as the only Orisha to tame Ogun and does so in this instance as well, by freeing them from their fetters.[60] Bilal's narrative is marked by the realism of a firsthand account, presumes that the journey across happened on the earthly plane. I assert that just as King Laro's daughters joined Oshun in her domain, the people of Ibo Landing found themselves at the bottom of the river as well.[61] Though from Bilal's perspective, the people of Ibo Landing never return to the surface, I assert that this represents another example of sinking burdens, and in this case the burden for the Ibo people was their flesh, their only tether to the trauma of enslavement. Submerging themselves confidently backed by the faith that freedom awaited them at the bottom of Ibo Landing, their bodies shackled in iron sunk, but their spirits remained buoyant, free of the weight of flesh and iron, and floated away.

Though Eula's recounting of the story at Ibo Landing as told to her by her own great-grandmother, differs from Bilal's account, the difference is one marked by faith, where Bilal's Islamic influence obscure other possibilities for interpretation of the story. Eula's account, however, is clearly influenced by her own close relationship to the "old souls" and her faith in their influence over her own life. Eula's rendition of the story of Ibo Landing, supplies one of the epigraphs for this chapter, given water's centrality to the narrative as a character all its own. Eula recounts this story after she and Eli both have visited the burial ground, and it is at Ibo Landing where she and her husband find solace. Eula enthusiastically tells this story to Eli, a story he must have heard many times before, as he wades out to the very same statue that visually separated their experiences in the burial ground. As Eula explains that "you wouldn't think they'd get very far seeing as it was water they were walking on.... They just kept walking, like the water was solid ground," Eli himself appears to be walking on water as he journeys out to embrace the wooden statue.[62] Even as he approaches the statue and kneels to get closer to it, there is a marked difference between Eli's ability to comfortably kneel on the water, in contrast to the statue's bobbing back and forth indicating the water's depth.

Eula narrates not only the journey of Ibo people past, but her and Eli's own journey toward healing and acceptance, and ultimately to freedom. After Eli embraces the statue and releases it to float on its own, he returns to shore to embrace Eula and his unborn child. Again, water punctuates ends and beginnings: an end to Eula and Eli's victimhood and suffering as a couple, which gives way for other cycles of trauma to end as well. Not only do the "old souls" choose Eula as a vessel not only for the first-born of the next generation, but also the message to be delivered before the Peazants departure to ensure that intergenerational trauma is addressed and given room to heal on the ancestral homeland in communication with and proximity to the ancestors and not carried with them as they begin anew in a strange land. I argue that Eula is specially situated to deliver this message because of her pregnancy. As Nana Peazant says, "[T]he ancestor and the womb are one and the same," and she is as close as is (meta)physically possible to egun.[63]

Eula's final monologue is prompted by Yellow Mary's surprising declaration of her desire to stay with Nana Peazant and return to her roots instead of heading for Nova Scotia. Haagar's (Kaycee Moore) criticism, "Oh, now how's she going to come and put her shame upon Mother Peazant?," prompts Nana's response, "I can't understand ... how me and Peazant put you children here on Earth to fight among yourselves. How you can leave this soil, this soil. The sweat of our love it's here in this soil. I love you 'cause you're mine. You're the fruit of an ancient tree."[64] The conflict between relatives regarding Yellow Mary's devalued status based on her "ruining" causes Nana Peazant severe emotional distress, as she confronts the reality of her offspring leaving her and many of her cultural traditions behind. Nana delivers this monologue while being embraced tightly by Yellow Mary and Eula on either side both as a comfort for themselves and to ensure that Nana remains upright. Nana's final groan in pain and disappointment triggers Eula to forcefully break free from the embrace while holding her head, as if she was taken over by an uncontrollable urge to address the Peazants in full regarding their retrograde thinking surrounding issues of rape and sexual assault and what it means to shame victims into perpetuity as models for bad womanhood, taking Yellow Mary's case as the prime example.

A gripping emotional moment, Eula begins by indicating the ways in which Yellow Mary has remained supportive of the Peazants even though many of them have failed her. "Hush, hush, hush! Hush all of you. Some of us aren't forgetting how Yellow Mary sent the money to get Cousin Jake out of jail last spring."[65] Eula is interrupted by Haagar, who insists on maintaining Yellow Mary as an outcast and insults her by saying "[n]ow, Nana, we ain't talking about no Cousin Jake here. A dog don't get mad 'cause you say he's a dog."[66] Haagar's character represents a point of contention throughout the entirety of the film as she is both an in-law relative and clearly set on leaving the old ways behind for the promise of refinement and upward mobility available on the mainland. She represents a stark counterpoint to Eula and Nana, and espouses a moral superiority over Yellow Mary and anyone who finds solace and efficacy in Nana Peazants ways. Beautifully staged, Haagar's interruption prompts Eli to encourage his wife to, "Say it!"[67] To say that which equally needs to be said by Eula, as the perfect messenger, and what needs to be heard by the Peazants.

Underscored by the sounds of the beach, waves crashing and seagulls squawking, Eula begins her monologue:

> If you're so ashamed of Yellow Mary 'cause she got ruined, what do you say about me? I'm ruined too? As far as this place is concerned, we never was a pure woman. Deep inside, we believed that they ruined our mothers and their mothers who has come before them, and we live our lives always expecting the worst 'cause we feel we don't deserve no better. Deep inside, we believe that even God can't heal

the wounds of our past or protect us from the world that put shackles on our feet. Even though you're going up north, you all think about being ruined, too. You think you can cross over to the mainland and run away from it? You're going to be sorry, sorry if you don't change your way of thinking before you leave this place. If you love yourself, then love Yellow Mary, because she's a part of you, just like we're a part of our mothers. A lot of us are going through things you feel you can't handle all alone. There's going to be all kinds of roads to take in life. Let's not be afraid to take them. We deserve them because we're all good women. Do you understand who we are and what we have become? We're the daughters of those old dusty things Nana carries around in her tin can. We carry too many scars from the past. Our past owns us. We wear our scars like armor for protection. Thick, hard, ugly scars that no one can pass through to ever hurt us again. Let's live our lives without living in the fold of old wounds.[68]

Throughout her monologue, Eula is only interrupted three times: once, in the beginning by her husband urging her on, in the middle by Viola exclaiming her love and faith in God, and toward the end by herself and the need to vomit brought on by the force of emotion in conjunction with her pregnancy. Eula forcefully attacks the fact that the thin line between Yellow Mary's criticism and her own acceptance is that her rape occurred after she had been married, whereas Yellow Mary's occurred before decreasing her marriageability substantially. Eula attempts to initiate a paradigm shift where there is an impossibility for ruin given the circumstances under which Black people were brought to America, and the inability for Black women to achieve purity archetypes womanhood by virtue of their Blackness. In American society, then as now, Black women are always already ruined, given their social inability to achieve womanhood as construct to the benefit of whites and the detriment of blacks.

On this, Saidiya Hartman eloquently writes that "virtue designates a racial entitlement not accorded to the enslaved [or the freed], then consent is nullified not only on the grounds of one's civil status but also on the bases of presumed sexual predilections."[69] Taking Haagar as a proxy, and the rest of the Peazants tacit agreement with her vitriol, these social contracts of virtue and ruin, or whore and holy one continue to be enforced. Hortense Spillers addresses this complexity in her seminal article "Mama's Baby, Papa's Maybe: An American Grammar Book," writing that "[f]irst of all, their [African peoples] New World, diasporic plight marked a theft of the body—a willful and violent (and unimaginable from this distance) severing of the captive body from its motive will, its active desire. Under these conditions, we lose at least *gender* difference *in the outcome,* and the female body and the male body become a territory of cultural and political maneuver, not at all gender-related, gender specific."[70] Here, both Eula and Yellow Mary's bodies represent a territories of cultural and political maneuvers vis-à-vis the Peazants desire to leave subjection on St. Simon's Island when they leave for the mainland. They symbolize an effort on behalf of the Peazants to expunge their shame, place it on to Yellow Mary and (albeit quietly) Eula, and separate themselves from the generational trauma of ruin by separating themselves from Yellow Mary and Eula. Navigating the interstices of blame and shame as detailed by Hartman—"the [Black] woman not only suffered the responsibility for her sexual (ab)use but also was blameworthy because of her purported ability to render the powerful weak"—Eula impresses on the family that their departure from the island does not ultimately indicate a departure from the trauma that informs their thinking regarding this issue, and that a paradigm shift is required to attain the freedom that they suspect is waiting on them on the mainland.[71]

Although the scene is captured at the campsite that is on the beach, closer to Yemaya's salty and temperamental waters, I assert that the gentle waters of Ibo Landing, Oshun's sweet water, prompt this discourse, as the plight of scorned women, especially the sexually exploited, is squarely within Oshun's realm of influence of feminine sex and sexuality. As mentioned above, there are instances where Oshun is characterized as a harlot, or *panshanga* (also *panshage, panchákara, and puchunga*) in Afro-Cuban parlance.[72] The term itself is fraught in terms of its interpretation based on its Yoruba etymological root, *pánṣága,* which Robert Farris Thompson translates to mean, "prostitute, adulteress, profligate man."[73] Conversely, the Afro-Cuban term is translated to mean "divine courtesan," and even accounting for the terms' connotative difference, they both describe a key characteristic of Oshun's personality: sexual agency/exploitation, which are not mutually exclusive. Not unlike her struggles with infertility, there are patakís that suggest that in times of struggle, Oshun turned to sex work to provide for herself and her children. Following the empathy she felt for barren women, Oshun too feels for women who are (sexually) vulnerable or labeled whores and comes to their aid. I assert that given Eula's consultation with the "old souls" (egun) and her trip to the river (Oshun) at Ibo Landing before her emotionally charged outburst regarding the nature of women's (de)valuation based on their sex, that she was equally influenced by both to deliver her message.

Finally, Eula's message covers a large swath of conceptual ground but lands solidly on an emphasis of healing old wounds and dispensing with the responsibility of carrying the weight of intergenerational turmoil thrust upon the women of the Peazant family that mediates their relationship with one another as well as their spouses. Eula's message shows the clear influence of Oshun, given her emphasis on transcending the old scars that no longer serve as armor, but as cages. Eula's plea to her family to relinquish their death grip on old wounds is not unlike Ibeyi's plea to carry away old and dead leaves. In fact, Eula's words usher in an end to a negative cycle, to clear room for a new cycle of prosperity as her family sets out, without her, to new territory. Beginning and ending at Ibo Landing, the story of the Peazants as explored through Yellow Mary and Eula's experiences of trauma and transformation is guided by the varying flows of the river and Oshun, and the Atlantic Ocean and Yemaya. Due to Eula's spiritual labor in proximity to the river, the Peazants can both stay on and leave St. Simons Island relating positively to their (maternal) genealogy, cultural traditions, and family ties, which ensures that the work of maintain these traditions on the mainland will "proceed smoothly," just as Oshun, "slithering gently," carries the family to their destination smoothly over her waters.

4

Honey in the Hive

Oshun and Yemaya in Celebration of the Black Feminine

> in the dream i am crowning
> osun,
> nefertiti,
> and yemoja
> pray around my bed
> —Warsan Shire, "I Have Three Hearts"

> You two are like honey and molasses. You pour very slowly together
> —Doña Tina, *She's Gotta Have It* (2019)

Lemonade, 2016: A Ripple Effect

Beyoncé continues the iconographic adoption of Yoruba culture broadly, and Oshun and Yemaya specifically, in the pregnancy photoshoot that celebrates the coming arrival of her twins. Posted on her website on February 2, 2017, the series titled "I Have Three Hearts," plays on the fact that she herself was pregnant with twins, which announced by an Instagram post on her verified account one day prior. The titular poem, also written by Warsan Shire, who adapted the poetry for *Lemonade,* calls Oshun and Yemaya by name, as is featured in the epigraph, anchoring what will continue to be an intimate relationship between the two goddesses in Beyoncé's work to come. The accompanying photoset, which is still available on Beyoncé's website, takes a cue from the poem and visually integrates Oshun and Yemaya's influences, most notably water, but also bright yellows (pupa), and deep blues (dúdú). Centering Beyoncé's baby bump, the photos place her underwater, again, while draped in different combinations of flowy yellow and maroon fabric to cover breasts and below her waist. Ethereal is the most apt descriptor of the photos, as one of them features Beyoncé in triplicate, just below the surface of the water which has been staged as the floor. Taken together with Oshun's own relationship to Kehinde and Taiwo (Ibeji), the pregnancy announcement follows the conceptual framework established by *Lemonade,* and extends the original iconographic adoption of Oshun's elements and generates new ones.

This is similarly true for her first performance after the announcement, the 2017 Grammy awards, where Beyoncé performed "Sandcastles" and "Love Drought." Dressed in a golden diadem, large gold earrings, a thick gold necklace, and an ornately beaded gold dress that accentuated her pregnancy with a likeness of her own face on the belly, Beyoncé opened the performance holding a similarly flowy piece of yellow fabric high above her head, which was blowing in the manufactured wind. Beyoncé's strategic use of this cloth simulates yet another feature associated with Oshun's dance in the diaspora: the *mantón,* a shawl often worn by dancing devotees when mounted.[1] Just as the shawl in dance transitions from laying delicately on the shoulders of the devotee, to becoming an indispensable accessory in the movements associated with Oshun to simulate the gentle rippling of water and her femininity, Beyoncé, too, operationalizes this fabric at times extending it high above her own head, at others draping it delicately over her head as a veil, and others draping it over her shoulders as cape to accentuate her regality.

Beyoncé's use of fabric in both "I Have Three Hearts," and the Grammy's performance also draws on the cultural import of cloth in Yorubaland. As mentioned above, Beyoncé is photographed with yellow fabric tied around both her bust and waist. It is custom in Yoruba culture for pregnant women to tie cloth, *òjá,* around their waist when pregnant, to protect their wombs from malevolent forces. According to Babatunde Lawal, this custom originates alongside the Gẹ̀lẹ̀dẹ́ ritual dance as an ẹbọ to Yemaya on behalf of a barren woman.[2] Considering that she names both Yemaya and Oshun in "I Have Three Hearts," and that she uses yellow fabric in both the photographs and the performance, Beyoncé creates and executes a multilayered iconographic adoption of the mantón, òjá, and Gẹ̀lẹ̀dẹ́, engaging the (spi)ritual and cultural significance of Oshun and Yemaya simultaneously, using her pregnancy as the visual framework to tie them together establishing that any celebration of the divine feminine, or the joy that accompanies it would be incomplete without acknowledging the joint work of the two Orishas together, a potential foreshadowing of what would come in *Black Is King.*

Visually stunning, the performance takes advantage of the advances in stage production to show Beyoncé on the stage, in person, and in prerecorded visuals that are choreographed to multiple poems featured in the visual album. Though in person she wears the floor-length gown described above, in the visual she wears a golden bikini, with a yellow cape that billows with every movement bringing the ethereal elements from "I Have Three Hearts," to the stage, and driving home the goddess energy, in this case Oshun, as a guiding force in *Lemonade* and the productions that follow it. In this performance, however, other goddesses are referenced, as the diadem makes clear references to the Virgen de la Caridad del Cobre, Oshun's Catholic identity. Additionally, in the instances where the special effects give Beyoncé multiple arms, references to the Indian goddess Kali are made. It is worth noting that her mother, Tina Lawson, introduced the performance, and projected images of three generations of women, Tina, Beyoncé, and her daughter, Blue, filled the stage, bringing forward the visual album's emphasis on intergenerational healing. Though she does not incorporate water into this performance, perhaps because of her pregnancy, there are many instances where her dancers, dressed in nude gowns and smaller diadems of their own, imitated the rippling waves of water in their choreography accompanied by blue backlighting to complement the movement. Beyoncé ends the performance standing elegantly on a bed of multicolored flower petals, surrounded by her dancers who kneel before her with their arms outstretched as if trying to touch her, but can't quite reach. Her performance of "Love Drought" ends with audio clip from the poem "Accountability," which reverberates, "you look nothing like your mother. You look everything like your mother," before she transitions into singing "Sandcastles." Not unlike the film, she ends the performance, centering healing, relying on Warsan Shire's poetry consistently, closing the performance with, "If we're going to heal, let it be glorious." As expected, Beyoncé follows closely to the framework established by the film, even considering the new elements she adds to improve the production value for the stage.

Additionally, Beyoncé maintained water as a foundational element (in conjunction with pyrotechnics which is common) to her performances in other instances, like her performance at the BET awards on June 26, 2017, which was after the Formation World Tour concluded. Here, Beyoncé is dressed in an ornate black, long-sleeved leotard with long braids and is notably barefoot, as are her dancers. She performs "Freedom" with Kendrick Lamar and her background dancers who must wade through the water on stage. Just as water punctuated the progression of the visual album, in this performance, water almost becomes a performer itself, as it is embedded deeply into the choreography. As Beyoncé's dancers run and leap behind her, they do so with the intent of splashing the water, and as water soars through the air, it creates yet another backdrop for Beyoncé in conjunction with the lights, the screen, and her dancers. Although Kendrick Lamar rises to the stage in front of the pool to perform his verse, at the conclusion even he joins Beyoncé in the water to stomp around in it himself, reinforcing the water's centrality to the performance, and perhaps to the overall structure of *Lemonade* and the creative developments in its wake.

On May 24, 2019, the long-awaited second season of *She's Gotta Have It* was released on Netflix and, as expected, continued exploring Nola Darling's burgeoning relationship with Orisha and Lucumí. Finding Nola in some very similar situations regarding love and relationships, financial instability, and her art, the season takes a different approach to centering and decentering Nola in her own story to allow Oshun and Yemaya's presence to be made known, with Nola crossing an ocean to find Oshun in another location, Puerto Rico. There Nola finds that to build on the growth and self-possession she achieved in the first season, she must lend her gifts and her voice to creating art that not only liberates herself but also her community at large. The complex interplay between egun, Oshun, and Yemaya's influence in the narrative's trajectory begs the question, What good is personal growth and success if it is not used for social change?

A little more than a year following the second and final season (2019) of *She's Gotta Have It,* Beyoncé released a single titled "Black Parade" that maintains intertextuality with *Lemonade,* her baby's birth announcement, and potentially answers the questions asked of Nola in *She's Gotta Have It* in its inclusion of egun, Oshun, and Yemaya as well as its celebration of peaceful protest. Released on Juneteenth 2020, a holiday originating with Black Texans to celebrate the abolition of enslavement, Beyoncé references simultaneously her own Houston roots and what marks the beginning of a new creative epoch centering diasporic Blackness in her lyrics and imagery, more broadly.[3] Though this song was a surprise release with no promotion, it itself became a teaser for the visual album to come, *Black Is King.* "If *Lemonade* represents Beyoncé's local return to her Black Southern roots, *Black Is King* represents her status as a global citizen, not just in her collaboration with diverse Afropop and Afrobeat artists but also in her collaboration with African directors as well as the different film locations around the world used to convey her vision for a Black Global community." "Black Parade" builds a bridge between them.[4]

Adapted from the soundtrack *The Lion King: The Gift* (2019), *Black Is King* represents a love letter to continental Africa in not just its iconographic adoptions but also its inclusion of African artists from across the continent. Playing during the end credits of *Black Is King* (2020), "Black Parade" functions much like "Formation" did to *Lemonade*, as both prelude and postlude, and not integrated into the larger narrative of the visual album. But unlike "Formation," it does not have its own accompanying visuals. Its addition to the end credits for the visual album underscores the broader narrative trajectory of the film encouraging African Americans to research and reclaim the greatness of their African heritage(s) to empower them to stand against social injustice. In a reversal, I will be treating my analyses of "Black Parade" first and not last (in part due to its earlier release) as the sonic bridge between *Lemonade*, *She's Gotta Have It*, and *Black Is King* as well as to elucidate the intimacy between Oshun and Yemaya in its celebration of the divine elements of Black femininity in its lyrics that are paralleled in the visual album.

"Black Parade": It's a Celebration

In the first verse of the song, Beyoncé follows the narrative structure and iconographic adoptions of Yoruba culture in *Lemonade* by immediately centering the South, ancestors (egun), and Orisha in her celebration of Blackness as well as the sweetness and abundance of Oshun's feminine archetype. "I'm goin' back to the South / I'm goin' back, back, back, back / Where my roots ain't watered down / Growin', growin' like a Baobab tree / Of life on fertile ground, my ancestors put me on game / Ankh charm on gold chains, with my Oshun energy."[5] Here, Beyoncé locates the South at large and Texas specifically as a source of power, just as Louisiana represented a character of its own in *Lemonade*. I interpret her reference not just to Texas because of the deliberate connection to Juneteenth and her actual roots, but also to the broader cultural landscape of African Americans whose ancestors were enslaved across the South, fought for liberation there, and built thriving communities and cultural institutions. It is worth noting that a key feature of many Juneteenth celebrations from the holiday's inception is a parade and pageantry.[6] In releasing the song on June 19 and titling it "Black Parade," Beyoncé completes a conceptual celebration of her heritage, her community, and her femininity all while looking toward the future.

Growth is a centralized theme in the first verse and hinges upon another one of Oshun's aspects: fertility. Whereas in *Lemonade*, Oshun's aspects, benefits, and drawbacks were limited to the individual trajectory of Beyoncé's character in the narrative, here they are expanded to highlight a more communal focus that is carried through *Black Is King* and *She's Gotta Have It*. It seems now that Beyoncé, the woman and the character, has successfully repossessed herself, she can turn her energy outward to reflect positive change in her community. She simultaneously references fertility as an individual challenge or aspiration achieved (as she has in other music) and shifts to broaden the scope of fertility using double entendre to metaphorically to engage why the South provides such ripe ground for personal and social change, as well as her own fecundity.[7] In the second verse she sings, "Go figure, me and Jigga, fifty 'leven children."[8] This is a notable growth from her comments regarding hope for more children after her miscarriage, as well as a clear reference to her own prediction of the birth of her second daughter using Warsan Shire's poetry in *Lemonade*. In "Black Parade," Beyoncé allows herself to take a victory lap and celebrate her maternity, which is but one interpretation of how she is embodying her "Oshun energy" in the context of the song.

Moving toward the communal interpretations of fertility in the same verse, Beyoncé shifts her attention toward the fullness of the social justice movement. In conjunction with being released on Juneteenth, "Black Parade" came on the heels of George Floyd's brutal murder at the hands of Minneapolis Police officers.[9] She seems to reference the murder directly in the lyrics. Singing, "Lay down, face down in the gravel / Woo, wearin' all attire white to the funeral," she recalls the gruesome way Floyd was made to lay face down on the concrete while officer Derek Chauvin knelt on his neck for almost nine minutes.[10] Fortunately, bystander footage captured the event and sparked national and international protests calling for the termination and indictment of the officers involved as well as widespread policing reform. Beyoncé captures this in the lyrics before and after the George Floyd reference: "You could send them missiles, I'ma send my goons / Baby sister reppin' Yemaya (Yemaya) / Trust me, they gon' need an army (Ah) / Rubber bullets bouncin' off me (Ah) / Made a picket sign off your picket fence (Ah) / Take it as a warning (Ah, ah)."[11] Her reference to her sister and Yemaya simultaneously further underscores her own commitment to embodying Oshun herself. In positioning her sister as representing Yemaya and as a "goon," Beyoncé replicates the dynamics of the divine sisterhood between herself and Solange, but also between Oshun and Yemaya. Though Yemaya is often characterized as the older of the two (and is often characterized as her mother instead), Solange has had a long public history of protecting her senior sibling despite their birth order. Though much of what has been written about the elevator incident wherein Solange attacked her brother-in-law after the Met Gala in 2014 is speculation, public and musical references to the incident characterize Solange as a fierce protectress of her sister, and in this instance, "goon" becomes synonymous.[12] These references not only reflect how the goddesses often work together for one another, but also for the benefit and protection of their children and society at large.

Beyoncé's continued reference to peaceful protests and rubber bullets highlight the ways participants in these marches are vulnerable to police brutality in a way that she isn't, allowing her to use music to interrupt cycles violence that affect Black people. These lyrics recall the imagery of the "Formation" video and its criticism of overpolicing, as well as honoring the long tradition of peaceful protest and civil disobedience in the Black community, and further *Lemonade*'s own honoring of mothers whose sons faced the same fate as Floyd. The intertextuality between "Black Parade" and *Lemonade* is strengthened by her reference to "[a]ncestors on the wall / let the ghosts chit-chat," and continuing to center white (funfun) clothing as having ceremonial import.[13] Further, Beyoncé attempts to disrupt commonly held ideas about the American dream and the perceived sense of safety provided by picket fences and all they represent: middle-classness, suburbia, and often, willful ignorance about injustice. In her clever use of this wordplay and imagery, she establishes the gravity of the circumstances by asserting that peaceful protest is only one response to the devaluation of Black lives, and that it is possible (and even likely) that civil unrest will follow if things aren't changed.

She continues this line of reasoning toward the end of the first verse: "Lil' Malcolm, Martin mixed with mama Tina (Woo) / Need another march, lemme call Tamika (Woo) / Need peace and reparation for my people (Woo)."[14] In describing her own political leanings using Malcolm X and Martin Luther King Jr. as representative examples of militancy and nonviolent direct action, she reinscribes the tension between picketing with picket fence posts as an effective course of action in its own right when heeded, as well as a harbinger of more radical courses of action when ignored. She also references her own incorporation of Black nationalist imagery during her Super Bowl L performance of "Formation," as well as her own incorporation of Malcolm X's "Who Taught You to Hate Yourself?" speech in *Lemonade* to anchor her criticism of how Black women are often treated in America. She also nods directly toward grassroots organizing by referencing Tamika Mallory, founder of Until Freedom, and co-chair of the 2017 Women's March.[15]

In addressing injustices that affect the entire Black community, Beyoncé still centers women and their work in attempting to restore balance to society, recalling Oshun's own role in the Irunmolé.

Though the song grapples with some of the heavier experiences of being Black in America, the celebratory tone of the song is not lost but, rather, is emphasized by the chorus: "Honey, come around my way, around my hive / Whenever mama say so, mama say / Here I come on my throne, sittin' high / Follow my parade, oh, my parade."[16] While surface-level readings of these lyrics lend themselves to references to Beyoncé's fan base, aptly named the "beyhive," the imagery also overlaps squarely within Oshun's domain as well and highlights the long-standing overlap between Beyoncé's own imagery and that of Oshun. While I assert that these parallels are there, I realize that the degree of intention behind them varies and that some might even be coincidental. However, Beyoncé's direct reference to her embodiment of Oshun's energy earlier in the song in conjunction with her pleas for the "motherland [to] drip on me" solidifies the intertextuality between Oshun's iconography, and Beyoncé's narrative choices post (and perhaps even before) *Lemonade* as one of Oshun's daughters, if only aesthetically speaking. As established in earlier chapters in the book, Oshun represents both the balance of the bitter and sweet elements of life and this song reflects that and emphasizes the necessity of Black joy and Black love. Where *Lemonade* focuses on the familial elements of finding healing, joy, and love, "Black Parade" and subsequently *Black Is King* turns outward to the diasporic Black community to find those things in the grandeur and majesty Black American history and African heritage. For Beyoncé, this has meant leaning heavily into the beauty and wisdom to be found in Yoruba cultural and religious iconography. Including Yemaya along with Oshun in her narrative expansion outward reinscribes uninhibited feminine energy as foundational to cosmic and social order, as well as the importance of women's work in striving toward that order by using their gifts to be change agents.

Black Is King: In Praise of the Divine Mother, Yemaya

Where *Lemonade* figured Beyoncé as synecdoche, one woman representing the stories of many women, *Black Is King* uses Beyoncé's interpolation of Disney's *The Lion King* to explore one boy's journey toward kingship (read: self) to represent a broader story about the liberational potential of Black people returning to African ways of knowing as a grounding force. At the end of the visual album, Beyoncé dedicated *Black Is King* to "[her] son, Sir

Carter. And to all our sons and daughters, the sun and the moon bow for you. You are the keys to the kingdom."[17] Quoting "Keys to the Kingdom," performed by Nigerian artist Tiwa Savage, Beyoncé establishes her commitment to generating images and music to inspire the next generation of Black children to seek themselves out. Despite the somewhat fraught relationship between Disney as a corporation with a checkered history of racism, (mis)representing Black people and Black stories, and mixed reviews about how Beyoncé chose to reconstruct images of Africa for a largely American audience, the pan-Africanist approach to diaspora is both Yoruba-centric and effective. And while the varied critiques of *Black Is King* and its political positionality are valid and worth discussion, my focus is to elucidate the Yoruba iconographic adoptions (though there are many from other ethnic groups), as well as the symbolic import of Oshun and Yemaya's prominence.[18]

In watching *Black Is King*, the similarities between it and *Lemonade* in narrative style and cinematography are apparent. Water is a central focal point and anchors the narrative development, this time through the Nile River. The opening monologue—"I feel like I'm not a king yet. But, like, I got potential for it, you feel me? But I'm not there yet, you feel me? Like, I know I got the capabilities to, but sometimes I don't know how to navigate"— characterizes the Nile River and water at large as the means by which the main character, the prince/Simba, comes to learn to navigate not only the world but also himself.[19] Adapted from *The Lion King*, instead of depicting literal exile from Pride Rock, this interpolation integrates vignettes of various stories of a prodigal son lost and returned, including Moses, layering the geographic importance of the Nile River and blending (if not syncretizing) Yoruba and Egyptian myth and cosmogony to develop a full foundation on which to build a new story in which returning to the self, or one's roots as in "Black Parade," is required for returning to the community to effect positive change.[20] Shifting from how a woman or women might do this for herself in *Lemonade*, Beyoncé comes to represent how a mother might facilitate this for a son in *Black Is King*. At once representing herself at times as Yocheved (Jochebed), Yemaya, and Oshun, she establishes the centrality of the queen mother in the healthy development boys who become men and princes who become kings that go on to lead their communities. In *Black Is King* the central plot points of *The Lion King* are expanded to represent being off the righteous path, lost, and found in a much larger cultural sense which allow "[t]he Orishas [namely, Oshun and Yemaya] to hold your hand through this journey" of self-rediscovery.[21]

After the opening shots of the Nile and its rushing current, a lone basket is captured floating down stream. Footage of the basket floating is intercut with diverse images of Black people while Mufasa's lecture to Simba about the circle of life, voiced by the iconic James Earl Jones, who narrates the journey. Taken together, the message that "we are all connected" seems to situate the yet unseen baby in the basket as representative of Africans who were set adrift during and after the transatlantic slave trade who are all connected to one another and their various places of origin.[22] The camera takes the viewer to a wide shot of Beyoncé along a coastline in a flowing white gown, first alone, and then again lovingly gazing at the child in her arms and walking toward two men also dressed in white prepared to bless the child with incense. Notably, the poetry of Warsan Shire punctuates significant moments in *Black Is King* just as it did in *Lemonade*.

Her poem welcomes and introduces the prodigal child as well as his task: "Bless the body, born celestial, beautiful in dark matter. Black is the color of my true love's skin. Coils and hair catching centuries of prayers, spread through a smoke. You are welcome to come home to yourself. Let black be synonymous with glory."[23] The poem provides a segue into the first song of the visual album, "Bigger," while women in white line the shore as Beyoncé and other mothers bring their children to be blessed with water from a calabash. The visual references to *Lemonade* are apparent, just as Yemaya's influence is present. "For instance, her shrine typically contains a pot from which water is given both to newborn babies and to women who come to beg for children," and this is replicated in *Black Is King* not at her shrine but at her shore.[24] Following my interpretation of the baby set adrift in the basket as representative of diasporic Africans, Yemaya's influence is ever stronger based on the widely held belief among Orisha practitioners that "Yemonja, who became Yemaya in the New World, was with them as a mother protecting her children" during the slave trade.[25] If Yemaya guided and protected her children on the treacherous journey to the New World, its stands to reason that she would guide and protect them as they find their way back.

This is supported Beyoncé next appearance in a majestic royal blue garment embracing her oldest daughter, Blue Ivy Carter, and then intermittently in a lagoon fed by a large waterfall. Replicating the seminal moment from *Lemonade* where she opens the door to release a cascade of water in the now-iconic yellow gown to embody Oshun as woman scorned, here she embodies Yemaya's as primordial mother, supported the lyrics of "Bigger": "Let mama let you know (let you know) / Mama's just tryin', I can't get no days off, I don't get no days off / Truly, I'm feelin' it, I had to say that thing twice / Tryin' to be a good wife, Still really hard, I can't lie / But I promised you I will fight, so I fight."[26] As the first song of the visual album, it situates Beyoncé not as the protagonist, but rather a supportive mother figure passing on the wisdom she's gained from her own journey not unlike Nana Peazant in *Daughters of the Dust*. Just as in *Lemonade* the lyrics allude to slippages between Beyoncé's character and her person as she refers to the difficulties is navigating her own roles as mother, wife, and businesswoman. Building a bridge directly from the previous visual album, her reference to forgiveness, the seventh chapter of *Lemonade* reframes that work as part of a "bigger" picture necessary not just for intergenerational healing, but also for any hope of unifying Black communities in a collective struggle against injustice. Beyoncé continues to express her unconditional love to her child, this time employing water in the lyrics as well as the imagery: "Let love be the water / I pour into you and you pour into me / There ain't no drought here."[27] Centering water adds to the fullness of Yemaya's iconographic adoption in conjunction with the intertextuality with *Lemonade* by referencing "Love Drought," which set the stage for "Forgiveness," which she now characterizes as key in the fight to "rewrite" history and its narrow depiction of African contributions to global cultural and technological development. Elizabeth Pérez reflects on another aspect of Yemaya, writing that "[t]he 'creative genius' of the foremother lies in finding means of combating oppression in a manner that ensures her charges' well-being and furthers the cause of their collective liberation."[28] In offering herself as "sanctuary" or haven in the difficult times to come, she also prioritizes the safety and success of her child. She offers these words as a gift and a prayer before sending him out into the world to face the obstacles that will meet him along the way and before the narrative shifts to follow the child.

Moving away from the beach to the desert and space to explore celestial and even Afro-futuristic elements of ancestors and bygone kings during the "Stars Interlude" and "Find Your Way Back," as well as to urban centers to explore danger, betrayal, death, and opulence in expansive compounds in "Don't Jealous Me," "Scar," and "Mood 4 Eva," and to the jungle for "Already," the narrative does not return to the imagery of the water goddesses until the child prince has grown up and is ready to meet his mate. The viewer is transitioned back into the significance of the feminine influence by two disembodied monologues, the first from a woman forcefully saying, "You can't wear a crown with your head down. I can't say I believe in God and call myself a child of God and then not see myself as a god. That wouldn't make any sense. I wear my Nefertiti chain every day. I never take it off. I know my history. I did the research. I'm a creator of all things."[29] This monologue transitions us to a close shot of the prince's love interest portrayed by Nandi Madida in an elegant fuchsia gown and low-cut fuchsia hair, which marks a thematic shift in the narrative, the wardrobe, and what it represents: Oshun's Vodoun counterpart, Erzulie-Freda.

This is followed by a male voiceover that extols the virtues of women by saying "Many times it's the women that reassemble us. A lot of my manhood training came from women. Men taught me some things, but women taught me a whole lot more."[30] This remark draws verbally on the visual emphasis on gender parity and balance captured in the visual album and calls on an ancient festival held in Ayede centered around a sacred calabash that requires the sitting king to honor Yemaya's power in seeking to restore his own.[31] The monologue, taken together with the images of Beyoncé in floating in open ocean wearing a crown of cowries and jewels very similar to one Yemaya is often depicted wearing as women stand along the shore in silver iridescent garments holding calabashes above their head, solidifies the iconographic adoption of the Yemaya Festival as well as what it represents. In doing this, "male and male power are balanced and complimentary. Male authority is legitimized by and dependent upon female support and cooperation."[32] The monologue in *Black Is King* acknowledges twofold the common circumstances of Black boys who are often raised (independently) by women who occupy the role of primary caregiver and the narrative priorities of the visual album to impress upon viewers that Black men and women need each other, that one is not more powerful than the other, and that the true power is in unification—of masculine and feminine energies, of course, but also of the African diaspora.

Celebrating the Fun in Feminine through Erzulie-Freda's Imagery

Warsan Shire's poetry follows the monologue and marks this dual return to the shore for the viewer, and to the self for the prince. Beyoncé recites, "You are swimming back to yourself. You'll meet yourself at the shore. The coast belongs to our ancestors. We orbit, make joy look easy. Cutlass and calabash. Earth and womb. Lost languages spill out of our mouths."[33] Shire's reference to the coastline and the ancestors neatly ties together the subtext of the narrative where the prince at once represents Simba in this adaptation of *The Lion King*, any young man lost in the world trying to find his way back home, as well as diasporic Africans at large reaching toward Africa, real and imagined. The completion of this journey of self-knowledge for the prince marks his readiness to step into the fullness of his power and become king, and perhaps more importantly, find his queen who has been introduced to the viewer but not to him. The monologue of another man transitions the film back toward the fuchsia tones foreshadowed by Madida's cameo. As he says, "Water signifies life. Water signifies purity. Water signifies hope. Water signifies the ability to be reborn," and the camera pans to Beyoncé on the shore in a billowy fuchsia tulle gown holding a woven basket overflowing with pink flowers.[34] This monologue and shot introduce the song "Water," which details the flirtation between two lovers who meet at the river to enjoy each other's company.

The lyrical and visual move away from the ocean and toward the fresh water of rivers and streams along with the aesthetic choices of pinks and florals lends itself to an iconographic incorporation of Erzulie-Freda, "the lwa of love and beauty. She is the ultimate woman, beyond compare and one whom every man desire and every woman aspires to be like,"[35] and in this way, she is similar to, but not the same as, Oshun. Erzulie-Freda's incorporation is a meta-diasporic occurrence by at once representing African cultural continuities found in Haiti, but also in Beyoncé own creole roots in New Orleans.[36] As the goddess of love, Erzulie-Freda's presence at the precipice of the burgeoning romance between the prince and his love is appropriate. Vacillating between bustling cityscapes, staged scaffolding for backup dancers, and plains, I want to focus on the setting of the creek that most closely aligns with Erzulie-Freda's iconography. Described as "the luxurious mulatta who loves perfume, music, flowers, sweets, and laughter," her characteristics are also reflected in her *veve* (religious symbol used to call lwas), an intricate heart. In *Black Is King* Erzulie-Freda is depicted and embodied true to her nature as a riverine goddess whose splendor is seductive.

Beyoncé is front and center in a satin gown as the leader of a line of dancers all in various shades of pink, creating an ombre from deep fuchsia to pale pink capturing the expansiveness of Erzulie-Freda and her attributes. Each woman carrying a woven basket with pink flowers on their heads as they dance, hips swaying, in ankle-deep water embodies the sensuality signature to Erzulie-Freda. The lyrics of the song situate presence in the courtship as Salatiel makes his plea in the first verse and the chorus: "Well, darling, if you leave, I'll go wherever you go / I'll wear your heart on my sleeve so everybody here knows / But if you tell me to stay, you'll never be on your own / So, baby, don't wait too long."[37] Salatiel's pursuit reflects the notion that when it comes to Erzulie-Freda, "[m]en are so enamored of her, that they give her the best they have to offer."[38] Further, his offer to wear her heart on his sleeve instead of his own directly references Erzulie-Freda's veve and begs Erzulie-Freda to come into the space in a different way. Beyoncé embodiment of Erzulie-Freda's *rada* (cool and benevolent) aspects in response further highlights her divinity, desirability, and power: "I'll bring you back the moon just so we got all night / I'll bring the sun down, too, so I can show you the light / Trust me, if you ever leave, I'll be right by your side, oh / For you, I will ride, ah."[39] A positive response that ultimately binds together the romance it scores between the prince and his love, it also expands on the at-times narrow conceptions of the lwa. Though Erzulie-Freda is often characterized as flighty in her flirtation, she has three husbands, exhibiting her ability to commit to the worthy.[40] Further, Erzulie-Freda's divine power is centered in Beyoncé's description of bending the cosmos as her whim, and for her own enjoyment. In this instance, joy and love are both made easy by welcoming Erzulie-Freda's presence and exhibiting the abundance of spiritual and material benefits of letting the African spirits that guide you take the lead.

Mirroring Oshun's Image

Though Beyoncé formally likens herself to the Oshun and the other characters and archetypes she embodies in *Black Is King* in the lyrics of "Mood 4 Eva," singing "I am Beyoncé Giselle Knowles-Carter / I am the Nala, sister of Naruba / Oshun, Queen Sheba, I am the mother," she doesn't visually capture her essence in the visual album until after her dalliance with Erzulie-Freda.[41] In the context of narrative progression, she has transitioned through divine mother, as represented by Yemaya, divine consort as represented by Erzulie-Freda, and lands back at Oshun to capture Black beauty both deified and personified. Marking this transition with Warsan Shire's poignant poetry, Beyoncé recites, "We have always been wonderful. I see us reflected in the world's most heavenly things. Black is King. We were beauty before they knew what beauty was," as Simba and Nala meet, first as children, then as young adults.[42] The camera pans over to the scene of a young girl awaiting her debutante ball while playing hand games with an older woman. Scored to "Brown Skin Girl" Black debutantes are captured frozen in poses capturing the finery of their gowns and the grace of their choreography.[43] The poem, together with the tableau vivant of the debutantes, signifies a shift in the narrative priority toward celebrating the beauty of

Black girlhood and womanhood based on the ancient archetypes that Oshun's "mythhistorical" archive provide. Through this imagery and the lyrics of "Brown Skin Girl," a veritable Black girl anthem, Beyoncé extends the self-reclamation she establishes in *Lemonade* to *Black Is King* and broadens it to invite all Black women to embrace and reclaim African understandings of beauty that uplift them and reject European ones that oppress them. Although there is an embedded irony in celebrating African conceptions of beauty against the backdrop of a debutante ball, a decidedly European (and perhaps sexist) ritual for young women coming of age, I choose to read this combination of images as visual and cultural syncretism. After all, the established priority of *Black Is King* is to represent the diversity of people, cultures, and spiritualities dispersed and developed throughout the African diaspora while emphasizing the proverbial roots of the tree representing Blackness. Consequently, Oshun worship in Cuba and the United States often incorporates the finery of European colonial dress and high culture including elaborate ball gowns, lace fans, expensive perfume, champagne, and classical music, particularly played by violins. Accordingly, a debutante ball is as fine a setting as any to celebrate how Oshun offers positive models of Black beauty that affirm Black women. To bring Oshun's energy and iconography into focus, Beyoncé returns to a readily recognizable goldenrod outfit with a flowing train, head wrap, and gold lipstick. Footage of her dancing and reclining near a river's edge is interspersed between footage of the debutante ball in progress, with guest stars Naomi Campbell, Kelly Rowland, Lupita Nyong'o, whom she mentions by name for their virtues in the song, and other notably dark-skinned Black women celebrating themselves and one another, as well as her mother and two daughters.

This complex combination of images serves to contribute meaningfully to digital discourses on colorism. The chorus below situates skin color as the site of harm that needs correction through celebration. "Brown skin girl / Ya skin just like pearls / Your back against the world / I'd never trade you for anybody else, say."[44] The director of the video, Jenn Nkiru, remarks that "as a Black filmmaker and as a Black woman filmmaker, a lot of the work I'm creating is readdressing gaps, just gaps, quite frankly"—in this case, the gap in representation of darker skinned Black women in television and film.[45] This video does this twofold in the broader narrative of *Black Is King*. First, through its casting and the lyrics, dark-skinned Black women are serenaded and given their flowers in a high-profile way. Second, using Oshun as a focal point in this way, deliberately or not, intervenes in the way color is used in her lore as well as Yemaya's in the New World. Where Oshun is often described as fair-skinned, or a mulattress, Yemaya is almost uniformly described as dark in complexion like the molasses that adherents use to propitiate her. Beyoncé's embodiment of both Orishas over the course of the visual album subverts these color comparisons not just because of Beyoncé's own complexion as a light skinned woman, but also because of her commitment to acknowledging the African origins of the goddesses in conjunction with various iterations throughout the Black Atlantic. This is commitment to African origins (and perhaps Yoruba-centrism) is supported by her prominent, though quick feature of Robert Farris Thompson's seminal book *Black Gods and Kings: Yoruba Art at UCLA* in "Mood 4 Eva." Centering Oshun in this celebration and affirmation of Black women and girls is a logical expansion on her celebration of herself in *Lemonade*.

Despite the narrative of *Black Is King* being centered on healthy masculine development, the inclusion of Yemaya, Erzulie-Freda, and Oshun establish the necessity for masculine and feminine energy to work in tandem for communal strength and social change. In a monologue between "Keys to the Kingdom" and "The Other Side," a woman's voice remarks, "It would be a much better world for all of us if kings and queens realized that being equal, sharing spaces, sharing ideas, sharing values, sharing strength, sharing weaknesses, balancing each other out, that is the way in which our ancestors did things, and that is an African way. The royalty in you is there for you to be a blessing to others. For you to leave a legacy that others can look to and find hope and find strength and find healing as well."[46] This comment expands the message of *Black Is King*: to return to African ways of knowing as a means of praxis, not just an exercise in celebrating cultural heritage. Just as Oshun provided an avenue for Beyoncé to tackle her own healing journey, here with her water goddess counterparts, that priority of healing the deep wounds of intergenerational trauma and redressing the imbalance between men and women (masculine and feminine) is expanded from the Knowles-Carter family to the African diaspora at large. And while *Black Is King* is in no way Oshun-centric when compared with *Lemonade*, it is an example of how Oshun demands generosity of her children so that the abundance her blessings might be "blessings to others."

"#IAmYourMirror": Nola Darling Reflecting the Change She Wants to See

Season 2 of *She's Gotta Have It* finds Nola Darling in a more self-possessed place, in a seemingly healthy romantic relationship with Opal Gilstrap (Ilfenesh Hadera), and in solid friendships with her male ex-lovers who still offer moral and financial support. Unfortunately for Nola, things, as they often do in her case, quickly deteriorate. She finds herself ill-suited as a stepparent to Opal's daughter Skylar (Indigo Hubbard-Salk), characterized as an immature partner, broken up with at her happy place, Coney Island, uninspired, and still unable to pay her rent on time. Though she has her fair share of external conflict—being accosted by Jamie's wife on the street, re-encountering Dean Haggin, and negotiating her relationships with Clorinda, earWave (a music-streaming company) co-opting her #MyNameIsn't street art for their ad campaign—the central conflict of the season is internal as Nola painstakingly works through what kind of person, and consequently, what kind of artist she is going to be. Instead of seeking out Lourdes for another spiritual consultation, the spirits seek Nola out by creating circumstances that send her from her beloved Fort Green to Puerto Rico for charity, and unbeknownst to her, a spiritual intervention. Lourdes and Mars getting evicted, not being able to reach their mother, and a natural disaster create a perfect storm of events to get her where she's going. Though the season has nine episodes, I will focus most notably on two, episode 7, "#OhJudoKnow," and episode 9, "#IAmYourMirror."

In "#OhJudoKnow," Nola, Mars, Lourdes, Shemekka, and Winnie (Fat Joe) arrive to the island for two separate established reasons: first, to distribute hurricane relief funds that they raised at Winnie's club; and second, for Lourdes and Mars to confront their mother about being evicted. Before the group sets out on their business, the audience is introduced to the syncretized nature of Puerto Rico through Noche De San Juan. Urged by Lourdes, the group runs into the ocean just before midnight to plunge themselves backward into the water seven times to "get cleansed of this negativity."[47] Though the annual celebration, which occurs on the night of the summer solstice between June 23 and 24 each year, done in honor of St. John the Baptist, many practitioners of Espritismo and Lucumí also participate as depicted in the episode.[48] Though the number of dives can vary from three to twelve, it is notable that Lourdes instructed the group to dive seven times, the number of her spiritual mother, Yemaya. Though we understand Yemaya in the context of the show as Lourdes's mother, this reengagement with her warrants a closer analysis of how her energy guides and interacts with Nola.

As mentioned in chapter 1, Yemaya, through her daughter Lourdes, brings Nola to meet Oshun, and that dynamic is mirrored in season 2 where she literally crosses an ocean (Yemaya's domain) and dives in before Oshun intervenes. After spending time distributing money to various charities, no doubt Oshun's work, Mars and Nola finally arrive in Santurce to meet with his mother about restoring the lease on their apartment. Rosie Perez reprises her role as Tina from *Do the Right Thing* (1989) and *White Men Can't Jump* (1992), now Doña Tina, Lourdes and Mars's mother. Guided into her sitting room by Lourdes, they are greeted by Doña Tina's Oshun shrine. Though the *sopera* is prominently displayed, the entire room, which is painted yellow, seems to belong to Oshun and is replete with peacock feathers and sun flowers. Doña Tina emerges from a back room wearing a white head wrap and a long dashiki-style dress. After admonishing Mars for shirking his responsibilities, she finally addresses Nola by saying, "You know, look what we got here. *La hija de Oshun* (Oshun's daughter)," and promptly tells her that "there are people who wanna talk to you."[49] After giving a food offering to a spiritual shrine, feeding her guests, and likening Nola and Mars to honey and molasses, another reference to the intimate relationship between the Oshun and Yemaya, she sends Mars and Lourdes on a store run to get them out of the house.

After they leave, Doña Tina immediately begins mediating the dialogue between Nola and the spirits who brought her to her door. Though they discuss Nola's relationship with Mars briefly, Doña Tina quickly redirects Nola to the heart of the matter by saying, "But the spirits didn't drag you all the way over here for me to talk to you about Mars. They wanna know why you're not serving your blessings.... And your blessing is to speak for those who cannot speak for themselves. That's what you are here to serve."[50] After receiving that message, Nola admits to being lost, uninspired, and unsure how to bring her voice and those she represents together. To that, Doña Tina offers her last bit of sage advice: "[L]et your eguns hold the map."[51] Opening herself up to that advice, Nola and Mars go exploring the island the next day and are taken with a beautiful mosaic of Oshun in progress. She is awestruck again when a woman dressed in all the trappings of Oshun walks by and greets her again as "la hija de Oshun." This serves as a pivotal moment in the episode by marking a turn for Nola as a smile of inspiration washes the awe from her face but also foreshadowing another encounter with Oshun and Yemaya later in the day.

Biking over to Río Grande de Loíza, an estuary where the river meets the ocean, Nola and Mars meet a fisherman on the shore dressed in yellow but wearing a blue crown with beads hanging down obscuring his face that clearly represents Yemaya. For the third time on her trip, she is greeted as a daughter of Oshun, and he allows her to take the first picture in what will become the solo art showing she's been planning. Nola and Mars continue their trip along the shore to meet Lourdes and the others at a drumming. She joins the dance circle and before long is guided over to *anya* (sacred) drums by a little girl in a blue head scarf. The drummers are flanked on one side a woman in a yellow shirt and white skirt and on the other by a woman in blue and white. This arrangement visually captures the geography of the river and ocean, of Oshun and Yemaya, coming together to greet Nola. As she reaches the drummers, they begin playing praise songs to Oshun. As the drummer picks up speed and intensity to call Oshun into the space, Nola is overcome by the energy, smiles, laughs, and dances her way back into the water. Perhaps physically moved by Oshun's energy, she faces the water and opens her arms in gratitude. Satisfied, she returns to dry ground, kneels, and warmly embraces the girl who brought her to the drums. This is the culminating moment of her trip and clarifies Oshun and Yemaya's influence on Nola's journey both to her and the viewer. She realizes that instead of being obsessed with her own work and voice, that she should see her art as a reflection of the responsibility given to Oshun's daughters: to do Oshun's work (providing healing, beauty, love, and compassion) in the world. Although Mars invites her to stay in Puerto Rico longer, she knows that part of her journey is complete and declines by saying, "I gotta get back. I got work to do."[52] Where she was lost, Oshun, Yemaya, and her ancestors found her and provided her with a mission and the tools to do it. She is tasked with using her artistic gifts for the greater good of her community and paying her spiritual blessings forward through social change.

Nola's growth in Puerto Rico is acknowledged quickly in episode 8, visually and verbally. Her singular Oshun candle has grown to a small table with offerings of fruit and flowers representing the expansion of the role of Oshun in her life. Additionally, Nola's godmother and landlord, Miss Ella (Pauletta Washington), remarks that "[y]ou've grown. . . . You're on a journey of your own choosing," which emphasizes Nola's conscious decision to heed the guidance of Yemaya, Oshun, and her ancestors.[53] The fruits of her choice, labor, and financial sacrifice are on full display episode 9, which shares the same name as her installation, "#IAmYourMirror." The name suggests that she took her designation as Oshun's daughter to heart and adopted the iconography of her mirror to emphasize her commitment to being a voice for the voiceless, telling her audience, "I hope you see yourself reflected."[54] Oshun and Yemaya's influence extend beyond the title of the installation. She wears a blue dress to the opening, which is a change from the yellow she's been wearing all season. Images of the woman she met dressed as Oshun and the fisherman in Puerto Rico line the walls, and a nude painting of Opal she worked on before they split has been converted into a painting of Yemaya is prominently displayed that bears a striking resemblance to Beyoncé's iconographic adoption in *Black Is King*. The painting provides a backdrop to a conversation between Opal and Nola where even Opal has to give Nola credit for her actual and artistic growth. Opal's comments represent the consensus around Nola's art except for what lies behind the curtain.

Even with all the growth she's undergone, Nola wouldn't be Nola without some controversy. Placing a portrait behind a maroon curtain to simultaneously highlight and obscure it, it becomes the focal point of the evening and the topic of much debate regarding its propriety or lack thereof. Fans, friends, and foes debate whether the portrait does more harm than healing. In an interesting turn of events, the artist behind Nola Darling's portraits, Tatyana Fazlalizadeh, appears as herself critiquing the painting in a monologue that says "Nola Darling's piece is part of a long tradition of transgression in Black art. She's using herself as a mirror to reflect back to America, its atrocities, not just against black people, but against black women in particular."[55] Fazlalizadeh uses language that connects back to Nola's iconographic adoption of Oshun's mirror, which is used for vanity as often as it is used to reflect the truth of a person or a situation, no matter how ugly. For truth fertilizes the foundation of change, and acknowledging ugliness is the first step toward transformation. The episode replicates the gallery-going experience for the viewer by withholding the painting until just a minute before the episode is over. After all the debate, and even protest regarding the painting, the viewer finally gets to decide for themselves if they see themselves reflected in the painting, a nude self-portrait of Nola hanging from a noose of her own braided hair with the American flag transposed over her body. And while the painting might not reflect the characters who disagreed with the vulgarity of her approach, it does reflect the oppressive conditions of Black women in America that need attention. For better or for worse, the painting generated important conversations that needed (and need) to be had about oppressive systems choking the life out of Black women and though the viewer doesn't get to see it, hopefully planted seeds for social change. Assuming Nola followed the map her ancestors provided, she learned that it can often be an arduous if rewarding path to walk. Guided by Oshun and Yemaya, at least she chose the journey leading to the greater good.

Conclusion

Reflections

Expanding the Journey to Healing: *4:44* (2017), *Everything Is Love* (2018), and *Black Is King* (2020)

After the album's release, Beyoncé announced that she would be taking her show on the road for the Formation World Tour during her Super Bowl L halftime performance on February 7, 2016. The tour started on April 27, bringing the spiritual energy as well as the iconographic salience of Oshun to the stage. Like most tours, the Formation World Tour maintained fidelity to the aesthetic elements that made the visual album striking, including those inspired by Oshun. In any given performance, the stage at some point would feature quite a few yellow or gold things, including garments, stage lighting and other accessories, which changed in one way or another at each venue. One consistency with the visual album that the tour took great care to maintain was the prevalence of water, Oshun's element, which I argue, carries more symbolic weight in this instance, as Beyoncé has incorporated yellow into her performances over the years. However, water, its connection to Oshun, and its narrative significance for *Lemonade* makes its emphasis in the performances during the Formation World Tour especially significant. It is important to note that there are instances where Beyoncé wears yellow while performing in ankle-deep water, allowing the water and the color yellow to work in tandem to anchor the iconographic adoption of Oshun's elements.

On June 30, 2017, over a year after *Lemonade*'s release, Jay-Z released an album titled *4:44*, which was widely received as a response to the previous album, if not a continuation of the narrative. The album provides Jay-Z's perspective on Beyoncé's commentary in *Lemonade* regarding their marriage and his infidelity. Unlike his wife, Jay-Z sat down for interviews to elucidate the album's meaning and eliminate the guesswork on behalf of consumers. On September 29, 2017, Jay-Z sat down with Dean Baquet, the *New York Times*'s executive editor, to discuss the album, race, fatherhood, and the transitions that were required to save his marriage. When asked about how Beyoncé's "confessional album" influenced his own work, Jay-Z responded,

> It actually started out we were working on material together and it became Lemonade. You know, she went off and did her thing, and it was like, it just felt like she should go first and she should share her truths with the world. So it wasn't based on I have to say something because this album, it wasn't even like that. It just was really honest. . . . We were using our art, almost like a therapy session and we started making music together. And then the music she was making at that time was further along, so her album came out as opposed to the joint album that we were working on. We still have a lot of that music and this is what it become. There was never a point where it was like, "I'm making this album." I was there. I was right there the entire time.[1]

Through these therapy sessions that he mentioned, as well as his own album, Jay-Z takes accountability for his actions and their implications, following the trajectory of *Lemonade*. Additionally, his commentary confirms intertextuality between the two albums, as well as the joint album to come. Jay-Z's interview also confirms the autobiographical/autoethnographic/biomythographic nature of the albums, as well as the centrality of healing in both albums. The primary difference between the two, however, is Jay-Z's interest in exploring his own intergenerational trauma and establishing a causal relationship between his own trauma and the pain he inflicts on his wife and, by extension, his children. Though the album covers a broad range of topics, including race, financial literacy, and fatherhood, the album finds itself centered on an apology, primarily to his wife but also to victims of his past crimes. Jay-Z continues in response to Baquet's question asking about their respective responses to the albums and the pain they elicited:

> Of course, very uncomfortable but sitting in that . . . the best place in the hurricane is like in the middle of it. We were sitting in the eye of the hurricane, maybe not use hurricane because so many people are being affected right now, but the best place is right in the middle of the pain and that's where we were sitting. And it was uncomfortable and [we had] a lot of conversations you know. And [I'm] really proud of the music she made, and she was proud of the art I released. And you know, at the end of the day, we really have a healthy respect for one another's craft. I think she is amazing. You know, most people walk away, and like, divorce rate is like fifty percent or something

because most people can't see themselves. The hardest thing is seeing pain on someone's face that you caused and then have to deal with yourself. So you don't, most people don't want to do that. You don't want to look inside yourself, so you walk away.[2]

Both on his album and in this interview (and others as he also sat down with David Letterman), Jay-Z strikes poignant intertextual chords with *Lemonade*, recalling the albums emphasis on confrontation with emotions, but especially with pain. This quote in particular draws on his own need to be vulnerable in the process of healing the relationship, as elucidated by the lyrics in Beyoncé's song "Sandcastles." Additionally, Jay-Z speaks of reflection and the difficulties of the process. Oshun's mirror, as operationalized in *Lemonade* to show Beyoncé her true sense of self after recovering from the devastation of betrayal, also required Jay-Z to look at himself as a perpetrator and who he could be beyond that. Ultimately, it is the reflective capacity of both Beyoncé and Jay-Z, as he describes, that saved the marriage and led to the production of three distinct but intertwined albums.

About one year after *4:44*'s release, the couple began the On the Run II Tour, performing music from both album and music that they have done together in the past. The tour itself became promotion for the joint album they released ten days into the tour on June 16, 2018, which they titled *Everything Is Love*. Though Jay-Z makes it clear that both *Lemonade* and *4:44* are retrospectives on issues they had done the work to address, *Everything Is Love* is presented as the manifestation of the work as well as a display of their ability to reap the benefits of that work, completing the trilogy and providing an end to the narrative trajectory toward healing. After two distinct albums that are rooted in the differences, the third represents a synthesis of the two, and the conclusion that healing provides a foundation for them to continue to work at the relationship, but also to enjoy it together on solid ground. The release of the album coinciding with the tour reinforces this notion as the performances themselves are marked by jovial repartee between the two, who have both expressed the extreme pleasure that performance brings them.

After the conclusion of the tour of their tour in October 2018, the duo headlined the Global Citizen Festival: Mandela 100, in Johannesburg, South Africa, on December 2, 2018. Here they performed together and separately, which is a custom for the pair, but Beyoncé solo performance engages yellow yet again, in a custom Atelier Versace jumpsuit with a matching hat, alongside a variety of other colors worn in a similar fashion by her dancers. Whereas Beyoncé's costuming has historically been monochromatic, this performance lit up the stage with an array of colors simulating a rainbow. Given her overall visual tribute to South Africa across the six costume changes in the performance, this wardrobe choice can be interpreted as a reference to Nelson Mandela's description of the country as a "rainbow nation" in his inaugural speech.[3] Also worth noting, given the intertextual connections I have made between Beyoncé and Ntozake Shange, is the costuming's striking resemblance to Shange's seminal choreopoem, *for colored girls who have considered suicide/when the rainbow is enuf.* This, like many of Beyoncé's other aesthetic choices can be read as a dual tribute to South Africa, and Mandela, the titular honoree of the music festival, as well as to Ntozake Shange, who died on October 28, 2018, just a little over a month before the performance. Additionally, Ntozake Shange's chosen Xhosa name represents a tribute to South Africa itself, one that Beyoncé carries on in her performance.[4] While she could have reasonably been wearing any color in the rainbow, she chose again to wear yellow.

This trajectory was continued (and perhaps culminated) with her releases of *The Lion King: The Gift* and the accompanying visual album *Black Is King* (2020), and the above summary events situates *Lemonade* and the subsequent albums in what became the Carters' trilogy as the foundation on which Beyoncé built out a larger aesthetic commitment to Oshun, Yoruba religious iconography, Africa, and its diaspora. Where *Lemonade* might have been considered an isolated incident, and indeed was criticized by bell hooks and Azealia Banks (a proud practitioner of African traditional religions) as an opportunistic if not exploitative take on African traditional religious iconography and concepts, the production of *Black Is King* (2020) solidified Beyoncé narrative priorities to create the beginnings a Black Atlantic cultural renaissance with her counterparts across the African diaspora.[5] In stark contrast to Azealia Banks's vocal advocacy and defense of African traditional religion, but characteristic of her commitment to privacy, Beyoncé has not claimed to be a practitioner of any African traditional religion.[6] Contra Azealia Banks, I do not believe it is important or necessary that she do so as it will not meaningfully change the cultural work she has done to honor and raise awareness about Yoruba religious systems or unravel the complex system of intertextuality she has woven using Oshun to thread the needle.

Oshun's Mirror and Me

While I did not originally conceptualize this project as an exercise in autoethnography, it has become as much about me, as it is about Oshun, her religious iconography, its symbolic import, and its cultural impact through *Lemonade* as a central text. I always saw it as a marriage between my academic interests and the fact of my practice of Lucumí, but I suspect that I only considered my positionality as a literal and figurative footnote in the broader exploration of Oshun's social capital in Black popular culture. Now that I am at the end of the writing process, which is accompanied by reflections of my own in conjunction with those regarding the research itself, I can ascertain the ways in which Oshun's energy facilitated my writing in very similar ways to the ones that I identify in *Lemonade, She's Gotta Have It, Sassafrass, Cypress & Indigo, Daughters of the Dust* (1991), and *Black Is King*. This project had been dedicated to Oshun from the outset, but I was not yet a daughter of Oshun myself when I started. Though I am that now that I have finished, this fact only strengthens my desire to do her work in the world and do justice to the community of practitioners I and this work represent.

In this book, I have accomplished my intervention into the broad fields of Africana Studies, anthropology, cultural studies, literary criticism, religious studies, sociology, and Yoruba Studies by not only drawing connection between them in the name and practice of interdisciplinarity but also by studying Oshun and Lucumí as cultural influencers that live beyond ritual practice or the sacred. Whereas studies of Lucumí and its practitioners have typically, though not exclusively been anthropological studies of ritual and practice, I have sought here to study Oshun and Lucumí autoethnographically, as I live them in the quotidian, without discrete boundaries between the sacred and secular or between theory and praxis. In fact, I would describe this work as study of the epistemology of Oshun, an explication of how the knowledge, or ways of knowing embodied in Oshun's mythistorical archive, and further, an application of them as tools to analyze cultural phenomena affected Black people broadly and Black women particularly.

Implications for Further Study

Like many researchers who have come before me—Robert Farris Thompson, Mercedes Sandoval, and Migene González-Wippler to name a few—I suspect that my perspectives regarding the iconographic adoptions of Orisha and their iconographies will shift with time and experience. Additionally, there is room to expand the academic discourse regarding Yoruba diasporic cultural influence in several directions, including the implications for public consumption of iconographic features of a private practice in a location like the United States, where even in 2019, the practice of Lucumí and other Yoruba-influenced spiritual traditions still largely remain "basement" practices hidden from the public. This is a distinct cultural phenomenon affecting practitioners in America since Orisha worship has made its way into the public cultural fabrics of Cuba, Puerto Rico, and Brazil, for example. Since many of the iconographic features of the religion maintain ritual significance, it is worth asking what the implications of iconographic adoption will mean for spiritual practices that are lifestyles and do not adhere to neat sacred-secular divisions. Like my godmother, Iya Gheri, says, popular interest in Lucumí comes in waves, like Yemaya and Oshun, and for different reasons. It is worth exploring academically what this wave (read: trend) will reveal or even obscure about the contemporary cultural significance of Orishas, Lucumí, and practitioners of African traditional religions at large.

Additionally, the mass exodus of young Black people (women in particular) from Judeo-Christian faith practices is connected to the cultural shift toward West African religions broadly, as many of the women leaving churches find themselves in the basements that often double as ilés for practitioners. This cultural journey of thus return is captured well by *Black Is King*, but certainly warrants further study. For example, what could broad cultural acceptance, if superficial, mean as it relates to offsetting social stigma related to African-centered spiritual practices, especially regarding their efficacy in addressing issues of trauma and facilitating healing in literature and in life. Accordingly, what changes are precipitated by marginal religious cultures moving to the center, if only for a moment. Importantly, along the lines of Omise'eke Natasha Tinsley's valuable work, there is more room to explore issues of gender fluidity in practice, as well as the conceptual difference that Yoruba diasporic socioreligious thought makes in understanding gender and gender queerness in Western societies from non-Western perspectives.

Finally, the transnational implications of Afro-Atlantic religions and the complexity of the cultural economy that exists between practitioners with varying access to information and materials and money would be worth exploring. After all, Beyoncé herself was accused of having capitalist priorities in choosing to include Yoruba religious iconography and concepts in her work. I am particularly interested in questions like how the advent of the internet in conjunction with increased demand for information about Yoruba religions in the wake of *Lemonade, She's Gotta Have It,* and *Black Is King* shifts economic and power dynamics between groups of practitioners internationally and in any given locale. Any of these questions represent ripe ground for continued interdisciplinary study.

GLOSSARY OF TERMS

àbíkú—literally, (child) born to die

abojúèjì—Mikelle Smith Omari-Tunkara defines this in conjunction with Ògúnwande Abimbola as a person who "participates in the culture for a while and then goes somewhere else"; also, a person who has "eyes and mind in two places"

àburò—younger sibling in a set of twins

adimu—food offering to Orisha

àjẹ́—the term is generally and traditionally used to describe powerful women, and usually those of an advanced age (postmenopausal)

Ajogun—purveyors of doom—death, disease, destruction and loss; also, sometimes referred as Osogbo

àlàfíà—peace or good health

anya—a drumming ceremony for Orìsà that uses consecrated sacred drums

aṣe (ashe/ache)—essential life force of all living creatures, spirits, and Orìsà as bestowed by Olódùmarè; also, used as a positive affirmation

àwòrán—a representation or spectrum

awòran—beholder or spectator

babalawo—male initiates into the secrets of Ifá

bembe—a general term for drumming ceremonies in the Lucumí tradition

Diloggún (Ẹẹ́rìndínlógún)—sixteen-cowrie-shell divination system

dúdú—black or any color similarly deep in hue

ẹbọ—an offering proscribed by divination to request the aid of Orisha for a favorable outcome

ẹgbọ́n—older sibling in a set of twins

egun—ancestors

egúngún—Yoruba masquerade honoring the ancestors

elekes—consecrated beads fashioned in the color and number of the Orisha they represent worn by Lucumí practitioners

ẹmí—spirit or soul

estera—a straw mat, often used to cover the floor for seating and divinatory purposes

ẹtò—progress

funfun—pure white

Gẹlẹdẹ—according to Babatunde Lawal, is a masquerade that includes art and ritual dance to educate, amuse, and maintain social harmony by celebrating motherhood; it's myth of origin is associated with Yemaya, who is considered the mother of all mothers

Ibeji (Ibeyi)—divine twins born from Oshun and Shango; refers to any twins

idé—bracelet; consecrate beaded bracelets fashioned in the color and number of the Orisha they represent worn by Lucumí practitioners

ìdílé—natal family

ikin—kola nuts

ikú—death

ikùkù—cirrus and cumulus clouds

ilé—spiritual house; can refer to both the physical location of worship as well as the community of people initiated into that particular spiritual house

ìran—spectacle

Irunmolé—seventeen primordial Orisha that descended from heaven to make the earth habitable for humankind

ìtàn—a memory-based oral art form

iyanifa—female initiates into the secrets if Ifa

iyawo—wife; in the Lucumí tradition, it is used to refer to newly initiated priests who are considered wives of the Orisha they have been initiated to jicará—coconut husk bowl of various sizes used in Lucumí ceremonial contexts

Lucumí (Regla de Ocha)—Afro-Cuban religion premised upon three Yoruba-derived religious tenets: ancestor veneration, belief in Olódùmarè as the creator, and Orisha worship

lwa (loa)—Haitian Vodun term for deity

mantón—a shawl often worn by dancing Lucumí priests when mounted by their Orisha

minkisi—small containers or sachets that hold spiritual substances in Ki-Kingo-based practices

Obí—a divination system employing four pieces of coconut; also refers to the Orisha Obí whose ashe is believed to be housed inside the coconut

ochá—the ceremony by which a Lucumí practitioner is initiated into priesthood

Odù Ifá—Yoruba divination system based on sixteen primary odùs (scriptures) as well as the combination of the sixteen, resulting in 256 possible outcomes in any given divination

ọfọ aṣẹ—the ability to pray effectively

Òjá—cloth tied around the waist of pregnant women to protect the womb from malevolent forces

ọkọ̀—husband; groom

ọpẹlẹ—a divination chain strung with eight kola nuts used to determine combinations of Odù Ifa

ọpọn Ifá—divination tray

orí—the head; also used to reference the essence of a person which would be located in the head

oríkì—praise poetry

Orìsà (Orisha)—benevolent deities in the Yoruba pantheon that intervene on behalf of human beings and serve as intermediaries between humans and the supreme god Olódùmarè

pánṣága (panshanga)—harlot; prostitute; adulteress

patakí—oral histories of Lucumí religion that are associated with odù verses and are used to glean wisdom during divination petro—term describing the pantheon Haitian lwas characterized by their hotness, aggression, and dangerous tendencies

pupa—red and similarly intense colors

rada—term describing the pantheon Haitian lwas characterized by their coolness and benevolence

santero/a—an initiated priest in the Lucumí tradition

sopera—covered porcelain vessel used to house Orisha

umbandisto/a—practitioner of the Afro-Brazilian religion of Umbanda, which is characterized by its syncretism, joining together Roman Catholicism, Spiritism, Indigenous Brazilian practices, as well as Yoruba deities, beliefs, and practices

veve—religious symbol used to call lwas in Haitian Vodoun

NOTES

Introduction

1. Caldwell, "I Came to Slay," 38.
2. Omari-Tunkara, *Manipulating the Sacred*, xxiii.
3. The term "Lucumí" is at times used interchangeably with "Santería." Some practitioners of the religion distinguish the two, arguing that Santería is syncretized with Catholicism but Lucumí is not.
4. Baudin and McMahon, *Fetichism and Fetich Worshippers*, 19.
5. Lovejoy, "Mapping Uncertainty," 128.
6. Cros Sandoval, *Worldview, the Orichas*, 50.
7. McKenzie, *Hail Orisha!*, 61.
8. Awolalu, *Yorùbá Beliefs*, 9.
9. Awolalu, *Yorùbá Beliefs*, 21–35.
10. Awolalu, 65.
11. Awolalu, 16–17.
12. Canizares, *Cuban Santeria*, 3.
13. Awolalu, *Yorùbá Beliefs*, 12–15.
14. Canizares, *Cuban Santeria*, ix.
15. Awolalu, *Yorùbá Beliefs*, 21–35.
16. Badejo, *Ọ̀sun Sèègèsí*, 68.
17. Ramos, *On the Orishas' Roads*, 53–54.
18. Ramos, 15.
19. Bascom, *Ifa Divination*, 3.
20. Abimbola, "Bag of Wisdom," 141.
21. Omari-Tunkara, *Manipulating the Sacred*, 38.
22. Omari-Tunkara, 38.
23. Sterling, *African Roots*, 47.
24. Thompson, "Orchestrating Water," 261.
25. Abimbola, "Bag of Wisdom," 151.
26. Hale, "Mama Oxum," 214.
27. Thompson, *Flash of the Spirit*, 19.
28. Abiodun, "Hidden Power," 16–18.
29. Ramos, *On the Orishas' Roads*, 24.
30. Ramos, 24.
31. Thompson, *Flash of the Spirit*, 85.

32 Thompson, 84–85.
33 Thompson, 84.
34 Olajubu, "Identity, Power," 82. See also Gleason, "Oya," 63.
35 Gleason, "Oya in the Company of Saints," 265.
36 Gleason, "Oya in the Company of Saints," 270.
37 Mason, *Orin Òrìṣà*, 168.
38 Mason, 168.
39 Mason, 168.
40 Oyewùmí, *What Gender Is Motherhood?*, 86.
41 Ogunbile, "Ẹẹrìndínlógún," 198.
42 Ogunbile, 205.
43 Ogunbile, 205.
44 Lawal, *Yoruba*, 27.
45 Washington, *Our Mothers, Our Powers*, 26.
46 Lawal, *Yoruba*, 26.
47 Lawal, 27.
48 Nuñez, *Santeria Stories*, 220.
49 Cabrera, *Yemayá y Ochún*, 71.
50 Adepegba, "Osun and Brass," 102.
51 Thompson, *Flash of the Spirit*, 79.
52 Thompson, "Orchestrating Water," 261.
53 Thompson, 261.
54 Thompson, 261.
55 Okediji, "Whither Art History?," 138.
56 D. Rowe, "Autoethnography as Object-Oriented Method," 229.
57 Rowe, 231.
58 Rowe, 230. Author's emphasis.
59 Rowe, 231.
60 Haile, "*Good kid, m.A.A.d. city*," 489.
61 Haile, "*Good kid, m.A.A.d. city*," 490.
62 Boylorn, "Bitter Sweet (Water)," 15.
63 New York Times, "Jay-Z and Dean Baquet."
64 Horvitz, "59th Annual Grammy Awards." See also Caldwell, "I Came to Slay," 59.
65 Baade et al., "Introduction," 18. See also Barber, "Conversation with Salamishah Tillet."
66 Okediji, "Whither Art History?," 123.
67 Okediji, "Semioptics of Anamnesia," 15.
68 Okediji, 15.
69 Okediji, 15.
70 Okediji, 15.
71 Lawal, "Àwòrán," 498.
72 Lawal, 516.
73 Okediji, "Semioptics of Anamnesia," 15.
74 Benston, "Aesthetic of Modern Black Drama," 62.

75 Senyonga, "Livable, Surviving, and Healing Poetics," 369.
76 Sterling, *African Roots*, 160–161.
77 Sterling, 160–161.
78 Awolalu, "Yoruba Philosophy of Life," 22.
79 Drewal and Drewal, "Composing Time and Space," 233.
80 Drewal and Drewal, 233.
81 Drewal and Drewal, 242.
82 Valdés, *Oshun's Daughter's*.

Chapter 1. When Life Gives You Lemons, Add Honey

1 Knowles-Carter et al., *Lemonade*, 00:00–00:03.
2 LaBorde, "Mapping the Louisiana Locations."
3 LaBorde. Initially built to protect New Orleans from attack during the War of 1812, Fort Macomb was later repurposed and occupied by Confederate soldiers during the Civil War.
4 Lawal, *Yoruba*, 27.
5 Washington, *Our Mothers*, 26.
6 Shire, "unbearable weight of staying."
7 Shaw, "Merging Past and Present," 122.
8 McKittrick, "Plantation Futures."
9 Zauditu-Selassie, "Women Who Know Things." See also Brodber, *Louisiana*, 148. Erna Brodber similarly centers embodied knowledge in *Louisiana*, suggesting that the only way to truly know something is to feel it.
10 Knowles-Carter et al., *Lemonade*, 01:57–02:29.
11 Lee, *She's Gotta Have It*, "#DaJumpoff," 31:50–32:00.
12 Lee, 32:05–32:11.
13 Lee, 32:34–32:39.
14 Fazlalizadeh, "Stop Telling Women to Smile."
15 Pikaart, "Meet the Brooklyn Artist."
16 Pikaart.
17 Lee, *She's Gotta Have It*, "#Bootyfull," 10:26–10:30.
18 Lila, "Oshun." See also Lee, *She's Gotta Have It*, "#Bootyfull," 31:00–31:50.
19 Lee, *She's Gotta Have It*, "#Bootyfull," 31:48–31:50.
20 Lawal, *Yoruba*, 26.
21 Alexander, *Pedagogies of the Crossing*, 312.
22 Lee, *She's Gotta Have It*, "#Bootyfull," 33:00–33:06.
23 Lee, *She's Gotta Have It*, "#HeGotItAllMixedUp," 17:32–17:35.
24 Shange, *Sassafrass, Cypress & Indigo*, 106.
25 Shange, 100.
26 Shange, 122.
27 Shange, 213.
28 Shange, 214.
29 Brodber, *Louisiana*, 98. A similar hair-related event occurs in *Louisiana*, mirroring the significance of hair-maintenance processes while undergoing physical and

spiritual changes. The protagonist of the novel, Ella Townsend, chronicles the ways in which the development of her mediumship influences the way she related to her physical body as a vessel, remarking that "[o]ther changes have been taking place. They are relatively small things. My hair for instance. I no longer press. I don't know if this represents spiritual or intellectual movement or just plain convenience but there it is: my hair is natural and untouched. And I wrap it."

30 Knowles-Carter et al., *Lemonade*, 04:37–04:53.
31 Lawal, *Yoruba*, 27.
32 Knowles-Carter et al., *Lemonade*, 05:00–05:28.
33 It is important to note that new initiates are referred to as iyawos regardless of gender identification or anatomical sex.
34 Welang, "Death and Resurrection of Oshun," 765.
35 Welang, "Death and Resurrection of Oshun," 751.
36 Gooch, "'Wave through the Waters,'" 81.
37 Omari-Tunkara, *Manipulating the Sacred*, xxvi.
38 See Morrison, *Paradise*, 262; this twinning of Beyoncé's self recalls the twinning of Consolata Sosa in the basement of the convent among her coven. Connie, having found Consolata, presents herself anew—same and different—to her convent-mates. Locating one's twinned-self guides both Consolata and Beyoncé to the truest versions of themselves, self-assured and confident.
39 Hale, "Mama Oxum," 214. While Candomblé is characterized by its fidelity to Yoruba traditional practice, Umbanda is characterized by its syncretism, joining together Roman Catholicism, Spiritism, Indigenous Brazilian practices, as well as Yoruba deities, beliefs, and practices.
40 Knowles-Carter et al., *Lemonade*, 05:56–6:00.
41 Shaw, "Merging Past and Present," 119.
42 Knowles-Carter, "Hold Up," in *Lemonade*.
43 Campbell, "Yoruba Shrine Painting Traditions," 104.
44 Brandon, "Ochun in the Bronx," 156.
45 Knowles-Carter et al., *Lemonade*, 08:36–08:42.
46 Lawal, "Àwòrán," 498.
47 Lawal, 516.
48 Knowles-Carter et al., *Lemonade*, 09:35–09:38.
49 Shange, *Sassafrass, Cypress & Indigo*, 214.
50 Badejo, *Ọ̀sun Sẹ̀ẹ̀gẹ̀sí*, 81.
51 McNeal, "Pantheons as Mythistorical Archives," 185–244.
52 Shange, *Sassafrass, Cypress & Indigo*, 216. When initiated, and sometimes sooner in one's spiritual journey, the sprits guiding one's life are revealed. It is traditional that regardless of whether the Orisha that one is crowned with is characteristically male or female, both parents, mother and father, are identified and are often require equal treatment. This evidences the tradition's own insistence on complementarity and is further driven home by Sassafrass's instinct to offer flowers to Oshun on the day of Shango's festivities so that she does not get jealous.

53 Isama, "10 Things You Need to Know." Aptly titled, the list included is, in my experience, quite accurate in the items included and in the order that they are listed. Santana Caress Benitez's contributions to the article serve as an excellent addendum to her role in *She's Gotta Have It*, as the shows incorporation of Yoruba spiritual practices sparked a lot of interest among viewers. Rather than leaving viewers to grope in the dark for answers about the practice, she contributed meaningfully to the discussion of how to discuss religious practices as their iconography grows more popular in the internet age. Perhaps most notably, to offset the narrative in the show, she adds that practicing the religion is not a quick fix but rather a long journey and at times a protracted struggle.
54 Isama, "10 Things You Need to Know."
55 Mbiti, *African Religions and Philosophy*, 230.
56 Shange, *Sassafrass, Cypress & Indigo*, 217.
57 Shange, 218.
58 Lee, *She's Gotta Have It*, "#LoveDontPayDaRent," 22:58–23:05.
59 Lee, *She's Gotta Have It*, "#LoveDontPayDaRent," 23:25–23:28.
60 Lee, 26:19–26:28.
61 Lee, 26:42–26:46.
62 Lee, 26:38–26:43.
63 It is very common that clients are directed to wear white for varying durations after the completion of a ceremony.
64 Lee, *She's Gotta Have It*, "#LoveDontPayDaRent," 26:58–27:02.
65 Iya Gheri (Lucumí priestess), in discussion with author, August 2018.
66 Lee, *She's Gotta Have It*, "#LoveDontPayDaRent," 27:08–27:27.
67 Lee, *She's Gotta Have It*, "#ChangeGonCome," 35:00. Audre Lorde is also known for calling on the spirit energy of Orishas in her writings.
68 Lee, *She's Gotta Have It*, "#ChangeGonCome."
69 Lee, 30:04–30:12.
70 Lee, 30:27–20:34.
71 Elizabeth Catlett (1915–2012) is an African American artist whose sculptures and prints predominantly featured African American women as subjects.
72 Littleton, "Netflix Renews Spike Lee's 'She's Gotta Have It.'"
73 Jones, "Queen Ya Ya."
74 Jackson, "Cultural Continuities," 144.
75 Shange, *Sassafrass, Cypress & Indigo*, 114.
76 Okediji, *The Shattered Gourd*, 59.
77 Knowles-Carter et al., *Lemonade*, 46:26–47:19.
78 Knowles-Carter et al., 47:50–47:55.
79 Knowles-Carter et al., 49:09–49:14.
80 Knowles-Carter et al., 50:20–50:44.
81 Knowles-Carter et al., 51:34–51:45.
82 Knowles-Carter et al., 50:45–51:29.
83 Badejo, *Ọṣun Sẹ̀ẹ̀gẹ̀sí*, 78.

84 Washington, *Our Mothers*, 15.
85 Knowles-Carter et al., *Lemonade*, 51:53–53:17.
86 Alexander, *Pedagogies of the Crossing*, 318.
87 Knowles-Carter, "All Night," in *Lemonade*.
88 Iya Gheri (Lucumí priestess), in discussion with author, August 2018.

Chapter 2. Don't Hurt Yourself

1 Bascom, *Ifa Divination*, 3.
2 Epega and Neimark, *Sacred Ifa Oracle*, x.
3 Bascom, *Ifa Divination*, 11. Whether Diloggún is derivative of Ifá will be explored further in the next section.
4 Ogunbile, "Ẹẹrìndínlógún," 196.
5 Love, *Divining the Self*, 109.
6 Wimbush, "Reading Scripture, Reading Darkness," 23.
7 Lee, *She's Gotta Have It*, "#Bootyfull," 32:00–33:06.
8 Abimbola, "Bag of Wisdom," 141.
9 Abimbola, "Bag of Wisdom," 148.
10 Abimbola, 147.
11 Abimbola, 149.
12 Abimbola, 150.
13 Oyewùmí, *What Gender Is Motherhood?*, 42–46.
14 Abiodun, "Hidden Power," 16–18. As point of clarification, the term "odù" is used interchangeably to describe both Orisha and divination verses. In the reproduction of Odù Ọṣẹ́túrá, the term is capitalized to indicate its reference to the Irunmolẹ́. Though the term at times appears with the diacritical mark indicating a low tone over the letter "u," this chapter follows that the diacritical critical mark indicating low tone uniformly refers to Orisha, so that even the title *Odù Ọṣẹ́túrá* is referring to the son Oshun bore, and Abiodun's reference to the "seventeenth Odù" is Oshun herself, the last of the Irunmolẹ́. Accordingly, the term used in reference to Orisha is both capitalized and appears with the appropriate diacritical marks. The term used in reference to the divination verses themselves is lowercase and appears with the appropriate diacritical marks.
15 Iya Gheri (Lucumí priestess), in discussion with author, August 2018.
16 Oyewùmí, *What Gender Is Motherhood?*, 46.
17 Abiodun, "Hidden Power," 18.
18 Òjó, "Names and Naming," 242–43.
19 Cuthrell Curry, *Making the Gods*, 65.
20 Valdés, *Oshun's Daughter's* 92. See also Cuthrell Curry, *Making the Gods*, 65.
21 Spielberg, *Color Purple*, 02:06:40–02:06:49.
22 Spielberg.
23 Spielberg.
24 Knowles-Carter et al., *Lemonade*, 12:55–12:58.
25 Knowles-Carter et al., 10:32–12:13.
26 Knowles-Carter et al., 10:32–12:13.

27. Knowles-Carter et al., 10:32–12:13.
28. Knowles-Carter et al., 10:32–12:13.
29. Knowles-Carter, "Don't Hurt Yourself," in *Lemonade*. It is worth noting that the song samples Led Zeppelin's "When the Levee Breaks" (1971), which I read as another meta-reference to New Orleans in its reference to Hurricane Katrina while recalling the centrality of water in the larger narrative. See also Tinsley, *Beyoncé in Formation*, 24.
30. Knowles-Carter et al., *Lemonade*, 13:35–13:50.
31. Knowles-Carter et al., 14:52–15:18.
32. Knowles-Carter et al., 15:17–15:18.
33. Patterson, "We Went to 'Beyoncé Mass.'" Published just over two years after *Lemonade*'s release, this article outlines that even churches have cashed in on Beyoncé's star power and fan base. Celebrities of her status are often deified, and her own devout fans have gone so far as to refer to her as "Beysus" as well as superimposing her face over a rendering on Jesus Christ on social media websites. See also Griffiths, "Beyoncé's Message."
34. Lawal, *Yoruba*, 27.
35. Tinsley, *Beyoncé in Formation*, 77.
36. Tinsley, *Beyoncé in Formation*, 78. See also Hayes, *Holy Harlots*.
37. Sterling, *African Roots*, 153.
38. Thompson, "Orchestrating Water," 260. This is discussed in more detail in chapter 3.
39. Courlander, *Tales of Yoruba Gods*, 23.
40. Beyoncé's dalliances with Erzulie will be further explicated in chapter 4. See also Olajubu, *Women in the Yoruba Religious Sphere*, 81.
41. Thomas, "Unenslaveable Rapture," 58.
42. White, "Espousing Ezili," 66.
43. Knowles-Carter et al., *Lemonade*, 10:32–12:13.
44. Knowles-Carter, "Don't Hurt Yourself," in *Lemonade*.
45. Knowles-Carter et al., *Lemonade*, 15:28–15:40.
46. Abiodun, "Hidden Power."
47. Senbanjo, "Sacred Art of the Ori."
48. Senbanjo, "Sacred Art of the Ori."
49. Okediji, *Shattered Gourd*, 33.
50. Yai, "In Praise of Metonymy," 30.
51. Okediji, *Shattered Gourd*, 33.
52. Senbanjo, "Sacred Art of the Ori."
53. Senbanjo.
54. Hutten and Burns, "Beyoncé's Black Feminist Critique," 320.
55. Knowles-Carter et al., *Lemonade*, 16:15–17:06.
56. Knowles-Carter et al., 16:15–17:06.
57. Adéẹ̀kọ́, "Oral Poetry and Hegemony," 182.
58. Yai, "In Praise of Metonymy," 30.
59. Knowles-Carter et al., *Beyoncé*.
60. Winfrey, *Oprah's Next Chapter*, "Beyoncé."

61 Lawal, Gèlèdé Spectacle, 51.
62 Knowles-Carter et al., Lemonade, 16:15–17:06.
63 Abiodun, "Hidden Power."
64 Knowles-Carter, "Sorry," in Lemonade.
65 Knowles-Carter.
66 Knowles-Carter.
67 Abiodun, "Hidden Power."
68 Knowles-Carter et al., Lemonade, 20:36–23:02.
69 Fatunmbi, Ìwà-Pèlé, 97.
70 Knowles-Carter et al., Lemonade, 24:00–24:02.
71 Knowles-Carter et al., 24:06–24:22.
72 Knowles-Carter, "6 Inch," in Lemonade.
73 Fanon, "On National Culture."
74 Knowles-Carter, "6 Inch," in Lemonade.
75 Knowles-Carter et al., Lemonade, 26:48–27:16.
76 Knowles-Carter et al., 26:48–27:16.
77 Knowles-Carter et al., 28:17–29:21, 30:03–31:00.
78 Knowles-Carter et al., 29:21–30:03.
79 Knowles-Carter et al., 30:03–31:00.
80 Knowles-Carter et al., 30:03–31:00.
81 Knowles-Carter et al., "Daddy Lessons," in Lemonade.
82 Knowles-Carter et al., "Daddy," in Dangerously in Love.
83 Iandoli, "Complete Timeline."
84 Knowles-Carter, "Daddy," in Dangerously in Love.
85 Knowles-Carter et al., Lemonade, 02:42–3:01.
86 Knowles-Carter, "Daddy Lessons," in Lemonade.
87 Knowles-Carter et al., Lemonade, 35:15–35:55.
88 Knowles-Carter et al., 01:57–02:29.
89 Knowles-Carter, "Love Drought," in Lemonade. I understand that the co-writer of the song, Ingrid Burley, was motivated by very different circumstances to write the song, and my analysis of it extends only to its positionality in the broader narrative of the visual album.
90 Knowles-Carter, "Love Drought," in Lemonade.
91 Knowles-Carter et al., Lemonade, 38:18–39:33.
92 The kintsugi bowl can be interpreted to visually represent Beyoncé's desire for her repair work to make her relationship stronger than it was before. Though kintsugi is a decidedly Japanese practice, in this context, the bowl being repaired and held together by gold hints at Oshun's iconographic and spiritual role in guiding Beyoncé through the necessary steps to be able to repair and hold her relationship together.
93 Knowles-Carter, "Sandcastles," in Lemonade.

Chapter 3. Water Always Returns to Its Source

1 Wande Abimbola, "Bag of Wisdom," 151.
2 Nuñez, Santeria Stories, 77.

3. Kincaid, "At the Bottom of the River," in *At the Bottom of the River*, 74–75.
4. Kincaid, "At the Bottom of the River," in *At the Bottom of the River*, 76–77.
5. Thompson, "Sign of the Divine King." See also Omari-Tunkara, *Manipulating the Sacred*, 77.
6. Translation by Adéléke Adéẹ̀kọ. See also Olajubu, "Identity, Power," 84.
7. The different avatars or roads of Oshun are said to be found at different locations at the river including the river floor, waterfalls, and riverbanks. These locations play a key role in the folk narratives of the respective roads of Oshun.
8. LettySetGo and Steel, "Inspiration behind Beyoncé's 'Lemonade' Imagery."
9. Desta, "How Beyoncé's Lemonade Helped."
10. Wardi, *Water and African American Memory*, 7.
11. Gooch, "'Wave through the Waters,'" 78.
12. Knowles-Carter et al., *Lemonade*, 00:00–00:03.
13. Olajubu, "Identity, Power," 81.
14. Olajubu, 81.
15. Zaru, "Beyoncé Gets Political."
16. Moorish culture has found its way into African American communities through both Islam and secret societies of Moorish rites/freemasonry. The fez is a visual marker of this in the video.
17. It is worth noting that Oshun is typically described as one of three consorts of Shango. Additionally, while Oshun is most popularly associated with Orunmila, Shango, and Ogun, there are patakís that reflect romantic/sexual relationships with other Orishas like Erinle, but they are less common. My reversal of this description, centering Oshun, is intentional.
18. Olajubu, "Identity, Power," 81.
19. Knowles-Carter et al., *Lemonade*, 01:01:15–01:01:17.
20. Knowles-Carter et al., 01:01:54–01:01:56.
21. Ibeyi, "River."
22. It is worth noting that both songs were released before their debut album on an EP titled *Oya*, on August 7, 2014.
23. Hobson, "Foreword," xiii.
24. Bascom, "Principle of Seniority," 37. See also Oruene, "Magical Powers of Twins," 211.
25. Bascom, "Principle of Seniority," 37–38.
26. Ibeyi, "River."
27. Ibeyi.
28. Ibeyi.
29. This scene bears striking similarities to one in João Daniel Tikhomiroff's film *Besouro*. After offering yellow flowers to Oshun to ask for her aid in an impending battle, the protagonist, Besouro, is also seen being lapped by water on the shore as an indication that his offering has been accepted by Oshun, as well as a blessing.
30. Knowles-Carter et al., *Lemonade*, 38:18–38:23.
31. Knowles-Carter, featuring James Blake, "Forward," in *Lemonade*.
32. Knowles-Carter, "Sandcastles," in *Lemonade*.

33 Dash, *Daughters of the Dust*, 02:35–03:17. See also Bobo, *Black Women as Cultural Readers*, 135.
34 MacRae and Parrott, "Thunder," 297.
35 Williams, "Thunder," 30.
36 Bonnefoy, "Yoruba Myths and Religion," 147.
37 Hale, "Mama Oxum," 217.
38 Ogunbile, "Ẹẹrìndínlógún," 195.
39 Abimbola, "Bag of Wisdom," 151.
40 Murphy and Sanford, "Introduction," 6.
41 Ramos, *On the Orishas' Roads*, 25–26.
42 Dash, *Daughters of the Dust*, 34:00–34:26. See also Mason, *Orin Òrìṣà*, 94.
43 Ramos, *On the Orishas' Roads*, 41–44.
44 Ramos, *On the Orishas' Roads*, 41–44. See also Mason, *Orin Òrìṣà*, 178.
45 Dash, *Daughters of the Dust*, 34:20–34:24.
46 Dash, *Daughters of the Dust*, 40:33–40:37.
47 Ramos, *On the Orishas' Roads*, 42. Saint Christopher is said to ferry passengers over rivers, delivering his passengers safely at their destination.
48 Dash, *Daughters of the Dust*, 40:39–40:45.
49 Washington, "'Sea Never Dies,'" 257.
50 Dash, *Daughters of the Dust*, 58:20–59:55. See also Mason, *Orin Òrìṣà*, 340.
51 Dash, 01:13:37–01:14:09.
52 Dash, 59:56–01:00:10. See also Mason, *Orin Òrìṣà*, 355.
53 Mason, *Orin Òrìṣà*, 355.
54 Dash, *Daughters of the Dust*, 01:09:53–01:10:38.
55 Dash, 01:10:40–01:11:15.
56 Mason, *Orin Òrìṣà*, 93.
57 Hartman, *Scenes of Subjection*, 85.
58 Dash, *Daughters of the Dust*, 19:34–19:37.
59 Dash, 01:30:25–01:30:44.
60 Ramos, *On the Orishas' Roads*, 29.
61 I assert the connection here with respect to the fact that Ibo people have their own spiritual understandings that at times converge and diverge with Yoruba ones. Here, Yoruba and Ibo understandings of the importance of riverine goddesses converge around the general venerations of Mami-Wata (also Mammy Wata), as well as specific river deities like Nne Mmiri and Ogbuide that share attributes with both Oshun and Yemaya. See Jell-Bahlsen, *Water Goddess*.
62 Dash, *Daughters of the Dust*, 01:16:54–01:17:24.
63 Dash, 19:34–19:37.
64 Dash, 01:33:41–01:34:19.
65 Dash, 01:34:20–01:34:36.
66 Dash, 01:34:38–01:34:44.
67 Dash, 01:34:48–01:34:49.
68 Dash, 01:34:52–01:38:38.
69 Hartman, *Scenes of Subjection*, 105.

70 Spillers, "Mama's Baby, Papa's Maybe," 67.
71 Hartman, *Scenes of Subjection*, 87.
72 Thompson, "Orchestrating Water," 260.
73 Thompson, "Orchestrating Water," 260.

Chapter 4. Honey in the Hive

1 Ramos, *On the Orishas' Roads*, 92.
2 Lawal, *The Gẹ̀lẹ̀dẹ́ Spectacle*, 41.
3 Warner, "Beyonce Drops Surprise Song."
4 Hobson, "Foreword," xvi.
5 Knowles-Carter, "Black Parade."
6 Wiggins, *O Freedom*.
7 See Balvin et al., "Mi Gente."
8 Knowles-Carter, "Black Parade."
9 Hill, "How George Floyd Was Killed."
10 Hill.
11 Knowles-Carter, "Black Parade."
12 Direct musical references to the incident include Beyoncé's own "Flawless" remix, Jay-Z's "Kill Jay-Z," and, as some speculate, most recently "Cozy" on Beyoncé's latest project, *Renaissance*. See also Petit, "JAY-Z and Solange's Infamous Elevator Fight"; and Chelsey, "Beyoncé Hints."
13 Knowles-Carter, "Black Parade."
14 Knowles-Carter.
15 Mallory, "About Tamika D. Mallory."
16 Knowles-Carter, "Black Parade."
17 Knowles-Carter, *Black Is King*, 01:19:02–01:19:17.
18 See Efoui-Delplanque, "Battle or a Conversation."
19 Knowles-Carter, *Black Is King*, 00:32–00:43.
20 In this sense, Beyoncé characterizes Christianity as an African religion or at least syncretizes it with one to visually relocate Egypt in Black Africa.
21 Knowles-Carter, *Black Is King*, 01:13:58–01:14:03.
22 Knowles-Carter, 01:52–01:54.
23 Knowles-Carter, 02:34–3:22.
24 Sellers, "Yemoja," 144.
25 Bridges, "Opulent Mother," 4.
26 Knowles-Carter, "Bigger," in *Lion King*.
27 Knowles-Carter, "Bigger," in *Lion King*.
28 Pérez, "Nobody's Mammy," 25.
29 Knowles-Carter, *Black Is King*, 42:53–43:16.
30 Knowles-Carter, 43:18–43:31.
31 Sellers, "Yemoja," 144.
32 Sellers, "Yemoja," 145.
33 Knowles-Carter, *Black Is King*, 43:34–44:24.
34 Knowles-Carter, 44:26–44:38.

35 White, "Espousing Ezili," 64.
36 Ward, "Where Circum-Caribbean Afro-Catholic Creoles," 124.
37 Beyonce Knowles-Carter, Pharrell Williams, and Salatiel, "Water," in *Lion King*.
38 White, "Espousing Ezili."
39 Beyonce Knowles-Carter, Pharrell Williams, and Salatiel, "Water," in *Lion King*.
40 Erzulie Freda is said to wear three wedding bands representing her connections to Damballah, Ogoun, and Agou-Taroyo. See Dayan, "Erzulie," 6.
41 Knowles-Carter, "Mood 4 Eva," in *Lion King*.
42 Knowles-Carter, *Black Is King*, 48:34–48:58.
43 Knowles-Carter, 50:00–50:34.
44 Blue Ivy Carter, SAINt JHN, Beyoncé Knowles-Carter, and Wizkid, "Brown Skin Girl," in *Lion King*.
45 McKenzie, "'Brown Skin Girl' Director."
46 Knowles-Carter, *Black Is King*, 59:05–59:35.
47 Lee, *She's Gotta Have It*, "#OhJudoKnow?," 05:31–05:33.
48 Morales, "Aging with Grace and Power," 54.
49 Lee, *She's Gotta Have It*, "#OhJudoKnow?," 11:22–11:27.
50 Lee, *She's Gotta Have It*, 15:32–16:10.
51 Lee, *She's Gotta Have It*, 16:28–16:32.
52 Lee, *She's Gotta Have It*, 31:24–31:28.
53 "#OnTheComeUpTheComeDown&TheComeRound," 17:10–17:23.
54 Lee, *She's Gotta Have It*, "#IAmYourMirror," 03:27–03:29.
55 Lee, *She's Gotta Have It*, "#IAmYourMirror," 24:51–25:04.

Conclusion

1 New York Times, "Jay-Z and Dean Baquet."
2 New York Times, "Jay-Z and Dean Baquet, in Conversation."
3 Mandela, "Inaugural Speech."
4 I would like to point out that I did make this connection when reviewing the costuming but would like to give credit to Shelby Ivey Christie, who tweeted about it as well. Tweeted by the user on December 18, 2018, at 1:34 p.m.
5 Brooks and Martin, "Introduction," 1.
6 Peréz, "Black Atlantic Metaphysics."

BIBLIOGRAPHY

Abimbola, Wande. "The Bag of Wisdom: Ọ̀ṣun and the Origins of the Ifá Divination." In Murphy and Sanford, *Oshun across the Waters*, 141–154.

Abiodun, Rowland. "Hidden Power: Ọ̀ṣun, the Seventeenth Odù." In Murphy and Sanford, *Oshun across the Waters*, 10–33.

Adéẹ̀kọ́, Adélékè. "Oral Poetry and Hegemony: Yorùbá Oríkì." *Dialectical Anthropology* 26, nos. 3–4 (2001): 181–192.

Adepegba, Cornelius O. "Osun and Brass." In Murphy and Sanford, *Oshun across the Waters*, 102–112.

Alexander, M. Jacqui. *Pedagogies of the Crossing: Meditations on Feminism, Sexual Politics, Memory and the Sacred*. Durham, NC: Duke University Press, 2005.

Awolalu, J. Omosade. *Yorùbá Beliefs and Sacrificial Rites*. Burnt Mill, UK: Longman, 1979.

Awolalu, J. Omosade. "The Yoruba Philosophy of Life." *Présence Africaine* 73 (1970): 20–38.

Baade, Christina, and Kristin McGee. *Beyoncé in the World: Making Meaning with Queen Bey in Troubled Times*. Middletown, CT: Wesleyan University Press, 2021.

Baade, Christina, Marquita Smith, and Kristin McGee. "Introduction." In Baade and McGee, *Beyoncé in the World*, 1–32.

Badejo, Diedre. *Ọ̀ṣun Sẹ̀ẹ̀gẹ̀sí: The Elegant Deity of Wealth, Power, and Femininity*. Trenton, NJ: Africa World Press, 1996.

Balvin, J., Willy William, and Beyoncé. "Mi Gente." Single. Paris: Scorpio Music, 2017.

Barber, Tiffany E. "A Conversation with Salamishah Tillet." *Black Camera: An International Film Journal* 9, no. 1 (2017): 205–216.

Bascom, William. *Ifa Divination: Communication between Gods and Men in West Africa*. Bloomington: Indiana University Press, 1991.

Bascom, William. "The Principle of Seniority in the Social Structure of the Yoruba." *American Anthropologist* 44, no. 1 (1942): 37–46.

Benston, Kimberly W. "The Aesthetic of Modern Black Drama: From Mimesis to Methexis." In *The Theater of Black Americans: A Collection of Critical Essays*, edited by Errol Hill, 61–78. New York: Applause, 1987.

Baudin, Planque, and Mary McMahon. *Fetichism and Fetich Worshippers*. New York: Benziger, 1885.

Bobo, Jacqueline. *Black Women as Cultural Readers*. New York: Columbia University Press, 1995.

Bonnefoy, Yves. *American, African, and Old European Mythologies*. Chicago: University of Chicago Press, 2008.

Boylorn, Robin M. "Bitter Sweet (Water): Autoethnography, Relational Ethics, and the Possible Perpetuation of Stereotypes." In *Doing Autoethnography*, edited by Sandra L. Pensoneau-Conway, Tony E. Adams and Derek M. Bolen, 7–17. Rotterdam: Sense Publishers, 2017.

Brandon, George. "Ochun in the Bronx." In Murphy and Sanford, *Oshun across the Waters*, 155–164.

Bridges, Eric M. "The Opulent Mother: Brief Discussion of Yemonja and Her Worship in Yorùbáland." In *Recovering the African Feminine Divine in Literature, the Arts, and Practice: Yemonja Awakening*, 3–10 Lanham, MD: Lexington Books, 2020.

Brodber, Erna. *Louisiana*. Jackson: University Press of Mississippi, 1997.

Brooks, Kinitra D., and Kameelah L. Martin. "Introduction: Beyoncé's *Lemonade* Lexicon: Black Feminism and Spirituality in Theory and Practice." In *The "Lemonade" Reader*, edited by Kinitra D. Brooks and Kameelah L. Martin, 1–4 New York: Routledge Press, 2019.

Cabrera, Lydia. *Yemayá y Ochún—Kariocha, Iyalorichas y Olorichas*. New York: Ediciones CR, 1980.

Caldwell, H. Zahra. "I Came to Slay: The Knowles Sisters, Black Feminism, and the Lineage of the Black Female Cool." In Baade and McGee, *Beyoncé in the World*, 35–64.

Campbell, Bolaji. "Yoruba Shrine Painting Traditions: Color, Cosmos, Process and Aesthetics." PhD dissertation, University of Wisconsin Madison, 2001.

Canizares, Raul. *Cuban Santeria: Walking with the Night*. Rochester, NY: Destiny Books, 1999.

Courlander, Harold. *Tales of Yoruba Gods and Heroes*. Greenwich, CT: Fawcett, 1973.

Cros Sandoval, Mercedes. *Worldview, the Orichas, and Santeria: Africa to Cuba and Beyond*. Gainesville: University Press of Florida, 2006.

Cuthrell Curry, Mary. *Making the Gods in New York: The Yoruba Religion in the African American Community*. New York: Garland, 1997.

Dash, Julie, dir. *Daughters of the Dust*. New York: Kino International, 1991.

Dayan, Joan. "Erzulie: A Women's History of Haiti." *Research in Africana Literatures* 25 (1994): 5–31.

Desta, Yohanda. "How Beyoncé's Lemonade Helped Bring a Groundbreaking Film Back to Theaters." *Vanity Fair*. August 22, 2016. www.vanityfair.com/hollywood/2016/08/daughters-of-the-dust-exclusive

Drake, Simone C. *Critical Appropriations: African American Women and the Construction of Transnational Identity*. Baton Rouge: Louisiana State University Press, 2014.

Drewal, Margaret Thompson, and Henry John Drewal. "Composing Time and Space in Yoruba Art." *Word and Image* 3, no. 3 (1987): 225–251.

Efoui-Delplanque, Raphaëlle. "A Battle or a Conversation: Imagining Africa and Its Diaspora in Beyoncé's *Black Is King* and *Lemonade*." *Amerikastudien* 67 (2022):199–218.

Epega, Afolabi A., and Phillip John Neimark. *The Sacred Ifa Oracle*. New York: HarperCollins, 1995.

Fanon, Frantz. "On National Culture." In *The Wretched of the Earth*, 206–248. New York: Grove Press, 1963.

Fatunmbi, Awo. *Ìwà-Pẹ̀lẹ́: Ifá Quest: The Search for the Source of Santería and Lucumí*. Bronx, New York: Original Publications, 1991.

Fazlalizadeh, Tatyana. "Stop Telling Women to Smile." Tlynnfaz.com. Accessed April 1, 2024. https://tlynnfaz.com/Stop-Telling-Women-to-Smile

Gaines, Zeffie. "A Black Girl's Song: Misogynoir, Love, and Beyoncé's *Lemonade*." *Taboo: The Journal of Culture and Education* 16, no. 2 (Fall 2017): 97–114.

Gleason, Judith. "Oya: Black Goddess of Africa." In *The Goddess Re-Awakening: The Feminine Principle Today*, edited by Shirley Nicholson, 56–67. Wheaton: Theosophical Publishing House, 1989.

Gleason, Judith. "Oya in the Company of Saints." *Journal of the American Academy of Religion* 68, no. 2 (2000): 265–291.

Gonzales, Erica. "Beyoncé's 'Love Drought' Isn't about Jay-Z: A Co-Writer Reveals the Song's True Meaning." *Harpersbazaar.com*. June 16, 2016. www.harpersbazaar.com/culture/art-books-music/news/a16167/beyonce-lemonade-love-drought-meaning/

Gooch, Catherine D. "'Wave through the Waters': Water Imagery in Beyoncé's Visual Album *Lemonade*." In *Bodies of Water in African American Literature, Music, and Film*, edited by Sharon A. Lewis and Ama S. Wattley, 77–88. Newcastle upon Tyne, UK: Cambridge Scholars Publishing, 2023.

Griffiths, Kadeen. "Beyoncé's Message during Her 2016 VMAs Performance Tore Down Her Godlike Reputation." *Bustle*. August 28, 2016. www.bustle.com/articles/181082-beyonces-message-during-her-2016-vmas-performance-tore-down-her-godlike-reputation

Haile, James B., III, "*Good kid, m.A.A.d. city*: Kendrick Lamar's Autoethnographic Method." *Journal of Speculative Philosophy* 32, no 3. (2018): 488–498.

Hale, Lindsay. "Mama Oxum: Reflections of Gender and Sexuality in Brazilian Umbanda." In Murphy and Sanford, *Oshun across the Waters*, 213–229.

Hartman, Saidiya. *Scenes of Subjection: Terror, Slavery, and Self-Making in Nineteenth-Century America*. Oxford: Oxford University Press, 1997.

Hayes, Kelly E. *Holy Harlots: Femininity, Sexuality, and Black Magic in Brazil*. Berkeley: University of California Press, 2011.

Hill, Evan, Ainara Tiefenthäler, Christiaan Triebert, Drew Jordan, Haley Willis, and Robin Stein. "How George Floyd Was Killed in Police Custody." *New York Times*, May 31, 2020. www.nytimes.com/2020/05/31/us/george-floyd-investigation.html

Hobson, Janell. "Foreword." In Baade and McGee, *Beyoncé in the World*, vii–xviii.

Horvitz, Louis, dir. "59th Annual Grammy Awards." CBS. Aired February 12, 2017.

Hutten, Rebekah, and Lori Burns. "Beyoncé's Black Feminist Critique: Multimodal Intertextuality and Intersectionality in 'Sorry.'" In Baade and McGee, *Beyoncé in the World*, 313–338.

Iandoli, Kathy. "A Complete Timeline of Beyoncé's Complicated Relationship with Her Father: Is Mathew Knowles the Other Person She's Singing about on *Lemonade*?" *Cosmopolitan*. May 2, 2016. www.cosmopolitan.com/entertainment/celebs/a57822/beyonce-mathew-knowles-timeline/

Ibeyi. "River." Track 4 on *Ibeyi*. London: XL Recordings, 2015.
Isama, Antoinette. "10 Things You Need to Know before Practicing Lucumí." Okay-Africa. January 3, 2018. www.okayafrica.com/10-things-you-need-to-know-before-practicing-lucumi/
Jackson, Joyce Marie. "Cultural Continuities: Masking Traditions of the Black Mardi Gras Indians and the Yoruba Egunguns." In *Orisa: Yoruba Gods and Spiritual Identity in Africa and the Diaspora*, edited by Toyin Falola and Ann Genova, 143–160. Trenton, NJ: Africa World Press, 2005.
Jell-Bahlsen, Sabine. *The Water Goddess in Igbo Cosmology: Ogbuide of Oguta Lake*. Trenton, NJ: Africa World Press, 2008.
Jones, Jessica Marie. "Queen Ya Ya of the Washitaw Nation Is the Mardi Gras Indian of #Lemonade." *Diaspora Hypertext.com*, April 28, 2016. https://www.newblackmaninexile.net/2016/04/diaspora-hypertext-queen-ya-ya-of.html
Kincaid, Jamaica. *At the Bottom of the River*. New York: Aventura, 1985.
Knowles-Carter, Beyoncé. "Black Parade." Track 17 in *The Lion King: The Gift (Deluxe Edition)*. New York: Parkwood Entertainment, 2020.
Knowles-Carter, Beyoncé. "Daddy." Track 15 on *Dangerously in Love*. New York: Columbia Records, 2003.
Knowles-Carter, Beyoncé. *The Gift*. New York: Parkwood Entertainment, 2019.
Knowles-Carter, Beyoncé, Blitz Bazawule, Jenn Nkiru, and Emmanuel Adjei. *Black Is King*. Burbank: Walt Disney Studios Motion Pictures, 2020.
Knowles-Carter, Beyoncé, Ed Burke, and Ilan Benatar, dir. *Beyoncé: Life Is But a Dream*. New York: Parkwood Entertainment, 2013.
Knowles-Carter, Beyoncé, Kahlil Joseph, Dikayl Rimmasch, Todd Tourso, Jonas Åkerlund, Melina Matsoukas, Mark Romanek, dirs. *Lemonade*. New York: Parkwood Entertainment and Columbia Records, 2016.
LaBorde, Lauren. "Mapping the Louisiana Locations in Beyonce's 'Lemonade.'" Curbed New Orleans. June 3, 2016. https://nola.curbed.com/maps/beyonce-lemonade-louisiana-filming-locations
Lawal, Babatunde. "Àwòrán: Representing the Self and Its Metaphysical Other in Yoruba Art." *Art Bulletin* 83, no. 3 (2001): 498–526.
Lawal, Babatunde. *The Gẹ̀lẹ̀dẹ́ Spectacle: Art, Gender, and Social Harmony in an African Culture*. Seattle: University of Washington Press, 1997.
Lawal, Babatunde. *Yoruba*. Milan: 5 Continents Editions, 2012.
Lee, Spike, dir. *Do the Right Thing*. New York: Criterion, 1989.
Lee, Spike, dir. *She's Gotta Have It*. Beverly Hills: MGM, 1986.
Lee, Spike, dir. *White Men Can't Jump*. Los Angeles: 20th Century Studios, 1992.
Lee, Spike, dir. *She's Gotta Have It*, season 1, episode 1, "#DaJumpoff (DOCTRINE)." Aired November 23, 2017, on Netflix.
Lee, Spike, dir. *She's Gotta Have It*, season 1, episode 2, "#Bootyfull (SELF ACCEPTANCE)." Aired November 23, 2017, on Netflix,
Lee, Spike, dir. *She's Gotta Have It*, season 1, episode 6, "#HeGotItAllMixedUp (DYSLEXIA)." Aired November 23, 2017, on Netflix.

Lee, Spike, dir. *She's Gotta Have It,* season 1, episode 8, "#LoveDontPayDaRent (If You Don't Know Me By Now)." Aired November 23, 2017, on Netflix.

Lee, Spike, dir. *She's Gotta Have It,* season 1, episode 9, "#ChangeGonCome (GENTRIFICATION)." Aired November 23, 2017, on Netflix.

Lee, Spike, dir. *She's Gotta Have It,* season 2, episode 7, "#OhJudoKnow?" Aired May 24, 2019, on Netflix.

Lee, Spike, dir. *She's Gotta Have It,* season 2, episode 8, "#OnTheComeUpTheComeDown&TheComeRound." Aired May 24, 2019, on Netflix.

Lee, Spike, dir. *She's Gotta Have It,* season 2, episode 9, "#IAmYourMirror." Aired May 24, 2019, on Netflix.

LettySetGo, and Lesley Steel. "The Inspiration behind Beyoncé's 'Lemonade' Imagery." Genius. July 27, 2017. https://genius.com/videos/The-inspiration-behind-beyonces-lemonade-imagery.

Lewis, Sharon A., and Ama S. Wattley. *Bodies of Water in African American Literature, Music, and Film.* Newcastle upon Tyne, UK: Cambridge Scholars Publishing, 2023.

Lila, Hamsa. "Oshun," Track 2 on *Gathering One.* N.p.: BRG, 2003. Compact Disc.

Littleton, Cynthia. "Netflix Renews Spike Lee's 'She's Gotta Have It' for Season 2." *Variety.* January 1, 2018. https://variety.com/2018/tv/news/shes-gotta-have-it-spike-lee-netflix-renew-season-2-1202650672/

Love, Velma E. *Divining the Self: A Study in Yoruba Myth and Human Consciousness.* University Park: Pennsylvania State University Press, 2012.

Lovejoy, Henry B. "Mapping Uncertainty: The Collapse of Oyo and the Trans-Atlantic Slave Trade, 1816–1836." *Journal of Global Slavery* 4 (2019): 127–161.

MacRae, George W., and Douglass M. Parrott. "The Thunder: Perfect Mind (V1, 2)." In *The Nag Hammadi Library in English,* edited by James McConkey Robinson, 295–303. Leiden: Brill, 1996.

Mallory, Tamika D. "About Tamika D. Mallory." *TamikaDMallory.com.* https://www.tamikadmallory.com/about-tamika-d-mallory (defunct).

Mandela, Nelson. "Inaugural Speech." Speech given in Pretoria, South Africa, on May 10, 1994. University of Pennsylvania–African Studies Center. https://www.africa.upenn.edu/Articles_Gen/Inaugural_Speech_17984.html

Mason, John. *Orin Òrìṣà: Songs for Selected Heads.* New York: Yoruba Theological Archministry, 1992.

Mbiti, John. *African Religions and Philosophy.* New York: Doubleday, 1969.

McKenzie, Joi-Marie. "'Brown Skin Girl' Director Jenn Nkiru Talks Creating an Unapologetic Video Celebrating Blackness." *Essence.* December 6, 2020. www.essence.com/entertainment/only-essence/brown-skin-girl-jenn-nkiru/

McKenzie, Peter. *Hail Orisha! A Phenomenology of a West African Religion in the Mid-Nineteenth Century.* Leiden: Brill, 1997.

McKittrick, Katherine. "Plantation Futures." *Small Axe* 17, no. 3 (2013): 1–15.

McNeal, Keith E. "Pantheons as Mythistorical Archives: Pantheonization and Remodeled Iconographies in Two Southern Caribbean Possession Religions." In *Activating the Past: History and Memory in the Black Atlantic World,* edited by Andrew Apter and Lauren Derby, 185–244. Newcastle upon Tyne, UK: Cambridge Scholars Publishing, 2010.

Morales, Selina. "Aging with Grace and Power: A Puerto Rican Healer's Story." In *The Expressive Lives of Elders: Folklore, Art and Aging*, edited by Jon Kay, 42–54 Bloomington: Indiana University Press, 2018.

Morrison, Toni. *Paradise*. New York: Vintage Press, 2014.

Murphy, Joseph M., and Mei Mei Sanford. "Introduction." In Murphy and Sanford, *Oshun across the Waters*, 1–9.

Murphy, Joseph M., and Mei Mei Sanford, eds. *Oshun across the Waters: A Yoruba Goddess in Africa and the Americas*. Bloomington: Indiana University Press, 2001.

New York Times. "Jay-Z and Dean Baquet, in Conversation." YouTube video. 35:09. November 30, 2017. www.youtube.com/watch?v=XbuQAbG2AZ0

Nuñez, Luis Manuel. *Santeria Stories*. Putnam: Spring Publications, 2006.

Ogunbile, David O. "Ẹẹrindínlógún: The Seeing Eyes of Sacred Shells and Stones." In Murphy and Sanford, *Oshun across the Waters*, 189–212.

Òjó, Akinloyè. "Names and Naming." In *Encyclopedia of the Yoruba*, edited by Toyin Falola and Akintunde Akinyemi, 242–243. Bloomington: Indiana University Press, 2016.

Okediji, Moyo. "Semioptics of Anamnesia: Yoruba Images in the Works of Jeff Donaldson, Howardena Pindell and Muneer Bahauddeen." PhD dissertation, University of Wisconsin–Madison, 1995.

Okediji, Moyo. *The Shattered Gourd: Yoruba Forms in Twentieth-Century American Art*. Seattle: University of Washington Press, 2003.

Okediji, Moyo. "Whither Art History? African Art and Language as Semiotic Text." *Art Bulletin* 97, no. 2 (2015): 123–139.

Olajubu, Oyeronke. *Women in the Yoruba Religious Sphere*. Albany: State University of New York Press, 2003.

Olaniyan, Tejumola. *Scars of Conquest/Masks of Resistance: The Invention of Cultural Identities in African, African-American, and Caribbean Drama*. Oxford: Oxford University Press, 1995.

Omari-Tunkara, Mikelle Smith. *Manipulating the Sacred: Yorùbá Art, Ritual, and Resistance in Brazilian Candomblé*. Detroit: Wayne State University Press, 2005.

Oruene, Taiwo. "Magical Powers of Twins in the Socio-Religious Beliefs of the Yoruba." *Folklore* 96, no. 22: (1985): 208–216.

Otero, Solimar, and Toyin Falola, eds. *Yemoja: Gender, Sexuality and Creativity in the Latina/o and Afro-Atlantic Diasporas*. Albany: State University of New York Press, 2013.

Oyewùmí, Oyèrónkẹ. *What Gender Is Motherhood? Changing Yorùbá Ideals of Power, Procreation, and Identity in the Age of Modernity*. New York: Palgrave Macmillan, 2016.

Patterson, Brandon E. "We Went to 'Beyoncé Mass' and It was Glorious." *Mother Jones*. April 25, 2018. www.motherjones.com/media/2018/04/grace-cathedral-beyonce-mass-was-glorious/

Peréz, Elizabeth. "The Black Atlantic Metaphysics of Azealia Banks: Brujx Womanism at the Kongo Crossroads." *Hypatia* 36, no. 3 (Summer 2021): 519–546.

Peréz, Elizabeth. "Nobody's Mammy: Yemayá as Fierce Foremother in Afro-Cuban Religions." In Otero and Falola, *Yemoja*, 9–41.

Petit, Stephanie. "JAY-Z and Solange's Infamous Elevator Fight: Everything They—and Beyoncé—Have Said." *People*. October 8, 2022. https://people.com/music/jay-z-solange-elevator-fight-everything-theyve-said/

Pikaart, Hannah. "Meet the Brooklyn Artist Who Lent Art-World Cred to Netflix 'She's Gotta Have It' Reboot: Tatyana Fazlalizadeh Takes Us behind the Scenes." Artnet.com. December 11, 2017. https://news.artnet.com/art-world/brooklyn-artist-shes-gotta-have-it-1163225

Ramos, Miguel W. *On the Orishas' Roads and Pathways: Oshún, Deity of Femininity*. N.p.: Eleda.org Publications, 2014.

Rowe, Desireé D. "Autoethnography as Object-Oriented Method." In *Doing Autoethnography*, edited by Sandra L Pensoneau-Conway, Tony E. Adams and Derek M. Bolen, 229–232. Rotterdam: Sense Publishers, 2017.

Sanchez, Chelsey. "Beyoncé Hints at Jay-Z and Solange's Elevator Fight in 'Cozy.'" *Harper's Bazaar*. July 29, 2022. www.harpersbazaar.com/celebrity/latest/a40731435/beyonce-cozy-song-lyrics-meaning-explained-renaissance/

Sellers, Allison P. "Yemoja: An Introduction to the Divine Mother and Water Goddess." In Otero and Falola, *Yemoja*, 131–149.

Senbanjo, Laolu. "The Sacred Art of the Ori." TED video. 08:41. April 2017. https://www.ted.com/talks/laolu_senbanjo_the_sacred_art_of_the_ori?language=en#t-332350.

Senyonga, Mary. "The Livable, Surviving, and Healing Poetics of *Lemonade*: A Black Feminist Futurity in Action." In Baade and McGee, *Beyoncé in the World*, 368–388.

Shange, Ntozake. *Sassafrass, Cypress & Indigo*. New York: St. Martin's Press of New York, 1982.

Shaw, J. Brendan. "Merging Past and Present in *Lemonade's* Black Feminist Utopia." In Baade and McGee, *Beyoncé in the World*, 110–133.

Shire, Warsan. "the unbearable weight of staying – (the end of the relationship)." *warsan vs. melancholy (the seven stages of loneliness)*. 01:34. Bandcamp. February 14, 2012. https://warsanshire.bandcamp.com/track/the-unbearable-weight-of-staying-the-end-of-the-relationship

Simpson-Wilkey, LaJuan, Shiela Smith McKoy, and Eric M. Bridges, eds. *Recovering the African Feminine Divine in Literature, the Arts, and Practice: Yemonja Awakening*. Lanham, MD: Lexington Books, 2020.

Spielberg, Steven, dir. *The Color Purple*. Burbank, CA: Warner Bros., 1985.

Spillers, Hortense. "Mama's Baby, Papa's Maybe: An American Grammar Book." *Diacritics* 17, no. 2: (1987), 64–81.

Sterling, Cheryl. *African Roots, Brazilian Rites: Cultural and National Identity in Brazil*. New York: Palgrave Macmillan, 2012.

Thomas, Valerie D. "Unenslaveable Rapture: Afrxfuturism and Diasporic Vertigo in Beyoncé's *Lemonade*." *Topia: Canadian Journal of Cultural Studies* 39 (2018): 48–69.

Thompson, Robert Farris. *Flash of the Spirit: African and Afro-American Art and Philosophy.* New York: Random House, 1984.

Thompson, Robert Farris. "Orchestrating Water and the Wind: Oshun's Art in Atlantic Context." In Murphy and Sanford, *Oshun across the Waters,* 251–262.

Thompson, Robert Farris. "The Sign of the Divine King: An Essay on Yoruba Bead-Embroidered Crowns with Veil and Bird Decorations." *African Arts* 3, no. 3 (Spring 1970): 8–17, 74–80.

Tikhomiroff, João D, dir. *Besouro.* Culver City: Columbia Pictures, 2009.

Tinsley, Omise'eke Natasha. *Beyoncé in Formation: Remixing Black Feminism.* Austin: University of Texas Press, 2018.

Valdés, Vanessa K. *Oshun's Daughter's: The Search for Womanhood in the Americas.* Albany: State University of New York Press, 2014.

Ward, Martha. "Where Circum-Caribbean Afro-Catholic Creoles Met American Protestant Conjurers: Origins of New Orleans Voodoo." In *Caribbean and Southern: Transnational Perspectives on the U.S. South,* edited by Helen A. Regis, 124–138. Athens: University of Georgia Press, 2006.

Wardi, Anissa Janine. *Water and African American Memory: An Ecocritical Perspective.* Gainesville: University Press of Florida, 2011.

Warner, Denise. "Beyonce Drops Surprise Song 'Black Parade' on Juneteenth." *Billboard.* June 20, 2020. www.billboard.com/music/music-news/beyonce-black-parade-juneteenth-9406188/

Washington, Teresa N. *Our Mothers, Our Powers, Our Texts: Manifestations of Àjé in Africana Literature.* Bloomington: Indiana University Press, 2005.

Washington, Teresa N. "'The Sea Never Dies': The Infinitely Flowing Mother Force of Africana Literature and Cinema." In Otero and Falola, *Yemoja,* 215–266.

Welang, Nahum. "The Death and Resurrection of Oshun in Beyoncé's *Lemonade*: Subverting the Institutionalized Borders of Western Christian Thought in American Popular Culture." *Journal of Popular Culture* 54, no. 2 (2021): 750–770.

White, Krista. "Espousing Ezili: Images of a Lwa, Reflections of the Haitian Woman." *Journal of Haitian Studies* 5, no. 6 (2000): 62–79.

Wiggins, William, Jr. *O Freedom: Afro-American Emancipation Celebrations.* Nashville: University of Tennessee Press, 1990.

Williams, Gaye. "Thunder, Perfect Mind; Reflections on a Moon Text." *Psychological Perspectives* 34, no. 1 (1996): 22–32.

Wimbush, Vincent L. "Reading Scripture, Reading Darkness." In *African Americans and the Bible: Sacred Texts and Social Textures,* edited by Vincent L. Wimbush, 1–48. Eugene, OR: Wipf and Stock, 2000.

Winfrey, Oprah, dir. *Oprah's Next Chapter,* season 2, episode 22, "Beyoncé." Aired February 16, 2013, on OWN.

Yai, Olabiyi Babalola. "In Praise of Metonymy: The Concepts of 'Tradition' and 'Creativity' in the Transmission of Yoruba Artistry over Time and Space." *Research in African Literatures* 24, no. 4 (Winter 1993), 29–37.

Zaru, Deena. "Beyoncé Gets Political at Super Bowl, Pays Tribute to 'Black Lives Matter.'" CNN. August 16, 2017. www.cnn.com/2016/02/08/politics/beyonce-super-bowl-black-lives-matter/index.html

Zauditu-Selassie, Kokahvah. "Women Who Know Things: African Epistemologies, Ecocriticism, and Female, Spiritual Authority in the Novels of Toni Morrison." *Journal of Pan African Studies* 1, no. 7 (2007): 38–57.

INDEX

Abdurrahamn, Umar, 95
Abimbola, Wande, 6, 50–52, 78
Abiodun, Rowland, 53, 56, 138n14
Abojúèjì, 31
"Accountability" (Shire), 104
Adéẹ̀kọ́, Adéléke, 64
Africa: Black beauty of women and girls, 115–16; Black Global community and, 105–6, 112–13; Christianity and, 30, 143n20; contemporary fabrics, 71; diasporic spiritual and cultural practices, 5, 7, 15, 30, 42, 63, 111, 127; heritage of, 106, 109–10; religious iconography, 125; return to, 109–10, 113–14; ways of knowing, 109, 117. *See also* Yoruba culture
African Americans: African-centered spiritual practices, 115, 126–27; drama, 15; Hurricane Katrina and, 85; injustice and, 50, 106–9, 112; intergenerational trauma, 22, 57, 70, 91, 96–97; Juneteenth and, 105–6; Moorish culture, 141n16; nihilism and, 70; peaceful protest by, 86, 105, 108; police brutality and, 85–86, 108; police murder of, 42, 90, 107–8; Southern cultural landscape, 106; spectator and spectacle in performance, 15; water as embodied memory, 82–83; ways of knowing, 63, 109–10, 117; Yoruba spiritual practice, 19. *See also* Black women
African Diaspora Studies, 19
Afro-Atlantic religion: "basement" practices, 30, 127; Black women and, 1, 19; Christianity and, 30–31; cultural influences, 19, 126; Elegba and, 7; generational trauma, 2; iconography of, 2, 5–7; transatlantic slave trade and, 4; transnationalism, 127. *See also* Lucumí

Aganju, 8, 93–94
Àjẹ́, 45
Ajogun, 8–9
AkileAshe, Iya, 35
Àláfíà (peace/health), 16
Alejo, 31
Alexander, M. Jacqui, 27
"All Night Long" (Beyoncé), 45
"Already" (Beyoncé), 112
Anderson, Adisa, 91
"Anger" (Shire), 57
Anthony, Cleo, 23
"At the Bottom of the River" (Kincaid): Oshun and, 81; relation to *Lemonade*, 2; semioptics and, 14; water imagery in, 18, 80–82, 89
Autoethnography: author positionality, 14, 126; Blackgirl, 12; *Lemonade* as, 12–13, 23, 123, 126; Lucumí religion and, 126; object-oriented, 11–12; Oshun and, 126; reflexivity in, 12–14
Awòran (beholder or spectator), 15, 33, 43, 58
Àwòrán (representation or spectrum), 15, 33, 43, 58
Ayede, 113

Baade, Christina, 2
Badejo, Dierdre, 3, 45
Banks, Azealia, 125
Baquet, Dean, 13, 122–23
Bascom, William, 48
Benitez, Santana Caress, 25, 35, 137n53
Benston, Kimberly W., 15–16
Bent, Lyriq, 23
Besouro (Tikhomiroff), 141n29
Beyoncé: accountability and amends, 50; ancestral memories, 22, 41–42, 44, 106,

108; anger and, 57–58, 60–62, 76–77; autoethnography, 12, 23; awòran/àwòrán,
Beyoncé (*continued*)
33, 43, 58; BET awards performance, 104–5; celebration of African heritage, 105–6, 109, 117; celebrity and fandom, 3, 33, 46, 58, 73–74, 139n33; centrality of Oshun, 1–3, 17–19, 125; on collective experience of Black women, 15, 59; diasporic Blackness in work, 105–6; Erzulie and, 61, 139n40; face/body painting, 38, 62–63, 74; father of, 71–72; forgiveness and, 74–77, 90, 112; garments of, 29, 32, 37, 88, 111, 122; generational trauma, 2, 13, 16–17, 43, 70, 75; Grammy performance, 103–4; hope and, 43, 65, 117; Jay-Z's infidelity and, 1, 29–30, 46, 57, 61–62, 64, 66, 72–73, 76; journey out of suffering, 23, 74, 83–84, 89–90; labor of music production, 67, 76; lemonade recipe, 44; on love, 32, 43, 58, 73–74; marriage to Jay-Z, 13, 46; mirror imagery, 30–31, 41–42, 68, 71; motherhood and, 64–65, 107, 111–12; New Orleans and, 12, 63, 71; occupation of the plantation, 22–23, 69; on power of ajẹ́, 45; pregnancy with twins, 102–3; rebirth and, 22, 29, 32–33, 43–44; reconciliation and, 1, 38, 45–46, 57, 65–66, 77; redemption and, 44–46, 57; religious identity, 30–31; repair of relationship, 75–77, 90–91, 140n92; (re)possession of self through Oshun, 11, 21, 30–33, 35, 43, 46–47, 107, 109; restoration of balance, 69–70; retribution and, 18, 31, 33, 50, 66, 76; semioptics and, 31; sense of self, 46, 68, 124; social justice and, 44, 49, 107–9; Southern roots, 30–31, 71, 105–7; Super Bowl L performance, 84, 108, 122; Texas and, 71, 105–6; tribute to South Africa, 124–25; twinning of self, 31, 136n38; on wisdom of grandmother, 12, 44–45; yellow and gold costuming, 29, 31–33, 62, 74, 89, 102–4, 111, 116, 122, 124–25, 144n4; Yoruba iconography and, 102–3, 106, 109, 125, 127–28. *See also Lemonade* (Beyoncé)
Beyoncé (2013), 65
Beyoncé in Formation (Tinsley), 2
Beyoncé in the World (Baade and McGee), 2

"Bigger" (Beyoncé), 111
Bilal Muhammad (character), 95–97
Bingham, Margot, 24
"Bitter Sweet(Water)" (Boylorn), 12
Blackgirlness, 12–13
Black Gods and Kings (Thompson), 117
Black Is King (Beyoncé): African diaspora and, 110–11, 113–14, 116; African ways of knowing, 109–10, 117; Black boys, 110, 113; Black femininity in, 106, 112–13; Black Global community and, 105–7, 109, 125; colorism, 116–17; Erzulie-Freda in, 113–15, 117; intertextuality with *Lemonade,* 112; masculine development in, 113, 117; motherhood in, 110–13; Oshun imagery in, 19, 103, 115–17, 125–26; relation to *Lemonade,* 2, 109–12; return to Africa, 109–10, 113–14; semioptics and, 14; water imagery in, 110–14; Yemaya in, 113, 115–17, 121; Yoruba spirituality and, 110, 128
Black Lives Matter movement, 86
"Black Parade" (Beyoncé): celebration in, 106–9; diasporic Black community and, 109; embodiment of Oshun, 19; fertility and growth in, 106–7; intertextuality with *Lemonade,* 86, 105–9; Oshun imagery in, 19, 105–6; social justice and, 107–9; Yoruba iconography and, 106
Black people. *See* African Americans
Black Power, 84, 108
Black women: African understanding of beauty, 115–16; Afro-Atlantic religion and, 19, 127; blackgirlness, 12–13; collective experience, 15, 59; divinity of, 59, 67; embodied cultural and political maneuvers, 99–100; embodied knowledge, 23, 26, 135n9; exclusion from ritual, 6, 18, 49–50; of God, 59–60; intergenerational trauma, 13, 22, 43, 57, 70, 81, 91, 99–101; maltreatment of, 59, 108–9, 121; Oshun and, 126; purity archetypes, 99–100; sexuality and, 1–2; significance of hair, 29; sons murdered by police, 42, 90, 108; street harassment, 24–25; suffering by, 17, 21; thingification of, 68; violence against, 23, 25
Black women authors, 2–3

Blake, James, 42, 90
Boylorn, Robin M., 12–13
Brandon, George, 32–33
Brass, 10–11
Brazil, 6, 19, 127, 136n39
Brodber, Erna, 1, 135n9
Brooks, Kinitra D., 2
Brown, Michael, 42
Brown, Queen Ya Ya Kijafa, 42
"Brown Skin Girl" (Beyoncé), 115–16
Bruce, Cheryl Lynn, 94
Burley, Ingrid, 140n89
Byrd, Thomas Jefferson, 23

Cabrera, Lydia, 10
Candomblé, 6, 136n39
Carr, Gwen, 42
Carter, Blue Ivy, 46, 72, 82, 104, 111
Carter, Sir, 109–10
The Carters, 124–25
Catlett, Elizabeth, 40, 137n71
Chauvin, Derek, 107
Christianity, 30–31, 89–90, 127, 143n20
Christie, Shelby Ivey, 144n4
Colorism, 116–17
The Color Purple (film), 57
Colors: Orisha lore, 7–8; Oshun and, 1, 5–6, 10–11; symbolic meaning, 10–11, 22, 26, 32; Victorian concepts of, 22; Yoruba culture, 9, 22, 26–27. *See also individual colors*
Consolata Sosa (character), 136n38
"Cozy" (Beyoncé), 143n12
Cuba, 4, 19, 116, 127

"Daddy" (Beyoncé), 71–72
"Daddy Lessons" (Beyoncé), 71–72
Dash, Julie, 2, 18, 81–82, 93–94. *See also Daughters of the Dust* (1991)
Daughters of the Dust (1991): ancestral memories and, 91, 95–97; color imagery in, 82; Ibo Landing in, 82–83, 91, 96–97, 100–101; intergenerational trauma and, 97–101; Ki-Kongo iconography, 93; Oshun imagery in, 126; rape and pregnancy of Eula, 95–100; relation to *Lemonade*, 2, 82; semioptics and, 14; sonic tributes to Oshun, 92, 95; tradition and, 94–95; water imagery in, 18, 81–83, 89, 91, 93–98, 100–101; Yemaya and, 91, 94, 100–101
Day, Cora Lee, 91
Destiny's Child, 71
Destrehan Plantation, 73
Diaz, Lisa-Kaindé, 87
Diaz, Naomi, 87
Dilogún: divination verses, 2, 6, 26–27; Ifá and, 6, 49–50, 52, 138n3; Oshun and, 50, 52; women practitioners, 49
Disney, 109–10
Divination, 6, 16, 50–52. *See also* Dilogún; Ifá; *Odù* (divination verse)
Doña Tina (character), 119
"Don't Hurt Yourself" (Beyoncé), 18, 50, 59
"Don't Jealous Me" (Beyoncé), 112
Do the Right Thing (1989), 119
Dreams, 23, 67
Drewal, Henry, 16
Drewal, Margaret, 16
Dúdú (black): in *Lemonade*, 22, 29, 60, 67–68, 102; symbolic meaning, 9, 22, 26; water imagery and, 29

Ẹbọ (sacrifice), 16, 41, 51, 89, 103
Egun (ancestors), 4, 8, 38, 41, 95
Egúngún procession, 42
Elegba, 7–8, 26, 35, 56–57
Elekes, 10, 26, 87
Eli Peazant (character), 91, 95–99
"Emptiness" (Shire), 83
Epega, Afolabi, 48
Erinle, 141n17
Erzulie-Freda, 19, 113–15, 117
Erzulie-Gé-Rouge, 61, 139n40
Eshu Elegba, 95
Espritismo, 118
Ẹ̀tò (progress), 16
Eula Peazant (character), 18, 81, 91, 95–101
Everything Is Love (Beyoncé), 13, 124

Face painting, 37–38, 62–63, 74
"Faithful" (Ndegeocello), 40
Fans, 6–7, 11
Fatunmbi Fasola, Awo Fategbe, 48
Fazlalizadeh, Tatyana, 24–25, 121
"Find Your Way Back" (Beyoncé), 112

"Flawless" (Beyoncé), 143n12
Floyd, George, 107
"Formation" (Beyoncé), 84–86, 89–90, 106, 108
Formation World Tour, 104, 122
Fort Macomb, 21, 41, 46, 72–73, 135n3
"Forward" (Beyoncé), 44
4:44 (Jay-Z), 13, 122–24
"Freedom" (Beyoncé), 43–44, 104
Fulton, Sybrina, 42
Funfun (white): African spirituality and, 42; associations with purity, 26, 61; in *Lemonade,* 60–61, 82, 84–85; Lucumí rituals, 30, 137n63; Mardi Gras imagery, 42; in *She's Gotta Have It,* 37, 40–41; symbolic meaning, 9, 11, 40

Garner, Eric, 42
Gender: complementarity in Yoruba religion, 50, 52, 136n52; divination and, 50–52; exclusion from ritual, 6, 18, 49–50, 52, 55–57; ritual practices, 6, 18, 49; in Yoruba Studies, 52
Gheri, Iya, 38, 56, 127
Global Citizen Festival: Mandela 100, 124–25
Gold: Beyoncé and, 29, 31–32, 41, 74, 103–4, 116, 122; Erzulie-Gé-Rouge, 61; in *Lemonade,* 5, 29; Oshun and, 6, 9–10, 89, 122; Super Bowl L performance, 122; symbolic meaning, 9–10, 29
Goldberg, Whoopi, 57
González-Wippler, Migene, 126

Haagar Peazant (character), 97–99
Hadera, Ilfenesh, 118
Haile, James B., III, 12
Hair, 29–30
Hale, Lindsay, 31, 92
Hamsa Lila, 25
Hartman, Saidiya, 99–100
Headley, Heather, 27
Healing: honey imagery, 11; *Lemonade* and, 15–16; Lucumí rituals, 21, 26–27, 34–35; Oshun and, 17–19, 21, 23, 28, 35, 73, 85, 88; reconciliation and, 31; as ritual process, 17, 33–35; water imagery in, 34, 37, 85, 88–90

Hicks, Tommy Redmond, 95
Hoch, Danny, 27
"Hold Up" (Beyoncé), 32, 62
Honey, 5–6, 11, 35–37
hooks, bell, 125
Hubbard-Salk, Indigo, 118

Ibeji, 7–8, 34, 87, 103
Ibeyi, 15, 87–90, 101
Ibo Landing: in *Daughters of the Dust,* 82–83, 91, 96–97, 100–101; floating/flying of enslaved Africans, 83, 91, 96–97
Ibo people, 96–97, 142n61
Ìdó, 78
Ifá: bag of wisdom and, 51–52; Diloggún and, 6, 49–50, 52, 138n3; gender exclusion, 55–56; healing practices, 27; masculinist, 50; navigation through, 49; orality of, 48; Òrúnmila and, 6, 50; Oshun and, 2, 50–52; sacrifice in, 51
"I Have Three Hearts" (Beyoncé), 102–4
"I Have Three Hearts" (Shire), 102
Intuition, 22–23, 31, 41
"Intuition" (Shire), 22
Iona Peazant (character), 91, 94
Ìran (spectacle), 15, 17, 33
Irunmolé: exclusion in, 53, 56, 65–66; feminine energy in, 49–50; Orishas in, 5; Oshun and, 17–18, 49–50, 57, 65–66, 75, 92–93, 109, 138n14
Ìtàn, 63–64
Iyawos, 30, 136n33

Jackson, Joyce Marie, 42
Jay-Z: accountability and, 61–62, 64, 69, 74, 123; elevator incident, 108, 143n12; emotional world of, 76; *Everything Is Love,* 13; fandom and, 46; *4:44* album, 13, 122–24; hounding by, 67; infidelity by, 1, 29–30, 46, 57, 61–62, 64, 66, 72–73, 76; ingratitude and, 75; intergenerational trauma and, 123; "Kill Jay-Z," 143n12; love and, 73–74; as magician, 46; marriage to Beyoncé, 13, 46; Oshun's mirror and, 124; response to *Lemonade,* 122–23
Juneteenth, 105–7

Kehinde, 87, 103
"Keys to the Kingdom" (Savage), 110, 117
Ki-Kongo iconography, 93
"Kill Jay-Z" (Jay-Z), 143n12
Kincaid, Jamaica, 1, 14, 18, 80–81, 89. *See also* "At the Bottom of the River" (Kincaid)
King, Little Freddie, 71
King, Martin Luther, Jr., 108
Kintsugi bowl, 75, 140n92
Knowing: African American ways of, 63, 109–10, 117; embodied, 23, 26, 135n9; intuition, 23; men's infidelity and, 23
Knowles, Matthew, 71
Knowles, Solange, 107–8, 143n12
Knowles-Carter, Beyoncé. *See* Beyoncé
Knowles-Lawson, Tina, 46, 71, 104

Lake Pontchartrain, 73, 82–83
Lamar, Kendrick, 104–5
Lane, Chyna, 27
Laro, King, 79–81, 88–89, 96
Lawal, Babatunde, 9, 15–16, 33, 65, 103
Lawson, Richard, 46
Lawson, Tina. *See* Knowles-Lawson, Tina
Lee, Joie, 23
Lee, Spike, 23–24, 34, 37–38. *See also She's Gotta Have It* (2017, 2019)
Lele, Ochani, 48
Lemonade (Beyoncé): accountability and, 50, 61–62, 64, 69, 72, 74; autoethnography in, 12–13, 23, 123; black (*dúdú*) imagery in, 22, 29, 60, 67–68, 84; Black femininity in, 59, 67, 106; compared with *Daughters of the Dust*, 2, 82; dance in, 5, 32–33; *egun* (ancestors) in, 41–42; emptiness and, 66; head and hair imagery, 29–30; healing in, 46, 57, 104; honey imagery, 11; intergenerational relationships, 13, 58, 69; intertextuality with *4:44*, 123; intertextuality with "Black Parade," 86, 105–6, 108; Lucumí iconography in, 16, 29–31, 62, 87; magic references, 17, 42, 44–46, 72; mirror imagery in, 30–31, 33, 41–42, 68; New Orleans imagery in, 1, 21, 23, 42, 63, 68, 70–72, 84–85, 139n29; Ọ̀ṣẹ́túrá and, 49–50; Oshun imagery in, 1–3, 11, 16–17, 43, 60–61, 102–4, 126; plantation imagery, 22–23, 69; police cruiser imagery, 84–89; reconciliation in, 45–46, 57, 65–66, 75, 90; red (*pupa*) imagery in, 29, 60, 66–68, 83–85; redemption in, 44–46, 57; retribution in, 31, 33, 66, 77, 85; rural to urban setting, 72–73; semioptics and, 2, 14, 31, 63; social justice and, 44, 75; spectator and spectacle in, 16–17, 33; things in, 11–12; transformational process in, 15–16, 31; as visual album, 1–3, 12–14, 41–42; water imagery in, 9, 18, 29–33, 43, 73–74, 80–90, 102–4, 139n29; ways of knowing in, 12–13; white (*funfun*) imagery in, 60–61, 82, 84–85; yellow and gold imagery, 9–11, 29, 31–33, 62, 89, 102–4, 111, 116; Yemaya imagery in, 102–3; Yoruba ritual and iconography in, 2, 16–17, 32–33, 62–65, 87, 102, 128. *See also individual songs*
Lemonade Reader (Brooks and Martin), 2
Letterman, David, 124
The Lion King: The Gift, 106, 109–11, 113, 125
"The Look of Love" (Simone), 75
Lorde, Audre, 39
Louisiana: Fort Macomb, 21, 41, 46, 135n3; *Lemonade* project and, 1, 42, 106. *See also* New Orleans
Louisiana (Brodber), 135n9, 135n29
Lourdes (character), 25–29, 34–35, 37–38, 41, 49, 118–19
"Love Drought" (Beyoncé), 73, 103–4, 112
Lucumí: Black women and, 1, 16, 126; Christianity and, 30–31; cultural influence of, 87, 126; *egun* (ancestors), 4, 8; healing practices, 21, 26–27, 34–35; iconography of, 16, 29–31, 62, 87, 127; initiation process, 17–18, 28–29, 62; *iyawos*, 30; Noche De San Juan, 118; Olódùmare as creator, 4–5, 9; Orisha worship, 4–8, 10; *patakís*, 6–8; ritual practices, 17, 21, 29–30, 32, 35, 37–38, 137n53; roots of, 4–6; sacrifice in, 89; Santería and, 133n3; significance of hair, 29–30; symbolic import, 3–10, 14; water rituals, 18, 30, 81, 90, 136n33; ways of knowing in, 16, 31, 126; Yoruba-derived religious tenets, 4–6, 19–20, 35. *See also* Afro-Atlantic religion

160 · Index

Madewood Plantation House, 22–23, 69
Madida, Nandi, 113–14
Mallory, Tamika, 108
Mami-Wata (Mammy Wata), 142n61
Mandela, Nelson, 125
Mantón, 103
Martin, Kameelah L., 2
Martin, Trayvon, 42
Matsoukas, Melina, 84
Mbiti, John, 35
McFadden, Lesley, 42
McGee, Kristin, 2
McKittrick, Katherine, 22
McNeal, Keith, 2
Menstruation, 66–67
Mercedes-Benz Superdome, 72–73
Mirrors: Beyoncé and twinning of self, 31, 136n38; *egúngún* procession, 42; in *Lemonade,* 30–31, 33, 41–42, 68; Nola Darling (character) and, 34, 40; Oshun and, 6–7, 11, 31, 121
"Mood 4 Eva" (Beyoncé), 112, 115, 117
Moore, Kaycee, 97
Mr. Snead (character), 95

Nag Hammadi manuscripts, 91–92
Nana Peazant (character), 91, 94–98, 112
Ndegeocello, Meshell, 40
Neimark, Phillip John, 48
New Orleans: autoethnography, 12–13; Beyoncé and, 71, 114; Hurricane Katrina, 84–85, 139n29; in *Lemonade,* 1, 21, 23, 42, 63, 68, 70–71, 84–85, 139n29; Mardi Gras imagery, 32, 42, 84; Moorish culture in, 84, 141n16; police brutality in, 85; in *Sassafrass, Cypress & Indigo,* 28; spiritual influence of, 28; Vodun and, 61
Nkiru, Jenn, 116
Nne Mmiri, 142n61
Noche De San Juan, 118
Nola Darling (character): ancestral memories, 38–39, 41; consultation with Lourdes, 26–27, 34, 37–38, 41, 49; face painting, 37–38, 62, 74; head and hair imagery, 29; honey imagery, 35, 37; lovers and, 24, 27–28, 39–40, 117–18; Lucumí religion and, 105; Oshun's interventions for, 11, 25–28, 40–41, 120–21; poster campaign, 24, 39; reconciliation of conflict, 38; (re)possession of self through Oshun, 21, 25–28, 35–41, 105; self-portrait, 36, 38–40; spiritual intervention, 118; street harassment, 24–25, 39; suffering by, 23–25; transformation of, 40, 117–21; vandalizing of poster art, 27; water imagery and, 34, 37; white imagery, 37, 40–41. *See also She's Gotta Have It*

O., Barbara, 91
Oba, 8
Obatala, 5, 11, 38, 95
Odù (divination verse): as allegories, 49; cartography of the self, 49; gendered, 52–55; Irunmolé and, 138n14; orality of, 48; Oshun in, 5–6; Yoruba culture, 48. *See also* Odù Ọ̀ṣẹ́túrá; Orishas
Odù Ifá, 6, 48
Odù Ògúndá Ìwòrì, 78
Odù Okanransode, 51
Odù Ọ̀ṣẹ́túrá: accountability and, 72; Elegba and, 7; gendered exclusion, 55–57; hierarchical positioning of Oshun, 17–18, 49–50; Irunmolé and, 77, 138n14; Oshun and, 5, 65, 77, 81; retribution and, 18; social justice and, 50, 52, 56–57, 75
Ogbuide, 142n61
Ogun, 50, 95, 141n17
Ogunbile, David, 53
Okediji, Moyo, 2, 11, 14–16, 42, 63
Olódùmare: bag of wisdom containing Ifá, 51; color imagery, 9; Lucumí religion and, 4–5; Odù Ọ̀ṣẹ́túrá, 52–57; Oshun and, 5, 51
Omari-Tunkara, Mikelle Smith, 31
On the Run II Tour, 124
"Orchestrating Water and the Wind" (Thompson), 6
Orí, 63
Oríkì (praise poetry), 2, 11, 64
Orisha Ibeji, 7–8
Orishas: bag of wisdom containing Ifá, 51–52; complementarity in, 136n52; Elegba and, 7, 26, 56–57; elekes, 10; feminist theory and, 3; guidance of, 28; iconography of, 4–8, 126–27; *iyawos,* 30; in *Lemonade,* 32; Lucumí religion and, 4–8, 20; masculinist,

Index · 161

56; metallic symbolism, 11; Oshun and, 50, 92; sacrifice and, 89; symbolic import, 4–8; veiled faces, 80; worship of, 127; Yoruba mythic history, 2, 34. *See also Odù* (divination verse); Oshun

Ọrúnmila, 6, 26, 50, 92, 141n17

Oshun: Black beauty and, 115–16; in Black popular culture, 2–3, 126; brass and, 10–11; dance and, 5, 32–33, 103; Diloggún and, 50, 52; divination and, 6; as divine feminine archetype, 3, 19, 92, 103, 106; epistemology of, 2–3; Erzulie and, 61; exclusion from *odù*, 52–57, 65–66; fair skin, 116–17; fan symbolism, 6–7, 11; fertility associations, 92, 106–7; garments of, 32; happiness and, 47; healing practices, 17–19, 21, 23, 28, 35, 46–47, 76, 85, 88; hierarchical and social positioning, 17–18, 49–50; honey imagery, 5–6, 11, 36–37; Ibeji and, 7–8, 87, 103; iconography of, 1–8, 16–19, 32, 61, 121, 126; Irunmolé and, 17–18, 49–50, 57, 65–66, 75, 92–93, 109, 138n14; masculine and feminine energy, 113, 117; as mediator, 30; mirrors and, 6–7, 11, 31, 121; mythistorical archive, 2, 116, 126; number symbolism, 6, 83; Ogun and, 50, 95, 141n17; Olódùmare and, 5, 51; Orisha of fertility, 92–93; Ọrúnmila and, 50, 141n17; physical attributes, 80–81; pleasure associations, 5–6; red imagery, 83, 85, 102; repair of relationships, 140n92; (re)possession of self through, 17, 21, 25–26, 28–32, 34–41, 105; sex and sexuality, 1, 5, 92, 94, 100; Shango and, 8–10, 34, 50, 85, 87, 136n52, 141n17; silence and, 93; social justice and, 49, 52, 56–57, 75; sonic tributes to, 78, 83, 92, 95; tradition and, 94–95, 101; water imagery, 1, 5–7, 18, 29, 31–32, 35, 37–38, 73, 78–82, 85, 88–90, 96, 101–2, 141n7, 142n61; wisdom of Ifá and, 51–52; worship of, 5, 93, 116; yellow imagery, 1, 5–6, 9–11, 32–33, 102, 111, 122, 141n29; Yemaya and, 19, 26, 37–38, 94, 102–3, 106–8

"Oshun" (Hamsa Lila), 25

Oṣogbo, 5, 79–81

Ọ̀ṣun, 6, 8, 56, 92

"The Other Side" (Beyoncé), 117
Oya, 8, 11, 38, 41, 86
"Oya" (Ibeyi), 87
Oya-yansa, 95
Oyewùmí, Oyèrónẹ, 53, 55–56
Oyo Empire, 4, 7

Patakís: color imagery, 9–11; honey imagery, 11; interpretation of, 56; Lucumí religion and, 6–8; Oshun in, 11, 50, 76, 79, 81, 83, 91, 93, 100; water imagery in, 83–84, 91, 93

Pérez, Elizabeth, 112
Perez, Rosie, 119
Plantations, 22–23, 69, 73
Police brutality, 42, 85–86, 90, 107–8
Pomba Gira, 60–61
"Pray You Catch Me" (Beyoncé), 22, 29, 66
Puerto Rico, 105, 118–20, 127
Pupa (red): in *Lemonade,* 29, 60, 66–68, 85; Oshun and, 83, 85, 102; in *She's Gotta Have It,* 40; symbolic meaning, 9–10, 32, 66–67, 83

Ramos, Anthony, 23
Ramos, Miguel W., 93
Red. *See Pupa* (red)
Renaissance (Beyoncé), 143n12
Retribution, 18, 31, 33, 50, 66, 76
Ritual: color imagery, 9–11, 22, 26, 37, 137n63; gender-based, 6, 18, 49; honey imagery, 11; intimate nature of, 34; in *Lemonade,* 2–3, 16–17, 30, 32–34; Lucumí, 17, 21, 29–30, 32, 35, 37–38, 137n53; Oshun and, 5–6, 9, 17, 32–33; water imagery, 7, 18, 34, 37, 62, 80–81, 83, 85–86, 88–89; Yoruba, 2, 14–17, 136n39
"River" (Ibeyi), 15, 87–88, 90
Rogers, Alva, 91
Rowe, Desireé D., 12
Royal Parking Garage, 21, 58, 60, 72, 83

Sacrifice: Beyoncé and, 73, 77; Black women and, 44–45, 75; Nola Darling and, 120; Odù Ọṣẹ́túrá, 57. *See also* Ẹbọ (sacrifice)
"Sandcastles" (Beyoncé), 76, 91, 103–4, 124
Sandoval, Mercedes, 126

Ṣango, 6
Santería, 27, 133n3
Sassafrass (character): honey imagery, 35–36; Orisha worship, 28; Oshun's interventions for, 11, 34; rebirth and, 36; (re)possession of self through Oshun, 21, 28–29, 34–36, 136n52; suffering by, 23; water imagery and, 34
Sassafrass, Cypress & Indigo (Shange): New Orleans imagery in, 28; Oshun imagery in, 23, 28, 34, 36, 126, 136n52; relation to *Lemonade*, 2; semioptics, 15; Shango imagery in, 34, 136n52; spells and recipes in, 44
Savage, Tiwa, 110
"Scar" (Beyoncé), 112
Semioptics, 2, 11, 14–15, 31, 63
Senbanjo, Laolu, 1, 62–64
Seriality, 16–17
Shange, Ntozake, 1, 125. See also *Sassafrass, Cypress & Indigo* (Shange)
Shango: children's names, 95; fiery disposition, 85; Oshun and, 8–10, 34, 50, 85, 87, 136n52, 141n17; ritual iconography, 7; wives of, 8
Shattered Gourd (Okediji), 42
She's Gotta Have It (2017, 2019): Black Global community and, 107; color imagery in, 26–27, 37, 40–41; divination in, 26–28, 49; head and hair imagery, 29; Lucumí religion and, 35, 39, 41, 62, 105, 118; New Orleans imagery in, 23; Nola's art, 36, 38–40, 121; Oshun imagery in, 19, 23, 25–27, 34, 118–21, 126; relation to *Lemonade*, 2, 23, 29; revision for Netflix, 23, 34, 41, 105; ritual in, 34; submersion in water, 34, 37, 118; transformation of Nola Darling, 40, 117–21; Yemaya in, 118–21; Yoruba spirituality in, 35, 118–20, 128, 137n53. See also Nola Darling (character)
Shire, Warsan: use of poetry in *Black Is King*, 111, 113, 115; use of poetry in *Lemonade*, 1, 22, 41, 57, 64, 83, 102, 104, 107
Silk & Soul (Simone), 76
Simone, Nina, 75–76
Sister Outsider (Lorde), 39
"6 Inch" (Beyoncé), 67

Social justice: Beyoncé and, 44, 49, 107–9; exclusion and, 52–57; Odù Ọ̀ṣẹ́túrá, 49, 52, 56–57, 75; Oshun and, 49, 52, 56–57, 75
Spectacle, 15, 17, 33
Spectator, 15–16, 33. See also Awòran (beholder or spectator)
Spectrum, 15. See also Àwòrán (representation or spectrum)
Speculation, 15
Spillers, Hortense, 99
"Stars Interlude" (Beyoncé), 112
Sterling, Cheryl, 15
"Stop Telling Women to Smile" project, 24
Super Bowl L performance: Black nationalist imagery in, 84, 108; "Formation" debut, 84, 108, 122; Oshun imagery in, 122; water imagery in, 122; yellow/gold imagery, 122
Swan Lake (Tchaikovsky), 63–64

Taiwo, 87, 103
Tchaikovsky, Pyotr Ilyich, 63
Thomas, Valorie D., 61
Thompson, Robert Farris, 6, 11, 100, 117, 126
Tikhomiroff, João Daniel, 141n29
Tinsley, Omise'eke Natasha, 2, 60–61, 127
Turpin, Bahni, 91
Twins: Beyoncé and, 46, 102–3; Ibeyi, 87; mirror imagery, 7, 31; Orisha Ibeji, 7–8, 34, 87; in Yoruba culture, 87–88

Umbanda, 136n39
Until Freedom, 108

Viola Peazant (character), 94–95, 99
Virgen de la Caridad Cobre, 92, 104
Vodoun, 19, 61, 113

Wardi, Anissa Janine, 82
Washington, Teresa N., 3, 45
Water: in African American cultural history, 82–83; in Beyoncé's performances, 104–5; in *Black Is King*, 110–14; in *Daughters of the Dust*, 18, 81–83, 89, 91, 93–98, 100–101; healing practices, 34, 37, 85, 88–90; imagery in *Lemonade*, 9, 18, 29–33, 43, 73–74, 81–90, 102–4, 139n29; Lucumí initiation

process, 18, 62, 81; Oshun and, 1, 5–7, 18, 29, 35, 37–38, 73, 78–82, 88–90, 96, 101–2, 141n7, 142n61; rebirth of women characters, 18, 29–30, 35, 43, 81–82; riverine goddesses, 1, 8, 114, 142n61; submersion in, 18, 34, 37, 80–81, 83, 85–86, 88–89; Super Bowl L performance, 122; underwater thumping, 83; Yemaya and, 91, 100–101, 111–12, 142n61

"Water" (Beyoncé), 114

The Weeknd, 67

Welang, Nahum, 30

What Gender Is Motherhood? (Oyewùmí), 52–53

White. *See Funfun* (white)

White Men Can't Jump (1992), 119

Wimbush, Vincent L., 49

Winfrey, Oprah, 65

Wise, DeWanda, 41

Women: exclusion from ritual, 6, 18, 49–50, 55–56; feminine archetypes, 3, 19, 106; intuition and, 23; Oshun's interventions for, 3, 26; rebirth and, 18; sexually exploited, 100; street harassment, 24–25; Victorian aesthetics, 22–23, 73; violence against, 23; virtues of, 113. *See also* Black women

X, Malcolm, 59, 108

Yai, Olabiyi, 63

Yellow: Beyoncé's costumes, 29, 31–33, 62, 74, 89, 102–4, 111, 116, 122, 124–25, 144n4; honey imagery, 11; in *Lemonade*, 9–11, 31–33, 62, 89, 102–4, 111, 116; object-oriented autoethnography, 11; Oshun and, 1, 5–6, 9–11, 32–33, 102, 111, 122, 141n29; Super Bowl L performance, 122; symbolic meaning, 10–11, 32

Yellow Mary (character), 18, 81, 91, 93–94, 97–101

Yemaya: African diaspora and, 5; in *Black Is King*, 113, 115–17, 121; dark skin, 117; in *Daughters of the Dust*, 91, 94; divination and, 27; as divine feminine archetype, 19; healing practices, 35; Oshun and, 19, 26, 37–38, 94, 102–3, 106–8; protection of children, 111; in *She's Gotta Have It*, 118–21; water imagery, 91, 100–101, 111–12, 142n61; worship of, 113

Yemaya Festival, 113

Yemọjá, 6, 95

Yoruba culture: *àbíkú*, 65; aesthetic practices, 80, 125; Beyoncé and, 102–3, 106, 109, 125; color meanings, 9, 22, 26–27; concepts of space, 15; *egúngún* procession, 42; iconography of, 1, 62–63, 87–88, 102–3, 106, 109–10; importance of cloth, 103; influence of diaspora, 5, 14, 19, 42, 63–64, 87, 127; Lucumí religion and, 4–6, 19–20, 35; menstruation in, 67; mythic histories, 34; Oshun and, 5–7; pan-Africanist, 110; religious gender complementarity, 50, 52, 136n52; ritual and rhetorical practices, 2, 14–17, 136n39; spiritual practices, 19, 142n61; textuality, 2; twins in culture, 87–88; ways of knowing, 13

Yoruba language, 11

Yoruba Studies, 52, 126

Zeppelin, Led, 139n29

Sheneese Thompson is associate professor of Afro-American Studies at Howard University. Her research focuses on the intersection between Afro-Atlantic religiosities, particularly Lucumí and other Yoruba-derived religious systems, and their representations in literature, television, and film.